# Peace in the Balance

## The Future of
## American Foreign Policy

*Eugene V. Rostow*

SIMON AND SCHUSTER
New York

*First printing*
*SBN 671-21322-9*
*Library of Congress Catalog Card Number: 72-83089*
*Designed by Irving Perkins*
*Manufactured in the United States of America*
*By H. Wolff Book Mfg. Co., Inc., New York, N.Y.*

*Portions of this book have appeared in*
*the* Sunday New York Times Magazine

Grateful acknowledgment is extended to the following for permission to quote from previously published works:

W. W. Norton & Company, Inc., for *Civilization and Its Discontents*, by Sigmund Freud. Copyright © 1961 by James Strachey; and for *History as a System*, by Ortega y Gasset. Copyright © 1941, 1961 by W. W. Norton & Company, Inc.

The Macmillan Company, for *Containment and Change*, by Carl Oglesby and Richard Shaull. Copyright © 1967 by Carl Oglesby and Richard Shaull.

Pantheon Books, a Division of Random House, Inc., for *American Power and the New Mandarins*, by Noam Chomsky. Copyright © 1967, 1969 by Noam Chomsky.

Penguin Books, Inc., for *The Peloponnesian War*, by Thucydides, translated by Rex Warner. Copyright 1954 by Penguin Books, Inc.

Praeger Publishers, Inc., for *A New Foreign Policy for the United States*, by Hans J. Morgenthau. Copyright © 1969 by Council on Foreign Relations, Inc.

Random House, Inc., for *The Arrogance of Power*, by J. William Fulbright. Copyright © 1966 by J. William Fulbright.

*To the memory of*
*Eyre Crowe and Robert Vansittart,*
*great Undersecretaries of State,*
*who understood that peace is the*
*supreme task of diplomacy, and, in*
*their day, struggled for policies*
*that could have prevented war*
*before it became too late to do*
*anything but fight*

# Contents

THE GREATEST WAR in the past was the Persian War; yet in this war the decision was reached quickly as a result of two naval battles and two battles on land. The Peloponnesian War, on the other hand, not only lasted for a long time, but throughout its course brought with it unprecedented suffering for Hellas. Never before had so many cities been captured and then devastated, whether by foreign armies or by the Hellenic Powers themselves;* never had there been so many exiles; never such loss of life—both in the actual warfare and in internal revolutions. Old stories of past prodigies, which had not found much confirmation in recent experience, now became credible. Wide areas, for instance, were affected by violent earthquakes; there were more frequent eclipses of the sun than had ever been recorded before; in various parts of the country there were extensive droughts followed by famine; and there was the plague which did more harm and destroyed more life than almost any other single factor. All these calamities fell together upon the Hellenes after the outbreak of war.

War began when the Athenians and the Peloponnesians broke the Thirty Years Truce which had been made after the capture of Euboea. As to the reasons why they broke the truce, I propose first to give an account of the causes of complaint which they had against each other and of the specific instances where their interests clashed: this is in order that there should be no doubt in anyone's mind about what led to this great war falling upon the Hellenes. But the real reason for the war is, in my opinion, most likely to be disguised by such an argument. What made war inevitable was the growth of Athenian power and the fear which this caused in Sparta.

—Thucydides, *History of the Peloponnesian War*†

---

*Some of these cities, after capture, were resettled with new inhabitants.
†Rex Warner trans. (Penguin, 1954), Book I, Chap. 1, p. 25.

# *Preface*

IT IS CONVENTIONAL to describe the bellicose literature about how to achieve peace as a "great debate." Like many features of the conventional wisdom, the phrase is misleading. There is disagreement to spare in that literature, but little or no debate.

The idea of a debate is piously invoked, it is true, by most of the gladiators, at least in democracies. In our scheme of values debating is a Good Thing. Surely responsible democrats ought to engage in courteous and rational debates with each other in an earnest effort to achieve a wise state of public opinion and the wise policy that might be built on wise opinion. But few of the protagonists read what their opponents write or listen to what they say. The knights thunder past each other, clad only in their slogans, shouting wild calls to battle. They rarely joust, however, or even collide.

Generally speaking, arguments are answered by epithets or clichés. The devotees of geopolitics, brooding about nuclear deterrence, dismiss their critics as amateurs, journalists, demagogues, dupes, or worse. Their critics return the compliment. Why should they waste time considering the ideas of fascists, war criminals, revisionists (or other lackeys of monopoly capitalism), or burned-out cases whose minds were paralyzed in Cold War postures twenty years ago? Many a syllogism is disposed of by labeling its author a communist, a member of the Establishment, a radical, a conservative, a chauvinist, or—the ultimate pejorative, apparently, —a liberal.

Contemplating our national priorities, I can think of nothing we need more urgently than a genuine debate about the ends and means of foreign policy. Until we come much closer to agreement on this primal question, we shall have little opportunity to deal with the others.

My hope for this book is that it will help to stir up such a debate. Its theme is the relationship of ideas and events affecting the possibility of peace. In method it is both an analysis and a memoir. The core of the book is an assessment of the main positions I have been able to identify in the literature about peace—a critical taxonomy of the alternatives in foreign policy, classified by major premise. But the argument is illustrated by personal recollections as well as academic judgments.

I have been interested in the problem of peace since my student days, when I began to understand that, like our fathers, we faced the probability of war. Looking back, I realize that I have never stopped reading and writing about the subject, however great the press of other interests. This preoccupation has led me into the foreign-affairs bureaucracy three times—once in the Secretariat of the United Nations and twice in our government. Inevitably this book will draw on my experience as a practitioner, and particularly on my clinical adventures during the last two and a half years of President Johnson's term.

My job in the Johnson Administration was Undersecretary of State for Political Affairs, the third position in the State Department. The post had been established for Will Clayton in recognition of his high specific gravity.

During my tour of duty Nicholas Katzenbach was "the" Undersecretary of State. He is an old friend and former colleague at Yale, who came to the State Department from the attorney generalship. "The" Undersecretary of State has major administrative responsibilities and many policy assignments as well. The incumbent of the undersecretaryship I held is regarded as a roving halfback and given a variety of duties, depending upon his interests, and the issues that happen to require attention at the political level (for a day, a week, or a year or two, as the case may be) during his period in office.

Under the statute the holder of the post could be designated either Undersecretary of State for Political or for Economic Affairs. While I was asked to supervise the economic activities of the Department, I chose the more political title because I thought the main economic problems we faced in 1966—the monetary and trade policy issues implicit in our complex relationships with Europe and Japan—were essentially political in character and could only be handled effectively by an officer who also had departmental responsibility for our NATO policy, for nuclear issues, troop levels, and other matters of that kind. In addition to these topics my ongoing agenda included economic-assistance programs, particularly those for India, Indonesia, and Pakistan; the Middle Eastern crisis; chairmanship of an Interdepartmental Task Force on Telecommunications policy; and some of the melancholy and abortive "peace" initiatives for Vietnam.

Like other veterans of President Johnson's embattled administration, I have thought a good deal about what went wrong— about what Johnson could have done or should have done differently to prevent the tragic division of the United States, and of the Western world, over Vietnam. Hindsight offers a few clues, of course, about alternatives, or at least about tactical alternatives, that seem plausible in retrospect.

It seems obvious that as a military operation the campaign in Vietnam was for a long time misconceived, despite the superb morale and generally superb performance of the troops under conditions of excruciating physical and psychological difficulty. Error in the higher direction of a war is hardly an unusual situation in military history, nor one that admits of ready remedies. The war in Vietnam was a new kind of war, at least for this generation of the American military. Of course guerrilla warfare is difficult to suppress, and of course the campaign in Vietnam presented daunting strategic, tactical, and political problems. But such problems are never insoluble. It would surely have been better if Johnson had followed Lincoln's example and dismissed generals and defense officials until he found men as good as Stanton, Welles, Grant, and Sherman. General Marshall used to say that his most important service to the United States was his work as Deputy Chief of Staff during the thirties, when he purged the list of officers in anticipation of war. It was a painful task, he re-marked, which would have been nearly impossible if he had been a West Point graduate. As a result, however, our fighting forces during World War II had fewer colonels and generals who had to be replaced in the field than was the case in any previous war.

There is much to be said for the theory that the heart of the trouble in Vietnam was purely military. In our preoccupation with "trends" and "social forces" as the building blocks of history we often forget the importance of military skill as an independent variable. France was not defeated in 1940 by her social divisions but by her own generals, and by the stupidity and weakness of her governors as war ministers. Israel has survived because her captains have been remarkable; the unity and devotion of the Israelis would not have been enough if they had been badly led. Without the brilliant achievement of General Ridgway, the outcome in Korea could well have been different. It may yet appear that General Abrams has played a comparable role in Vietnam.

When governments employ military force they ignore at their peril its inexorable predicate—victory—and the classical standards for wisdom in its use. In this perspective, measure is nearly as vital to success as professional artistry. Neither is so important as will. The uncertain trumpet cannot command.

But American policy in Vietnam, and American opinion about Vietnam, were hesitant and uncertain from the beginning. This, I think, and not the indifferent direction of the war effort alone, was the fatal flaw. For the hesitation in our minds—the hesitation in our political policy, and in our perception of the issue—had an effect also on our willingness to face the military problem as such, for all its thorniness.

I conclude, therefore, that in its main lines the tragedy could not have been avoided; that its causes lie deep in our history as a people, and in the sickening experience of the Western world with war and near war since 1914; and that there is only one way to seek a cure: the nation should re-examine the foundations of its foreign policy before its foreign policy destroys the nation.

When I spoke of what went wrong with Johnson's foreign policy I did not mean to suggest that it failed as a matter of substance or of historical insight. In my view Johnson's conduct of our foreign relations ranks with Truman's. Neither my imagination nor my lexicon reaches much farther into the high register. Both men made important mistakes, but their right decisions outweigh their errors, and by a great deal.

But foreign policy was nonetheless their nemesis. Naturally both Truman and Johnson had troubles other than Korea and Vietnam. But they were trivial in comparison. I believe that Korea and Vietnam were the decisive causes of their political failure. Foreign policy wrecked their political careers, weakened their party, and perhaps weakened the presidency as well.

Johnson's tragedy, like Truman's, was that his foreign policy revived a division within the country—an intellectual and emotional division so intense as to make the President's withdrawal from politics a desirable step toward national reconciliation. Thus Truman stepped down in March 1952, before the storm over Korea, as Johnson did sixteen years later, before the storm over Vietnam. In each case, I am convinced, the President could have had his party's nomination for a second full term.

President Nixon has been enmeshed since 1969 in the same conflict between what he sees as inescapable, in his daily struggle with the cables, and the public yearning for relief from the troubles of the world. Making a virtue of necessity, he has stated the problem as a matter of principle. He will do what has to be done, he has said, even if it means being a one-term President.

We ought not to put our Presidents to such a test. After all, some of them might not meet it. There is something unnatural in expecting a politician to take positions that will surely harm his own political interests and perhaps hasten his retirement. And it is dangerous to run a government on the assumption that our Presidents will invariably elect the heroic course, come what may.

But there are reasons against the practice beyond those of elementary fairness and prudence.

The destruction of an American President is hardly a minor ripple in the stream of history. Johnson's reputation will doubtless recover, as Truman's did. My concern here is not with justice to reputations, but with the impact of the fate of these two Presidents on the pattern of the future. Together the experiences of Truman and of Johnson pose a fateful question about the condition of the American mind: Must an American President expect to walk the plank if his administration follows the kind of policy the United States followed in Korea under Truman, and in Vietnam under Johnson?

Abroad the question creates doubts, hopes, and anxieties which are fundamental to each nation's foreign policy. What will America do, and what will it not do, to protect its own security and those whose security is bound up with its own? What can people count on as fixed points in the spectrum?

At home the question measures tension in the mind of every President—and every other American politician and bureaucrat—when there is conflict between what he regards as the imperatives of national security and the glittering appeal of his own career. Against the background of these events any American President will use force, or threaten its use, most reluctantly, and only when he believes—rightly or wrongly—that his duty to the nation absolutely requires such action.

This constellation of doubt and tension is in itself a major causal factor in world affairs. The history of our tragic and brutal century is a chronicle of miscalculation about intent. In 1914 the leaders of Wilhelmine Germany thought Britain would not fight for Belgium, and would be a negligible—a "contemptible"—military force if it did; and they were confident America would never enter the war. Hitler fell into the same traps. Those who planned and initiated hostilities in Korea believed that the United States, which had just withdrawn its forces from South Korea, would not resist the take-over of that country by force. And it is reasonable to suppose that the men who made the comparable decisions in Vietnam gave far too much weight to the popular American slogan of the times, "No more Koreas."

That slogan dominated the electoral campaign of 1952. But a few years later President Eisenhower, with the full support of Congress, entered into a series of treaties and other commitments putting the military power of the United States behind the security of many countries and regions of the world threatened by Soviet or Chinese or (later on) by Cuban policies of expansion, or by policies of expansion supported by those countries. One of President Eisenhower's commitments was SEATO, the immediate source of our involvement in the bitter and difficult Vietnam campaign.

The election of 1968 was dominated in turn by the slogan "No more Vietnams." But in the spring of 1970 President Nixon attacked hostile bases in Cambodia, and later in that year convincingly intervened in the Jordanian crisis by threatening the use of force.

In short, there is dissonance between what officials believe they have to do and widespread, perhaps even prevailing, views as to what American and Allied foreign policy ought to be. The tension between reality and public opinion, between the pattern of action and the pattern of thought, is much too great for safety in the United States, in Western Europe, and in most of the nations of the Commonwealth as well.

That tension is the subject matter of this book. After the ordeals of Korea and Vietnam, the United States and the Western world as a whole are re-examining the premises of their foreign policies —their notions about what foreign policy is for, and about what it can and should accomplish. A number of propositions are competing for support, ranging from the absolutism of the United Nations Charter, at one extreme, to the grim vision of Fortress America, Fortress Europe, and Fortress Japan at the other.

In the light of events, the problems of choice among the competing theories of foreign policy raise difficult and novel questions, for which I offer no dogmatic answers. I am convinced, however, that there is little hope for peace unless they are faced, and weighed, for what they are. What is fundamental in this array of competing theories, to my way of thinking, is the bundle of questions about how to organize international society—questions about the structure of that society and about the ideas that should govern its patterns of behavior. As I define the word, these are problems of "law."

This cycle of questions suggests another, still more fundamental. What forces in society and what aspects of man's personality have made war and near war so notable a feature of the human condition in this century, as compared with the last one? What repressed impulses have been released, what social, political, and psychic controls dissolved, to produce the horrifying roster of mankind's experience with violence and tyranny during the last sixty years?

There is an outcry about foreign policy in the United States, exacerbated by the cost and anguish of the war in Vietnam. Wherever one goes men talk vehemently of a "new" foreign policy that could liberate us from the burdens we have had to bear since 1945. There must be something wrong with the idea of small wars to prevent big ones, they say, if it produces consequences as ghastly as the campaigns in Korea and Vietnam. Many Americans are frustrated and resentful, convinced that there must be a magic formula, a program not yet tried, that would permit us to bring the boys home, and return to "normalcy."

In Europe and in other parts of the world the words are different, but the music is the same. There is deep and often bitter dissatisfaction with the condition of international politics, and a certainty that if only the United States were not so stupid, so stubborn, so naïve about international problems, so much the prisoner of Cold War illusions, peace would prevail, NATO and other expensive rituals could be abandoned, and men could concentrate, as they should, on the happy pursuit of progress, culture, and the arts of leisure.

There is much in this protest to recall A. J. P. Taylor's brilliant, funny, and heartbreaking books, *The Trouble Makers.* I came upon it as I was finishing this manuscript. Its theme is closely related to mine. *The Trouble Makers* is a compassionate account of the arguments against the official foreign policy advanced by some of the finest spirits in British life since the time of Fox. Every chapter echoes themes one meets today in modern dress: the demand that England intervene abroad to right every wrong and unseat every tyrant, coupled with stern injunctions to remain aloof and isolated; the contention that England's safety required no more than naval supremacy, coupled with an adamant refusal to vote naval appropriations; vehement objections to alliance with undemocratic governments, coupled with silence or a reversal of positions when the balance of power was really threatened and association with undemocratic governments became important in preventing a war or winning it; and above all, the curious psychological quirk that has led generation after generation of English dissenters and radicals to blame Britain, and excuse her enemies, for every crisis of modern history. Even when they were right, Taylor shows, these paragons of decency and virtue were in nearly every case right for the wrong reasons. The debate of the thirties is the climax of Taylor's book. It is still difficult to believe that well-meaning and intelligent men were so obtuse. In the echoing sentence of Sir Denis Brogan, "Innocence is not enough."

After examining the literature of protest and experiencing its impact at first hand, both as an official and as a civilian, my conclusion is that the outcry is for the most part about the state of the world, and not about the state of American foreign policy. There is no magic formula, no hiding place, no easy option. The American government under five Presidents has made mistakes since World War II, including several major mistakes. But it has been on the right track. In my view it has had no real alternative to the general course it has pursued. While it should be possible to achieve improvements in the execution of policy through more sophisticated military and political tactics, and a more equitable sharing of the burden among the Allies, I cannot discover a new theory for our foreign policy that could assure us security without tears.

A few of the dissenting and radical critics of American foreign policy do offer genuine alternatives to the approach that has been followed: the pacifists, for example; the true isolationists; those who favor all-out ideological war to extirpate the heresy of communism; and those who in fact believe that the goal of the foreign policy of the United States should be not peace but the sword of "revolution," especially in the Third World, and, for some, in the United States itself. These views apart, however, I submit that the remaining critics have failed to define an alternative foreign policy. Their vocabulary is different from that of Dean Rusk and Henry Kissinger. Their books ring with eloquent and scathing denunciations of nearly all that has been done since 1945. Many who claim they are proposing a new policy are simply expressing the impatient restlessness of the young, their perennial—and altogether normal—eagerness to take over control from those presently in charge. Of course to them their own policy *is* new.

When one reads the fine print and puts aside the rhetoric, however, the literature divides itself into two classes. Some writers never succeed in articulating a coherent policy at all. The others, for all their anger, turn out to be advocating in fact the same policies that have been pursued since World War II—the patient, costly efforts to organize coalitions that could achieve a balance of power in world politics, and a system of peace at least partially consonant with the Charter of the United Nations—a system that could permit most independent nations to pursue their own political and social destinies without fear of international coercion.

It is tempting to conceal this somber conclusion in the costume of a new vocabulary, or at least to deck it out with a few novel words or phrases. It is difficult—perhaps it is impossible—for men to accept reality when it conflicts with ideas enshrined in their collective memory. Why not make the process easier by coating the pill a little and pretending that there really is something new and less disagreeable that could be done?

There is a reason for avoiding this course beyond that of personal preference. The problem of peace is a very old problem, integral to the study of the social process. It has been analyzed in comparable terms by the greatest minds in the history of human thought. There is nothing to be gained, and everything to be lost, by pretending that millennial difficulties in controlling the abuse of power can be solved by waving a wand or reciting a few sacred words.

For the society of nations, as for any other society, peace is not the automatic by-product of natural forces, but an achievement of law. By "peace" I do not mean the peace of the cemetery; or the wary silences of life in the First Circle; or a Roman peace, enforced by the will of a single ruler. This book is addressed to the possibility of peace in the world we know—a world of nation-states that have endured a certain history and are governed by certain habits and certain ideas. In this world, the world of reality, there will be anarchy, or rule by fear alone, unless an accepted system of law maintains a wide dispersal of authority and effective restraints on the use of force. Nations can be independent, just as men can be free, only if they are protected against the risk of domination by an overwhelming concentration of power. Procedures to safeguard the autonomy of nations and to promote justice among them, like the comparable procedures of municipal law within a society, can be expected to flourish only if the state system has a structure compatible with peace, and ordered by shared ideas about the limits of rivalry. Unless these conditions are met, men will cry peace, but peace will not be imposed upon the turbulence of history, and upon man's propensity for violence.

If I am right, or half right, in this bleak view, it follows that we should examine the issues in the debate about foreign policy as dispassionately, and as analytically, as our temperaments permit. For I remain of the conviction, despite ten years as a university administrator and six in the American government and the United Nations, that reason should be an important source of policy. In my opinion most of the really catastrophic errors of our recent experience have been intellectual errors—errors of theory and of analysis, not errors of intention, of arrogance, or even of pride.

If this be rationalism in a romantic age, the reader is duly warned.

But a disciplined intellectual examination of reality is our most acute need. In much of the literature about peace there is a disquieting mood of revolt against reason itself, a turning inward, a disinclination to consider the possibility of trouble ahead. Men have renewed their skill in resisting bad news. In many ways the moral and intellectual climate recalls that of the decade before 1914 and of the thirties, when general opinion refused to recognize the super-obvious danger of war until it was too late to do anything but fight. Far too often one is reminded of Ionesco's vision of hell in *The Rhinoceros*, where decent men, one after another, begin to eat geranium leaves, and turn into the obedient beasts of mass tyranny.

The American temperament resists the acknowledgment of

error. We like to think that success is our hallmark. My colleague C. Vann Woodward recently made American failure the theme of a series of public lectures. Reconstruction was his subject. In that titanic effort, he argued, the nation failed. It is good for us, he contended, good for our characters, good for our tendency to the sin of pride, to realize that we, too, can fail.

Woodward is surely right. And his moral applies at least as much to the study of our foreign policy as it does to the history of our domestic affairs. Some of the finest and strongest men our culture has produced—Charles Evans Hughes and Henry L. Stimson, as Secretaries of State, and Franklin D. Roosevelt, as President, to take only the spectacular examples—misjudged the course of world politics and the nature of our stake in it. They could have prevented the Second World War and all that flowed from it. But they did not do so.

Foreign policy, after all, can be the nemesis for interests more serious than reputations and careers.

This book originated in a talk given at Dartmouth College in the spring of 1969, when I had the honor of delivering the Harold J. Tobin Memorial Lecture under the sponsorship of the International Relations Program and the Department of Government. I am indebted to my hosts on that lively occasion, Professor Richard W. Sterling and several students whose names are unavailable, to my regret, either in my memory or in my files and those of Dartmouth College. I am sorry for this lapse, for the student officers who presided at the meetings did yeoman work with courtesy and aplomb, and led a discussion I found interesting, informative, and spirited. Articles drawn from the manuscript have appeared in the October 1970 issue of *Affari Esteri*, of Rome; in the *Proceedings of the American Society of International Law* for September 1970; in the April 1971 numbers of *International Affairs*, *Esquire*, and *The Round Table;* in the September 1971 issue of *Art International;* in *The New York Times Magazine* for April 23, 1972; and in the *Texas Law Review* for May 1972.

I tested and developed the argument of these pages in the purifying crucible of domestic conversation, where my wife and children—and several loyal and long-suffering friends—contributed immeasurably to its substance and tone, and sought valiantly, if not always successfully, to save me from error; in talks with many Yale law students, after my return there in January 1969, and especially with H. F. Shattuck and Stephen Cohen, who read and thoughtfully criticized an early draft, and with F. M. Kail, who commented on a later one; and, during the fall of 1970 in lectures and discussions at Oxford, where I was the George Eastman Visiting Professor for 1970–71. I particularly thank Carroll Kilpatrick, who carefully criticized a full draft; W. Averell Harriman, George F. Kennan, and John M. Blum, who performed the same service for Chapter 4; and Michael Howard, with whom I shared a bracing seminar at Oxford and many probing and helpful conversations on these themes. I owe special appreciation to William Whitworth, an exemplary journalist, whose fair and probing —and far from "naive"—questions helped me to understand many doubts and anxieties about foreign policy; and to John Fischer, who first urged me to turn my Dartmouth lecture into this book, and to Edward Buckingham, who helped check and recheck the text.

My intention here was to start where *Law, Power, and the Pursuit of Peace* (1968) finished. But it has not proved possible to avoid some duplication. I apologize to any reader who may be inconvenienced or annoyed.

E.V.R.

*New Haven, Connecticut; Peru, Vermont;*
*Balliol College, Oxford; Chateau d'Hodoumont, Belgium.*
*January 15, 1972.*

*Peace in the Balance*

# I

## *In Search of a Major Premise*

WHEN THE DELEGATES assembled in San Francisco to draft the
charter of the United Nations in 1945 their minds were dominated by visions that have suddenly lost their power to command.

The figure of Emperor Haile Selassie stood reproachfully before them, as he had stood in the palace of the League of Nations
ten years earlier asking in vain for help against Mussolini's aggression. With equal shame, they remembered China, which had also
met silence when it besought the League to stop Japan. If the
world had acted promptly, and in concert, would Japan have conquered Manchuria, and gone on to wage general war against
China, and then against others? Would Italy have attacked harm-
less Ethiopia, an ancient nation then hardly touched by the twentieth century? Would Germany and Italy have made war against
Spain by sending arms and men to support Franco's revolution?
Would the Rhineland have been occupied, Austria and Czechoslovakia invaded? In short, could the drive toward war have been
stopped earlier, before its momentum became irresistible?

To the men of 1945 the answer to these questions seemed self-
evident.

The theme of the first volume of Churchill's memoirs was "The
Unnecessary War." The war could have been prevented, Church-

ill argued, if Britain and France had taken Churchillian measures against aggression, firm and bold, and above all, in good time. Britain and France were certain then that Churchill had been right, and Baldwin and Chamberlain wrong. If only they had had the will to use force, they thought, or convincingly to threaten the use of force, in 1933, 1935, 1936, or 1938, while they still had military superiority, the tragedy could have been averted—and averted, moreover, by their efforts alone, without stirring either the American or the Russian giant from its cave.

By 1945 most Americans had grimly concluded that it was more dangerous for the United States to stay out of world politics than to participate in them. The United States had been dragged most unwillingly into the whirlpool of two great wars. The experience convinced America that it could no longer escape into isolation. Americans felt a sense of guilt about their refusal to follow President Wilson's advice after World War I. That austere and prophetic figure had urged his people to join the League of Nations and enter into a security treaty with France. To most Americans in 1945 it seemed obvious that they should have done so, and played an active and responsible part in the effort to preserve and consolidate the peace by political means. In the mutation of American foreign policy after World War II there was an element of penance to President Wilson's ghost.

Shaped by these convictions, the Charter of the United Nations asserted again the principle of the Covenant of the League and of the Kellogg-Briand Pact—that war be outlawed as an instrument of national policy, save for ancient rights of self-defense and assistance to those who are exercising their right of self-defense.[1] Indeed, the Charter went further. It condemns "force," not "armed force" alone. The men of 1945 stated the idea as a rule of law. They decreed not only that international society should be organized on the rock of this commandment but that it already

[1] The Charter also contemplates the use of force not as an instrument of national policy alone but pursuant to the authorization of competent organs of the United Nations, and pursuant also to decisions of regional organizations, although there is grave doubt whether regional organizations should be deemed to have broader authority than that of self-defense.

was so organized. And they underlined the finality of their view in some of the rulings of the Nuremberg tribunals.

The aspirations of the Charter were addressed to an international society built on quite different lines. The state system as it emerged from the holocaust in 1945 was the product of a history ruled by ideas, experiences, conditioned reflexes, memories, and fears quite alien to the clear prescriptions of the Charter. In Franck's words, "The United Nations Charter . . . bears little more resemblance to the modern world than does a Magellan map." [2]

The state system had gone through catastrophic convulsions since 1914. Societies had been weakened, and the self-confidence of their governors impaired, by the ghastly slaughter of the two wars; by the release of taboos against violence those wars had accomplished; and by the specter of the brutal tyrannies that had emerged in the wake of war.

The Concert of Europe had kept the general peace reasonably well for a century before 1914. By 1945 it had vanished even as an idea. The continental societies were exhausted by defeat, occupation, or the fear of the unmentionable in themselves. They had perforce to concentrate on recovery and moral rebirth. Britain was almost equally exhausted by victory. She found herself a medium-sized nation among very large ones. With the empire in liquidation and America in the wings, Britain wondered why she should continue to bear the costs and burdens of an imperial role.

The withdrawal of Europe from empire was a general trend affecting all the empires, save only the Russian and the Portuguese. As Bernard Lewis has remarked, "The so-called 'liberal imperialism' of Great Britain" (and he could have added, mutatis mutandis, that of France, Belgium, and the Netherlands as well) had "unnerved its servants, encouraged its opponents, and organized its own decline and fall." [3] The result was the emergence of

---

[2] T. M. Franck, "Who Killed Article 2(4)?," 64 *Am. J. Int. Law* 809, 810 (1970). See also Louis Henkin, "The Reports of the Death of Article 2(4) Are Greatly Exaggerated," 65 *Am. J. Int. Law* 544 (1971).

[3] "Russia in the Middle East," *Round Table*, No. 238 (July 1970), p. 257, at p. 263.

many new nations, each eager to master the secrets of modern wealth, nearly all vulnerable to take-over from within or without.

While these related processes were occurring, often under conditions of sustained turbulence, communist movements surged forward to bid for power, as they did after the First World War. But on this occasion their efforts were supported by the arms, prestige, and will of the Soviet Union, and later of China and Cuba as well. The Communist party of Lenin had conquered power in defeated and disorganized Russia in 1917. Now parties calling themselves Communist controlled other nations and asserted their ambitions in many parts of the globe. From the moment the war ended—indeed, well before the end of the war—the Soviet Union sought to establish political and military control not only in a cordon sanitaire around its borders but in more and more distant places, far from its marches. And, in order not to compromise its political freedom to pursue a policy of expansion, it rejected both the Baruch Plan for the international control of atomic energy and two formal American offers of economic assistance and cooperation: the first under the Lend-Lease Act, made during the war; the second, that of the Marshall Plan, in 1947. As Professor Lewis comments, Soviet leadership in this generation seems to have "the appetite, ferocity, smugness and sense of mission which are the essential components of the imperial mood, and which in the West have given way to satiety, guilt, and doubt." [4]

To these vast flows of change the United States, the nations of Western Europe, and Japan reacted first with concern and then with fear. When it became clear that the promises of Yalta and Potsdam about Eastern Europe would not be kept—after the threats to Iran and Turkey, the stronger pressures in Greece and Berlin, and the coup d'état of 1948 in Czechoslovakia—the conviction emerged that communist expansion had to be stopped in Europe and in Asia; that it could be stopped by the United States, hopefully in alliance with Europe and Japan, and indeed with other like-minded nations, as soon as such action became feasible

[4] Ibid.

for them; and that after a period of "containment" the communist countries would come to accept the logic of "détente" and "peaceful coexistence," so that mankind could beat its swords into plowshares and live according to the rules of the United Nations Charter. The symbolic meaning of this policy was underscored by the presence of Ethiopian troops in Korea: in the Korean case, men thought, the international community was doing what it should have done when Italy invaded Ethiopia in 1935.

Was there any hope then, is there any hope now that the Charter could be made to dominate the habits, memories, and processes of history, and the ancient prerogatives of the nation-state?

The prescriptions of the Charter had their own roots in the history of international affairs, particularly in the history of the nineteenth century. The system of Concert and Congress launched at Vienna in 1815 was the immediate ancestor both of the League and of the United Nations.

The European system that was given institutional shape in Vienna was something new in political history—a set of habits, and a set of procedures, which worked pretty well for nearly a century to harmonize the policies of the European states, and to avoid major war. Men differed as to whether its goal was to prevent war, or revolution, or both; to protect legitimacy; to organize the conditions of peaceful change, or to suppress them. The system collapsed finally under the pressures of epidemic nationalism, and especially German nationalism. Even the victors at Waterloo could not long suppress the national principle given so much momentum by the wars of the Napoleonic epoch. Prussia became Germany, and Piedmont Italy, through a series of little wars; Austria became a shell. When ultimate crisis came, the leaders of the system lacked the insight or the vitality to restrain Wilhelm, who, unlike Bismarck, sought victories incompatible with the general peace.

The dominant idea of nineteenth-century diplomacy was the balance of power, as it was in the eighteenth century, but the balance of power with a difference.

In the eighteenth century men thought that every nation had an equal interest in achieving and preserving a balance of power. In such an environment each could feel reasonably secure against the risk of rule by foreigners. In planning its policies each state would have to take the reaction of its fellows into account. Any move toward hegemony by one nation would call into being a coalition of the others to frustrate a trend that would inevitably menace them.

The principle of the eighteenth-century balance of power remained altogether valid to the minds that directed the Congress of Vienna. But the procedures of the eighteenth century—its hidden harmony of uncoordinated responses—had failed to prevent the conquests of Napoleon. Therefore the Concert of Europe no longer relied for efficient counterweights only on the parallel and automatic responses of nations to danger. The diplomacy of relatively frequent congresses; the recognition of a special responsibility for the general peace lodged in the large states; the insistence on seeking peaceful methods for resolving disputes before force was used; the practice of mobilizing the diplomatic influence of the entire community to prevent too strong a swing in any one direction—such were the ideas and experiences that later became the background of the League of Nations and the United Nations.

These principles constituted a force for restraint in the relations among states as customs, or "rules," more and more generally accepted as right. They were not, of course, universally effective. In the shadow of Vienna the conjuncture of powerful threat with weak and uncertain response proved to be quite as disastrous as the failures of eighteenth-century methods. Thus Wilhelm II and Hitler defied the rules of Vienna by undertaking to master Europe. While NATO was established in time to deter the Soviet Union from seeking the same goal by the same means, it remains to be seen whether the Western powers have the insight and will to persevere in their course.

Thus far, however, these ideas represent all men have dared or wished to accept, or deemed it feasible to articulate as hopes for a political system of nation-states. In broad terms, they are the principal elements of the ideal of peace with which world politics has struggled since 1815. It is a limited ideal. Its terms are that each nation should accept a restraint on its sovereign freedom to make war at will against its neighbors, without, however, qualifying its freedom for internal self-government. A great coalition fought twice since 1815 to prevent Europe from being unified under German control, and it has threatened to fight again to prevent the same result from being achieved by the Soviet Union. A Napoleonic solution for Europe, and for the world, could perhaps solve the problem of international war for a time, but at the cost of making the nations conquered provinces of a new Caesar. International war would then be renamed civil war. That is not an ideal for the future of international law and politics that I can bring myself to regard as necessary, desirable, or inevitable.

The system that evolved from the Congress of Vienna posited the notion that the international community, acting through its stronger members, should maintain a balance of world power and, through changing coalitions, enforce minimal rules of public order. The dominating idea of the system was that the collectivity would ensure all states their right to survive, and guarantee them also against the risk of a new Napoleon, a hegemonial power that would threaten their autonomy. Its chief methods were persuasion, diplomacy, consultation, conference, and compromise, reinforced by the occasional and limited use of force. That system had many shortcomings and blind spots, above all in the dynamics of colonial rivalry. But on the eve of the First World War, as Dr. Ian Brownlie points out, the world "had more of the attributes of a community of states than at any previous period." [5] The influence of shared principles was felt in the political life of the world community, stressing the idea that force should be viewed as the ultimate recourse of states, confined to situations of self-defense, and used only after peaceful modes of settlement had failed.

When Wilhelm II and his advisers broke the rules of the Concert of Europe they destroyed a network of habits that could well

[5] *International Law and the Use of Force by States* (1963), p. 49.

33

be described as a system of law. The political leaders of the fateful decades before both world wars, most particularly in Britain, failed in their responsibilities for peace. Thus far men have been unable to bring order out of the chaos the prewar leaders did not prevent, and establish a new system of peace nearly as effective as the one those men allowed to be destroyed. In their efforts, however, they have been guided by the set of ideas about peace which has evolved since 1815 and was codified in an ideal form by the Charter of the United Nations.

The Charter did not assume that men were angels. It contemplated the possibility that its rules might not soon become the effective law of the international community. It made provision for regional security arrangements, and reaffirmed rights of individual and collective self-defense. These provisions would be needed only when permanent members of the Security Council disagreed about the enforcement of the Charter by the Security Council as the preferred method for keeping the peace. When the great powers are divided, the Charter does not lapse or become inoperative. But it can then be enforced only by the methods of Vienna—by the action of a single nation, or by the formation of coalitions of nations, to counter the threat or the fact of aggression deemed substantially to imperil the equilibrium of peace. In either situation, balance of power diplomacy is not an alternative to the rule of the Charter, but the only available means to achieve its goals.

In facing the phenomenon of war after 1945 the Western nations soon acknowledged an exception to the nominal universality of the Charter. Save in the case of Yugoslavia, they made no attempt to enforce the Charter in behalf of the nations of Eastern Europe, which were tacitly acknowledged to be beyond their protection within a Soviet sphere of influence accepted as inevitable. Even in the period of American nuclear monopoly, the Western nations, striving for an understanding with the Soviet Union, were not disposed to insist on the Soviet promises made at Yalta and Potsdam about the political independence of the nations of Eastern Europe.

In instances of international coercion outside this area, however, the principle of the Charter was asserted to protect Iran, Greece, Turkey, Berlin, Korea, and South Vietnam. It was also invoked in some conflicts not directly involving communist states or communist proxies—namely, in the Suez crisis of 1956 and that of Kashmir in 1965.

Now a more general exception to the Charter is being claimed for situations like that of Spain in the thirties—situations (often described by the magic word "revolution") in which international assistance is given to insurrectionary forces within a state. In such instances the yearning for change challenges the Charter. The formal structure of the international state system is built on the principle that each state is autonomous and independent and has the right in its internal affairs to be free of international acts of coercion—that is, acts of coercion committed or assisted by other states. Such acts have always been considered acts of war. The rule is basic to the possibility of international law. It does not, of course, qualify the freedom of the inhabitants of any state to press for social or political change within that state by any means open to them. Indeed, coups d'état happen at the average rate of twice a month in international society today, and other forms of serious domestic turbulence are even more commonplace. But the rule codified in the Charter distinguishes internal processes of social change, whether democratic or violent, from the international use of force. What the Charter prohibits, with the sanction of the Nuremberg principle behind it, is aggression, not revolution. Article 2 of the Charter enjoins all members to settle their international disputes by peaceful means in such a manner that international peace and security, and justice, are not endangered, and to refrain in their international relations from the threat or use of force against the territorial integrity or political independence of any state.

The primary concern of the Charter, then, is international peace, not the internal affairs of member states. In the absence of compulsory procedures for accomplishing peaceful change, men heatedly claim the right to use international force to remedy what they regard as injustice enshrined in the pattern of history. Some popular sentiment supports the view. But, as Dr. Brownlie concludes, "there is even greater agreement and community of interest behind the proposition that, in the era of nuclear and thermonuclear armament, self-help involves intolerable risks." [6]

II

Since 1945 the men who have had responsibility for the policies of the American government have reacted to the condition of world politics in roughly the same ways. Whatever they thought, or said, or wrote before they entered the White House, they did very much the same kind of things while there. From Tehran and Yalta to Camp David, Glassboro, Warsaw, and beyond they have persistently sought understandings with the Soviet Union and with China; with equal persistence they have sought to deter and contain the expansion of Soviet and Chinese power beyond a point deemed threatening when understanding proved to be a will-o'-the-wisp.

There have been differences among the postwar Presidents, of course—differences of temperament, of ability, of style, and of luck. Some had a keener insight and a better focused instinct for action than their fellows. Few reached the level of decisiveness of Truman when the Soviets sought to keep the Allies from Berlin. At a meeting of his Cabinet immediately after the Soviets initiated their blockade one of his colleagues wondered whether Berlin was really so important after all. Truman remarked sharply that that was not the issue before him. The only question, he said, was whether we supplied Berlin by ground transport or by air.

But for all the differences among the five Presidents since 1945, the pattern of American action has been remarkably consistent and clear.

Policy was explained in a bewildering variety of ways. The

[6] Id., p. 436. The finest modern analysis of the law governing the use of force by states is M. S. McDougal and F. P. Feliciano, *Law and Minimum World Public Order* (1961). It reaches the same conclusion Brownlie does, pp. 190–196.

spokesmen of American policy talked of protecting freedom and democracy; of "containing" (or indeed of "rolling back") Communism, or the expansion of the Soviet Union, or of China, or Cuba; of demonstrating that aggression would not be tolerated; or promoting or assisting social progress; of insisting on respect for the United States, or even on respect for the presidency. They spoke as well of even more intangible goals—the "mission" of great powers, for example.

But the code of what in fact they did corresponds to no such rule. The United States and its allies did not become the universal policemen of the Charter. There has been no anticommunist crusade, no ideological opposition to "Communism" or "revolution" as such, no "globalism"—whatever that may mean. Many acts of aggression were ignored. Help was given to some states—Iran and Yugoslavia—that were not democracies; and some democracies—Czechoslovakia, for example—were abandoned to their fates. No serious attempt was made after 1945 to unseat Communist regimes in Russia, China, Eastern Europe, or indeed even in Cuba (where the foray of the Bay of Pigs was halfhearted, to say the least), or otherwise to remake the world in the American or the Western image. American policy did not bespeak the arrogance of power, nor yet hegemonic ambition. It was—and is—guided by a nonideological, nonimperialist, and manageable concept of the national interest.

Military power was used, or its use threatened, by the United States mainly to prevent an extension of Soviet, Chinese, or Cuban control through the international use of force. The threat of force has also been employed to deter international attacks on the territorial integrity and political independence of Middle Eastern states in a sensitive area of great importance both in itself and in relation to the security of Europe. When Communists came to power through elections, as in Chile, or through what seemed to be a purely internal coup d'état, as in Cuba, the United States was prevented by its own conception of the law from taking effective countermeasures. And cognate forces within the national mind prevented the effective diplomatic use of nuclear power as a threat in any of the situations of conventional war or near war since 1945, even during the period of American nuclear monopoly.

Thus far in the postwar period, then, and at great cost, the United States and its allies have almost instinctively followed a line of policy as old as the history of international affairs. They have used force, or threatened its use, in order to achieve and preserve a balance of power in the world, and the reciprocal acceptance of rules of restraint in the conduct of international conflict. In taking such action, each American President knew he would lose votes and alienate support. The only political question in his mind was how much support he would have to jettison in order to do what he thought had to be done. For public opinion, the source of authority in a free society, has been dubious and uncertain about American foreign policy since 1947, and sometimes hostile. And when foreign policy has involved the use of force or the threat of force, large segments of opinion have turned very hostile indeed.

American policy will not be credible, either to friendly countries or to the other kind, until the American people come much closer to agreement on the nature of their national interest in world politics and on what they should do to protect that interest. The same proposition holds for many other nations that have been protected by American power for twenty-five years and are still reluctant, despite their recovery, to take a proportionate share of responsibility for their own safety.

The American language has not yet achieved a vocabulary for explaining the nature of international society and defining America's security interest in its affairs. For all practical purposes the United States developed without a foreign policy for the century before 1914. In that period the nation was relatively safe within a worldwide system of order organized and maintained by the nations of Europe. There was no occasion to establish an American vocabulary about foreign policy. In the tradition of John Bright, Cobden, and Gladstone, Americans habitually use the language of evangelism in talking about the problem of power.[7] As President

[7] See A. J. P. Taylor, *The Trouble Makers* (1957).

Johnson once wrote of America's entry into the First World War, "Our slogans rallied the nation to fight tyranny and make the world safe for democracy. But we were really fighting to protect a national interest most Americans at that time did not understand—our interest in the balance of power."[8]

After Yalta, President Roosevelt told Congress that the United Nations would provide an alternative to "the system of unilateral action, the exclusive alliances, the balances of power, and all the other expedients that have been tried for centuries—and have always failed." His own confusion on this fundamental problem was a tragic flaw in his perception of world politics, and in the policies he pursued.

The problem of a rational and understood vocabulary for analyzing the problem of peace is not peculiar to the United States. As Michael Howard has acutely remarked, "The flower of British and French manhood had not flocked to the colours in 1914 to die for the balance of power."[9] Their passions were engaged by the poetry of patriotism, not the cool calculus of political theory, or the cooler principles of international law. Even Thomas Mann saw the First World War as a heroic, splendid affair, a worthy war of the European peoples.

Since 1945 Americans have tried to develop a rational foreign policy without benefit of an accepted intellectual foundation for such a policy. They were not clear about the forces in world politics that made it impossible for them to revert to isolation in 1945, as they did in 1919. Nor was there clarity, either, about how much American participation in world affairs was required by a policy of not being isolated. But there was then, and I believe there still is, a tenacious, if inarticulate and instinctive, majority opinion in America in favor of engaging in international politics sufficiently to minimize the risk of general war. The source of that opinion is the conviction, underlined by the events of 1917 and 1941, that when the pillars of the familiar world crumble, there is no way for a large nation to avoid involvement.

[8] *Encyclopaedia Britannica Book of the Year* (1969), p. 19.
[9] *Studies in War and Peace* (1970), p. 105.

What does that conviction imply? Is it in the national interest of the United States to rally a coalition that could insist on the full enforcement of the Charter provisions against war, or the use or threat of force more generally? Or, in an imperfect world, not yet worthy of the Charter, does the American national interest require something less—opposition to some but not all international acts of force that violate Article 2, Section 4 of the Charter?

If the second approach is chosen, should the United States and its allies regard themselves as bound by the rules of the Charter against the use of force? Manifestly, it could be suicidal to conduct international life for long on the basis of two sets of rules—those of the Charter for one group of countries, and those of the jungle for the others.

If the national interest of the United States requires only limited opposition to aggression, how should we decide which countries to help and which to abandon? Should the United States protect only great centers of power and wealth such as Europe and Japan, in the interest of preserving a balance of ultimate power in the world? Only countries populated by white people who speak English? Only countries of a European population? Only "democracies," or near democracies, or countries seeking to become democracies? Could any such distinction be made, and then carried out as a practical matter, at least in instances of coercion where one of the centers of Communist power is involved, directly or indirectly? And if any such rule were to be formulated, would it leave the weaker nations naked before their enemies, exactly in the position of China in 1931, Ethiopia in 1935, and Spain between 1936 and 1939? Would such a policy release aggression from all restraint and allow it to become a tidal wave threatening to engulf the world, as it did in 1914–18 and 1939–45?

On the other hand, has the development of nuclear weapons transformed the problem of American national security? In a nuclear age, is concern for the balance of power obsolete and irrelevant, as some contend? Could America be safe at home, behind a nuclear shield, and wash its hands of the costly and often tragic problems of recent international life, like the security of Europe, the Middle East, Korea, Japan, and Vietnam?

III

The import of these questions was brought into focus for me by a conversation with a colleague after a seminar at Oxford during the winter of 1971. The seminar had examined the morality of Britain's decision to fight on in 1940. Taking into account the costs and consequences of five more years of war, one of the participants in the seminar had suggested that it would have been morally preferable for Britain to have made peace with Hitler after the fall of France and accepted German hegemony in Europe, in the hope that German power, following the scenario laid down in *Mein Kampf*, would then have been extended into Russia, the Middle East, Africa, and Asia, leaving Britain in peace. Is the human odiousness of Hitler's regime the critical factor in such a moral calculation? Or was the moral problem for Britain the same when the threat of hegemony was asserted by Napoleon in the name of the principles of the French Revolution, or by the Kaiser's Germany in 1914? Was it just and moral on all three occasions for Britain to fight for the balance of power—that is, for a system of international order within which the British could govern themselves without fear of coercion from abroad? Or was the morality of the British decision in 1940, at least in the moral universe of the modern world, decisively affected by the monstrous character of Hitler's philosophy and policy?

Most of the students and faculty members who took part in the seminar reacted to the question with feeling. The discussion was conducted at a level of instinct and intuition that could not be confined by the rules of a utilitarian approach to ethics—the prevailing theme of the seminar. That theory would make the greatest good for the greatest number the sole test for the moral rightness of an action. It would have required the British government in 1940 to base its decision—to fight on or to surrender—on an inconceivably precise estimate of costs and benefits rather than on

41

traits of the British character developed over two thousand years of shared experience. In the seminar, however, men and women asserted claims of moral rightness that had no basis in utilitarianism: the inherent rightness of fighting back when attacked or threatened; and equally absolute claims of an inherent right to fight against slavery and tyranny, and for the survival of the nation in its familiar pattern, without regard for costs. One could hear Churchill's growl in the room, and the pride of his sardonic comment, "Some chicken, some neck."

As we came away from the seminar a friend remarked, "In 1914 men felt the same way about war as they did in 1940. But wasn't the war in 1914 unjust?"

I commented that I thought it impossible to judge the moral rightness of an international war, as distinguished from an internal revolution, by the moral character of the regime one was opposing. Where would such a rule leave us before the spectacle of Stalin's Russia, or Haiti, or other tyrannies, past and present? Were Britain and the United States really under a moral obligation to root out all the regimes in the world some of us, or all of us, thought were unjust, or extremely unjust? The only moral consideration I could discover to justify ordering troops into battle was one of national interest in the preservation of peace.

"To put the problem in its most provocative form," I said, "I should contend that the idea of the balance of power is the only test for the justness of war, once one gets beyond cases of invasion."

"Ah," my friend replied, "but that idea assumes the possibility of war."

I fully agreed. "It does, of course. But is there an alternative? Can one rationally assume the impossibility of war?"

"Is there no way," he asked, "to get the nations to deal directly with that problem, perhaps after a period of peace, when they can all see their common interest in peace, and thus eliminate the possibility of war?"

"That's what they did, in effect," I replied, "in 1815, 1919, and

1945, after periods of experience with war, if not of peace. But the ideas of those settlements have not yet fully succeeded in controlling the aggressive impulses of man. What should we do in the meantime?"

# 2

# *The Great Debate:*
# *Parkinsonian Phases*

THE FURY OVER Korea and Vietnam, which destroyed Truman and Johnson, and the corresponding turbulence over Nixon's foreign policy reflect a prolonged and thus far inconclusive national effort to assess the problem of national security in the light of changes taking place in the structure and substance of world politics.

Perhaps the first modern stage in the process was the election of 1916. The decisive element in that close election was Wilson's campaign slogan, "He kept us out of war."

The repudiation of President Wilson after World War I constitutes the second. That swing of the pendulum lasted until the mid-thirties and was characterized by the complete victory of those who advocated a nearly hermetic return to the policies of the past. The United States government avoided even the appearance of contact with the League of Nations, as if the mild and inoffensive League were the source of a contagious illness that might sully American purity. The policy of total noncooperation with foreigners extended beyond the political realm. In the economic sphere we refused to work effectively with other nations,

44

either in clearing away the burden of war debts and reparations or in taking the steps of commercial and monetary policy that might have restored the integrated international economy of the pre-1914 period. The Smoot-Hawley Tariff of 1931 and the London Economic Conference of 1933 were landmarks of monumental folly on the road to war.

By 1935 or 1936, however, the emergence of Hitler and the warning bells of German, Italian, and Japanese policy began to arouse the nation about foreign policy again in a third cycle of troubled discussion. But, like Britain, the United States hesitated, and hesitated fatally, before the threat.

The fourth round swirled around President Truman's programs of reconstruction and deterrence in the Middle East and in Europe, and culminated in the opposition to his course in Korea. Henry Wallace ran for President in 1948, it should be recalled, in protest against the Marshall Plan and Truman's policy of preventing Soviet take-overs in Iran, Greece, and Turkey.

The American mind has been intermittently and inconclusively preoccupied with these problems since the turn of the century. At that time a few perceptive men began to warn their countrymen that the condition of world politics was changing and that we could not expect much longer to be able to live in isolation according to rules supposedly laid down by President Washington and Secretary of State John Quincy Adams. The men who made these arguments were dismissed as dreamers, visionaries, jingoes, or worse as the country clung to the attitudes toward foreign affairs on which it had long been nurtured. Our forefathers had come to America to escape the wars and the power politics of the Old World, hadn't they? So, like sleepwalkers, Americans chose to pursue their destiny on the continent in peace, unique among the nations, e pluribus unum, a beacon of progress and of proud isolation from the mean and selfish quarrels of the imperialists. They were convinced that America was safe whatever happened in the world, because the oceans were broad and her republican principles impeccable.

Such is the stuff of collective memory, which still dominates America's emotional approach to world affairs.

It is hardly a matter for wonder that the United States has had such a difficult time accepting the fact of change in the architecture of world politics. It takes extraordinary effort to accept reality when it is in conflict with cherished perceptions of oneself and of the external world, and when an acceptance of reality would require unpleasant and even dangerous exertions. It is much easier to hope that the problems we dimly and unwillingly perceive will go away.

Our dispersed educational system, ruled by the elective principle, has not helped Americans to resolve the conflict. It permits many students to graduate with little training, or none at all, in the hard questions of power and peace. The absence of a sense of history is the greatest single weakness of American education, and therefore in the American outlook toward foreign affairs. In recent years American education has probably fallen behind in providing students an opportunity to study the problems relevant to their responsibilities as American citizens in an unstable world. In this respect American education, and the American outlook, share the weaknesses of British thought during the last hundred and fifty years. Well-meaning Englishmen, trained to translate Horace at sight, were unprepared to protect their realm without enduring the agony of two world wars.

The press and television have not offset the shortcomings of American education and scholarship. Such a feat would be too much to expect even from the Lochinvars and Don Quixotes of the media. I went through six years of public service with undiminished faith in Jefferson's view of the importance of a free press to the success of democratic government. Abuses there are, of course, a good deal of laziness, and some confusion between the function of the press and the function of the government. Many of our pundits regard themselves as statesmen, not journalists. But they are products of the same education and experience which also formed the minds of politicians and bureaucrats. Save in exceptional cases, their insights cannot be expected to differ markedly from those of the men whose work they are reporting and criticizing.

Other people face comparable problems in reconciling reality to the stuff of their collective unconscious. The British and the French are living through difficult adjustments to the changed scale of world politics, and to the delineation of new roles and new responsibilities that flow from those changes. Germany, Italy, and Japan live with nightmares, never quite free of the fear that their lives might be engulfed once more by the black tides of the human spirit. Many of the new nations of the world are finding it hard to rid themselves of the psychological baggage of their colonial past. And the nations governed by Communist parties are being forced to weigh national concerns against ideological zeal in a world that since the time of Alexander and before has invariably destroyed those who sought universal sway for a creed, or prince, or power, whether of light or of darkness.

It is hardly surprising, therefore, that the ideas about foreign policy in competition for influence within the American mind are not theories of logical precision. It is probably undesirable, and in any event it is impossible to examine these problems as an exercise in pure reason. They are freighted with intense emotion—the risk of war, and of nuclear war, and the shame of having one's government identified with policies that are often labeled "militarist" and even "imperialist"—hard words for the descendants of George Washington.

Chapter 3 of this book sets out the rival theses about the goal of foreign policy abstractly, as if they were axioms of plane geometry. The five subsequent chapters discuss particular theories of protest in some detail. In this chapter I wish to review some of the more general features of the literature of dissent as a whole, and the psychological factors that determine its quality and its tone.

II

The literature of protest against American and Allied foreign policy fascinates an official—and even a former official—for large parts of it indulge in a game he cannot play. Many of those who criticize what the United States and its Allies have done since the war are expert in the modes of reasoning Parkinson described with his usual mastery in "Function of Folly," [1] where he distinguishes "skill," "folly," and "incompetence" from "ability," a quality always in short supply. He defines "ability" as the capacity to get things done, measured in large part by catastrophic events that do not take place.

Instead of proposing a feasible and peaceful solution for a situation of impending violence, for example, some of the protesters solemnly conclude, in the best Parkinsonian style, that we should have done something else ten, twenty, or even fifty years ago. "The Balfour Declaration was a great mistake," they say; "Stalin was a tyrant, and we never should have helped him against Hitler"; or "We should not have ratified the SEATO treaty" or made some other national commitment of the postwar period. These propositions may or may not have weight on the Day of Judgment. But they are hardly contributions to the decisions a President has to make every morning. Undoing a mistake is never as simple as avoiding it in the first place. And sometimes the mistakes of the past turn out to be irrevocable.

Nor can an official escape from the telegrams he has to answer by invoking the United Nations—a favorite and superbly Parkinsonian ploy for many critics of established policy. They write and speak as if the United Nations were a place apart, a separate sovereignty, something more than the code of the Charter, and a meeting place for diplomats, where peace-keeping is concerned.

That sentence does not disparage the United Nations. A respected legal code is an influence on behavior even when it is not always or completely obeyed. And the procedures of the United Nations generate powerful, if not always effective, pressures for peaceful compromise. As for peace-keeping, the United Nations was not intended to function as a peace-keeping agency when the great powers are seriously divided. Nor, usually, can the United Nations as such generate enough pressure to persuade one or an-

[1] C. Northcote Parkinson, *In-Laws & Outlaws* (1962), p. 96.

other of the nations involved in a quarrel that following the rule of the Charter is preferable to war. Under such circumstances it is not a mean or trivial function to be the place where Foreign Ministers must assemble at least once a year, and where comparatively senior diplomats are always available. But the United Nations was not conceived, and has not developed, as a substitute for the foreign policies of the powers, great and small. It is, rather, one of the forums within which those policies can be expressed and reconciled.

An official cannot evade his problem by concluding solemnly, as so many civilian pundits do, "the solution for this controversy is to negotiate a fair agreement with the Russians or the Chinese" —or the Syrians or the North Koreans, as the case may be; the official knows that the United States and its allies have tried and tried again to reach such agreements, and that the most dangerous problems in the world arise because some people refuse to meet about them or to negotiate in fact when they do meet.

Nor is it always open to an official to slip by a particular crisis by concluding that we should protect our interests by political and economic means, but not by force, for he knows that force is sometimes used by those who oppose peace, and that it can only be deterred, or met, by force or the threat of force.

There are other ringing Parkinsonian formulae popular in the debate about foreign policy, but unavailable to officials—"Tear up our treaties," for instance. This cynical view is particularly popular among men who describe themselves as "idealists" and reproach all who disagree with them, and society at large, for immorality, materialism, deception, and like sins. Officials know— indeed they are never allowed to forget—that the world does not start fresh every morning, and that nations, like men, lose influence if their word cannot be trusted.

About Vietnam, for example, Johnson said, "Ike has made a promise. I have to keep it." The SEATO treaty, and all that lies behind it, was the key to Johnson's Vietnam policy. Ike's promise was a powerful force in Johnson's mind for a number of reasons: because he is that kind of man; because he believes the United

States should be a nation whose word is good, as he said over and over again, notably in his Baltimore speech of 1965; and because he knew that the SEATO treaty is the essence of the Vietnam problem as a matter of international politics.

It has recently become fashionable, for obvious reasons, not to mention SEATO in talking about Vietnam. But our silence on the subject, even in high places, does not conceal the problem from our friends or from our adversaries. Nor does it alter the fact that the credibility of an American guaranty is a critical feature of the Vietnam maze, and that the outcome of the affair will be felt wherever political arrangements depend upon the deterrent power of America's promises. Senator Fulbright's important proposal that the United States guarantee a peace agreement in the Middle East could not have much impact on events if SEATO, or any other American promise, turns out to be worthless.

Being an optimist, I often bet with myself when I read books, articles, or speeches about foreign policy. Will the author face the issue head-on, or find a formula of evasion? The moment of truth comes as he reaches the climax of his argument, when all the preliminaries are dealt with and the problem has been set out, when I think he is going to have to choose one alternative or the other and cannot find a way to escape. I usually lose the bet as the author slips past the issue in a paragraph of impenetrable prose whose viscosity measures the fact that the challenge of choice has left him exhausted. "Let us improve our relations with Communist China," he cries, but fails to mention the efforts in that direction the United States has undertaken, especially since 1966, or the problem of Formosa. "The arms race is a menace, and must be stopped," he says with feeling. The arms race is indeed a menace —a cancer, in fact. But it can only be stopped by agreement, and nine out of ten orators on the subject become opaque indeed as they approach the intricacies of the problem of negotiation and assurance which is the heart of the matter.

Sometimes the involution of these arguments is breathtaking. My witty friend Professor J. Kenneth Galbraith, for example, is surely, and justly, the most celebrated agricultural economist in the world, an engaging diarist and litterateur, and a minor novelist of charm. He has recently outlined a "new" foreign policy which he thinks could safeguard the United States and restore the Democratic party to power and glory. Despite formidable competition, his thesis easily won the Non Sequitur Prize for 1970, with palms.

After dismissing the Cold War as a myth from the beginning, Galbraith concluded (1) that the United States should never again intervene in Asia, Africa, or South America, except (2) that America should "strongly support collective resistance to armies marching across frontiers" even in Asia, Africa, and South America.[2]

Galbraith's Law would not only require the United States and its allies to repeat what the author regards as the disaster of Korea, should a similar episode occur, but would have required military intervention in Czechoslovakia in 1968 and in Hungary in 1956.

The learned ambassador, it is true, would have the United States ignore the phenomenon called "Wars of National Liberation," that is, "guerrilla" attacks on one country mounted from another, like those to which Israel and South Vietnam have been subjected, or assistance given by one country to a revolution within another, like the situation of Spain in the thirties or of Vietnam and many other countries more recently. Unfortunately, however, Professor Galbraith does not discuss the rule of international law that has for many centuries treated attacks by regular and irregular forces as legally identical, and the powerful reasons of policy and experience behind the principle that a government is responsible for the use of force on or from its territories.

Another former government official, Townsend Hoopes, achieves nearly comparable distinction by arguing that we must cease to be prisoners of the Cold War mentality, which no longer corresponds to reality, if it ever did, and recognize that we can withdraw unilaterally from Indochina without losing the capacity

2 "Who Needs the Democrats?," *Harper's Mazagine* (July 1970), p. 43, at p. 60.

to carry on the Cold War in other theaters where our interests are greater and the Cold War even more of a threat.[3]

During the first year or so of my recent Washington tour we were at pains to point out to senators and congressmen that their current "peace" proposals, which made headlines for them in their home states, were climaxed, after the usual ritual denunciations of the government, either by meaningless gimmicks ("Go to the United Nations"; "Reconvene the Geneva Conference") or by solemnly admonishing the President to do what he was trying to do in any event, namely, to induce the Soviet Union to cooperate in reaching a settlement, as it did finally in Korea, or to find other ways to get a genuine negotiating process under way. Their reply usually ran along these lines: "Look, the President has to do what has to be done. We know that. But we have to be elected. And in my state I am not strong enough to risk . . ."

After a time we tended to avoid such conversations. They recalled, all too painfully, Bertrand de Jouvenel's comment that politics is not a game.

One common feature of the fashionable temper is stated by Arthur M. Schlesinger, Jr., introducing a new edition of *The Vital Center*, first published in 1949.

Twenty years ago Professor Schlesinger was one of the leaders of the non-Communist Left and helped to rally public opinion against the outward push of the Communist nations, and particularly of the Soviet Union. Professor Schlesinger views "the modern crisis" as one of anxiety produced by the velocity of history and the impact of rapid change on man's peace of mind. In 1949, he writes, he believed that

> "the fact that the contest between the U.S.A. and the U.S.S.R. is not the source of the contemporary crisis does not, however, alter the fact that the crisis must be met in terms of this contest." I still think this was probably true in 1949, but it is obviously no longer true today . . . Those who know only the seedy and mediocre Soviet Russia of the 1960s would be quite wrong to see Stalin's Russia in the same image. And those who know only the frag-

[3] "Legacy of the Cold War in Indochina," 48 *Foreign Affairs* (July 1970), 601.

mented international communist movement of today would be equally wrong to suppose that Stalin did not have relatively firm control over the communist parties of the world a generation ago . . . Stalin died in 1953; and in the years since, nationalism has shattered the international Communist movement.[4]

The argument makes strange reading. Despite divisions within the revolutionary movement, parties calling themselves Communist are active in many parts of the world. Many of them obtain some support from fraternal parties and governments abroad. And without the benefit of full control over these parties, or unity of dogma among them, the Soviet Union is steadily taking advantage of every opportunity for expansion. In that process it acts as a national power and also as a spokesman for an ideology of revolution which appeals to some groups within every country of the West and of the Third World. The ideological element in Soviet policy varies in importance from time to time, but it never vanishes.

The sectarianism of radical movements persuades some that ideology is irrelevant, like the glittering coinage of Samuel Butler's musical banks. Before Titoism, Castroism, Maoism, revisionism, adventurism, dogmatism and infantilism they conclude that ideology is absurd, and (strange leap of thought) therefore of no consequence to policy. Both as a national power and as a force in the internal politics of many countries, Soviet power is skillfully advancing throughout North Africa and the Middle East and taking up positions in Asia, Africa, and Latin America, three years after the far-from-seedy invasion of Czechoslovakia.

This is not to suggest a return to the naïve dogmas of the doctrinaire Cold Warriors of the forties and early fifties, who saw Communists under every bed. But Schlesinger's view is quite as naïve. He comes close to saying that the Soviet Union is a passive and pacific factor in world politics and that the pressure of its ambitions is an illusion. The problem for Western policy in evaluating Soviet and Chinese intentions and capabilities is a problem of

[4] " 'The Vital Center' Reconsidered," *Encounter* (Sept. 1970), p. 89, at p. 92.

reality far more somber, and more difficult, than Schlesinger would have us believe.

But the extraordinary notion that the threat of Soviet (or of Chinese) expansion has vanished because the world Communist movement is no longer centrally controlled is often asserted, and it represents a considerable body of current opinion. That opinion is not less important as a political fact because it is without foundation. Soviet concern about possible hostility from China should be a factor inducing some caution in Soviet policy toward Europe and the United States; Chinese concern about Soviet mobilization in Siberia and Soviet penetration of Southern Asia—including North Vietnam—should have a corresponding effect on Chinese policy toward the United States and the West generally. Such is the ancient logic of the balance of power. But in the relations of China, the Soviet Union, and the United States and its allies, the promise of that benign force in world politics is barely manifest, as these lines are written during the winter of 1971–72. Even if skillful diplomacy should succeed in managing the tensions of that triangle to achieve stalemate and restraint, it could hardly become infallible magic. It has not yet even led the Soviet Union to do in Vietnam what it did to wind up the Korean war. On the contrary, concern about the possibilities of rapprochement between the United States and China led the Soviet Union to answer Nixon's trip to Peking with extraordinary ferocity, through its support of North Vietnam's full-scale invasion of South Vietnam in the spring of 1972. That event was a brutal message for China, and for every other nation in the world whose security depends upon American power. And the same concern about the possible menace of Chinese policy five years hence seems to have given a new urgency to Soviet policy in Europe and the Middle East, where it has been hard and inflexible. Nor, on the other side of the equation, has the fear of Russia as yet induced China to go much past its delightful symbolic gesture of a table tennis match, so far as public knowledge is concerned, by way of rapprochement with the United States. As this book goes to press, China has accomplished no visible change in Indochina, although surely a Korean-type solution in Vietnam, and the withdrawal of hostile forces from Cambodia, Laos, Burma, and Thailand are minimal terms for American support in deterring the Soviet Union.

### III

It is commonplace to say that Truman's fall, and Johnson's, stemmed in major part from flaws in their own characters and capacities. Thus Louis Halle and other students of recent foreign policy stress that Truman was not eloquent,[5] and the same judgment is generally applied to Johnson, at least for his formal speeches. These men, it is said, failed to explain their policies persuasively to the American people and to the people of the world. Public opinion became confused, and the President lost the support of the one force every President needs most. A gap developed between the people and their President—a "communications" gap, a "credibility" gap, a gap of sympathy and of empathy.

It is of course true that neither Truman nor Johnson has ever been near Churchill's class as a public orator. Very few men possess such a gift. But Churchill himself, for all his rhetorical power, could not rouse Britain and America from their trance during the early and middle thirties, when the Second World War could still have been prevented. Roosevelt, at the height of his influence, stirred a storm when he hinted obliquely that the United States should take some responsibility for "quarantining" aggressors. And Wilson, a genuinely great orator, spoke to the wind when he pleaded with his people to join the League of Nations.

The fact is that public opinion has a formidable power to resist information and advice it does not want to hear, even when they are conveyed in the tongue of angels—or of Cassandra. All politicians understand this; therefore many do not risk trying to lead opinion.

[5] *The Cold War as History* (1967), p. 117.

Recent years have witnessed many instances of the phenomenon.

One of the most dramatic occurred in 1967.

The Egyptians were using Soviet poison gas—including nerve gas—and some Soviet aviators as well in their prolonged war in the Yemen. The International Red Cross is a body reluctant to enter into controversies of a political character. But it was so outraged by the affair that it published a factual report on the use of gas in the Yemen, illustrated with horrendous photographs of the victims. The world press duly reported the facts without fanfare. The stories appeared briefly and stirred little interest.

There is, of course, a double standard in world opinion. Imagine the outcry if the United States had used nerve gas in Vietnam.

But there was another reason, I believe, for the absence of reaction. Like so much that has happened on Europe's Mediterranean flank, the event was contrary to the widely shared conviction that the Cold War is over; that the Soviets have abandoned policies of expansion and accepted the idea of peaceful coexistence; and that the continuation of tension is due only to the blindness and the Cold War mentality of American officials whose view of the world crystallized in the forties.

There are many other recent occasions when public opinion screened out facts inconsistent with the theories to which it was committed. A considerable number concern "missed" opportunities for peace in Vietnam.

In the years 1965, 1966, and 1967 the United States followed up a number of hints that talks leading to a reasonable peace in Vietnam could be started through secret meetings in unlikely places. The government chased every rabbit down every hole. We anguished over the drafting of telegrams and the conduct of dusty and inconclusive conversations behind a thousand potted palms. It was apparent that many of these leads were fakes. But they were all pursued relentlessly, and each one was treated as if it might uncover the key to the casket. Inevitably stories leaked to the press about some of these diplomatic efforts. Books and articles were written and political speeches made charging that Johnson

had "missed" a dozen chances for peace. Yet when Wilfred Burchett, the well-known spokesman for Hanoi, told the press in
New York in December 1968 that one of the most famous of
these peace efforts ("Marigold") was a hoax concocted by "well-
meaning friends" and never authorized by Hanoi, the story did
not appear at all in *The New York Times* and only made an inside
page of the *Washington Post*.[6] Its publication had no effect on
the flow of mythology about missed opportunities for peace.
Norman Cousins wrote one of the most critical of the articles
dealing with the episode on which Burchett commented. Mr.
Cousins' article appeared after the Burchett interview, but made
no reference to it.[7] Prime Minister Harold Wilson, in his memoirs, similarly charged Johnson with missing an opportunity for
peace through his handling of Marigold.[8] Wilson was convinced
that Kosygin wanted peace. But he never considered whether
Hanoi had authorized Kosygin to act for it.

I described the end of the spectacular Marigold episode in these
terms in *Law, Power, and the Pursuit of Peace*:[9]

> When in December, 1966, efforts through an intermediary to
> arrange meetings with Hanoi failed, and the bombing pauses over
> the Christmas and New Year's period resulted only in dramatic
> increases in infiltration into South Vietnam, direct contacts were
> established with the North Vietnamese. The substantive ex-
> changes of repeated contacts in January and early February were
> summarized in messages we conveyed in early February to Chair-
> man Kosygin and Prime Minister Wilson, heads of the Soviet and
> British governments, the Co-Chairmen of the Geneva Conference,
> who were meeting in London.
>
> We informed the British and Soviet representatives that we
> were ready to stop the bombing of North Vietnam if Hanoi
> would agree to stop infiltration of the South. In addition, we
> would also promise not to increase the size of our forces in the
> South. These assurances could be exchanged secretly, so that the
> continued suspension of the bombing would appear to be unilat-

[6] *Washington Post*, December 5, 1968, p. A-26.
[7] "Vietnam: The Spurned Peace," *Saturday Review*, July 26, 1969, p. 12, at
pp. 59–60.
[8] *A Personal Record, The Labour Government, 1964–1970* (1971), pp. 345–
366.
[9] Pp. 70–71.

eral. We said we should welcome British and Soviet support for this approach.

Although Hanoi had known of this basic position of the United States government for at least three months, on February 8, in an effort to avoid misunderstanding, President Johnson reiterated it in a letter to President Ho Chi Minh, emphasizing that these acts of restraint on both sides would make it possible to conduct serious private discussions leading toward an early peace. Such a meeting, the President stated, could take place in Moscow, Burma, or elsewhere.

Ho Chi Minh's reply on February 15 was harsh and unyielding —halt the bombing "definitely and unconditionally," cease all other acts of war, withdraw all American forces from Vietnam, recognize the Liberation Front as the sole legitimate representatives of the South Vietnamese people, and let the Vietnamese settle their problems themselves. In short, it was a formula for turning South Vietnam over to the Communists and to Hanoi's control.

To slam the door more completely, Hanoi then published President Johnson's letter, though not the communications which had preceded it.

Chester Cooper gives a more vivid although less complete account of these and related efforts in Chapter XIII of his *Lost Crusade*. His chapter brilliantly recaptures the atmosphere of strain and anxiety as men all over the world groped cautiously through the confusion of war and sought to find in Hanoi's silences, or occasional sharp signals, the hope they wished so desperately were there.

Cooper makes no reference to Burchett's statement, although he was himself inclined to believe that at most the North Vietnamese had given the Polish intermediary "a hunting license rather than any definite commitment when he was in Hanoi." [10]

Although Cooper's chapter reports instance after instance in which the highest officials of the administration spent hundreds of hours on the strategy and tactics of peace efforts and the drafting of messages, Cooper also says that as of late 1966 and early 1967 the administration was "just not interested in negotiations to the extent necessary to prevent military actions from interfering with or even negating diplomatic initiatives." [11]

[10] *The Lost Crusade* (1970), p. 342.
[11] Id.

## The Great Debate: Parkinsonian Phases

My own experience does not correspond to Cooper's. I, too, worked on "Marigold," and had many private talks about it with Rusk and other senior officials. They were of course wary, as we all were, of another trap or trick, and chagrined when routine bombing operations, long authorized for days when the weather was favorable, seemed to affect the climate for diplomacy, at least in the American and West European press. But the senior officials pressed, as the President and his staff did, to elicit every possible response from Hanoi. In the papers that lay behind Marigold the United States had offered Hanoi two concessions for one on Hanoi's part—an aspect of the affair Cooper does not mention, although to Hanoi it may well have been a fatal sign of weakness, indicating (correctly) that if they waited, more American concessions would come. Above all, however, it is difficult to understand how military operations could frustrate a diplomatic initiative that, as Burchett points out, and Cooper suspects, had no foundation in the intentions of Hanoi. That being the case, was Cooper right in calling his chapter on the subject "A Tragedy of Errors"? "Caught in a Snare" would seem closer to the facts.

The explanation for the famous scene of confusion in England over the Kosygin-Wilson phase of the peace attempt following on the Marigold affair emerges clearly in the books by Cooper, Wilson, and Johnson. In good faith, the British had given Kosygin a version of the Phase A-Phase B plan that did not exactly correspond to the one Hanoi had received from us directly several months before, or to the variation on it we had given the British, in the light of subsequent developments, before the Kosygin visit. Johnson writes:

> At the outset of the London talks, it became clear to me why the Soviets were willing to discuss Vietnam. Kosygin was pressing Wilson hard to use his influence to persuade us to accept Hanoi's vague offer of possible talks in exchange for a bombing halt. When the Prime Minister asked for our reaction to this proposal, I replied: "If we are asked to take military action on our side, we need to know what the military consequences will be—that is, what military action will be taken by the other side." I concluded my message to Wilson by saying: "I would strongly urge that the

two co-chairmen [of the Geneva Conference] not suggest a stoppage of the bombing in exchange merely for talks, but instead appeal to Hanoi to consider seriously the reasonable proposals we are putting before them, which would take us not merely into negotiation but a long step towards peace itself."

We had informed the British that I was going to tell Ho Chi Minh that if he agreed to "an assured stoppage of infiltration into South Vietnam," we would end the bombing and also stop increasing our troop strength in the South. I told Wilson that he could talk with Kosygin on the same basis if he wished, in full confidence that this represented our official position. We thought that the sequence was clear: Hanoi would first stop infiltration; we would then stop the bombing and, in addition, we would agree not to increase our troop strength in Vietnam. That is what I told Ho Chi Minh in my letter. I recognized, of course, that the new proposal altered the Phase A-Phase B plan we had discussed earlier with the British and had offered to Hanoi. Instead of asking the North Vietnamese to promise to take steps to reduce the fighting after the bombing ended, I wanted them to begin cutting down their actions against the South before we stopped the bombing. I felt strongly that this change was justified by the hard fact that during the bombing pause then underway very large southward movements of men and supplies were taking place in the area above the demilitarized zone. I refused to risk the safety of our men in I Corps by stopping air strikes before Ho Chi Minh had acted. On the other hand, I went further than ever before by proposing to freeze U.S. troop levels in the South.

The British read our message differently. They considered it a restatement of the Phase A-Phase B plan, with which they were familiar—that Hanoi would have to agree to halt infiltration but would not actually stop until after the bombing was suspended. When Wilson discussed this with Kosygin, the Soviet leader asked for the proposal in writing. The British gave a document to him without specific approval from Washington, which was an error, though I am confident that they acted in good faith. The result was a diplomatic mix-up for which we shared a certain amount of the responsibility. The British, with some embarrassment, had to go back to Kosygin with the revised, and correct, version of our proposal. That was the evening of February 10.

Meanwhile, the Tet truce period was running out. It ended on February 11, but with Kosygin still in the United Kingdom, we agreed to extend the bombing stand-down until he returned to Moscow on the 13th. At their final meeting with Kosygin on February 12, the British made a new proposal: If the Soviets could obtain North Vietnam's assurance that infiltration into the South would end the next day, the British would get U.S. assurance that the bombing, which then had been stopped for five days, would not be resumed and, further, that the build-up of American forces would end. We had agreed to this British approach before it was put to Kosygin. The Soviets in turn passed the offer on to Hanoi. By the time Kosygin left London the following day, there was still no word from Hanoi. Nor was an answer waiting when Kosygin got back to Moscow.

Prime Minister Wilson felt that we had given him and the Russians too little time to get an answer, but Hanoi had had several months to study and consider the Phase A-Phase B plans—and the proposal Wilson made to Kosygin was but a variation of that idea. It does not take all that long to cable "yes" or "no" or "we are giving it serious study," even from as far away as Hanoi. As a matter of fact, Hanoi did not have to send a cable at all. We had already carried out Phase A; the bombing had been stopped. If the leaders in Hanoi wanted to move toward peace, they knew that all they had to do was to take some visible step to cut back their half of the war. That step could have taken many forms—stopping infiltration or sharply reducing it, pulling back some of their units from advanced positions, cutting down the number of attacks, almost anything significant that would have reflected an honest desire on their part to reduce hostilities. We would have quickly recognized such an action and would have responded to it—as we had said time and time again. The hard but unfortunate truth was that the leaders in Hanoi had snubbed the two-phase approach before the Wilson-Kosygin sessions, and they turned it down again late in 1967. So I could not share the Prime Minister's feeling, which he expressed in the House of Commons, that "a solution could now be reached." [12]

Later, at Glassboro, Johnson did agree to a proposal from Hanoi, which Kosygin transmitted, to stop the bombing in exchange only for talks, provided the war around the 17th parallel was stabilized and the talks proved serious. This suggestion, also, produced no response.[13]

Despite the political costs of his silence in the face of charges that he had fumbled an opportunity for peace, and the provocation of Hanoi's step in publishing part of the correspondence, Johnson refused to authorize a white paper on the subject of

---

[12] Lyndon B. Johnson, *The Vantage Point* (1971), pp. 253–255.
[13] Id., pp. 256–257.

peace initiatives, or to allow even the most tendentious stories to be answered, on the ground that it was essential to maintain silence in preparation for the day when genuine peace feelers were made under the cover of secrecy and in reliance on our promise of secrecy.

One of the wisest of our French friends, a man of great experience in Indochina and an intimate of Ho Chi Minh, advised a senior American diplomat that the Vietnamese style was secrecy and that no public moves on their part would be serious. When they were ready for negotiations, he told us, they would arrange to meet our representative "at midnight in some village hotel." That counsel impressed Johnson. I was given the same advice by my Yale colleague Professor Paul Mus, a French scholar of great sagacity who had spent years in Indochina and knew the Communist leaders there well.

There is reason to believe that Burchett's disclosure applied to all the peace feelers of that period.

But American public opinion is inclined to accept the accusation that opportunities for peace were missed. Our politics are based on accommodation. It is difficult for Americans to believe that there are people in the world who prefer war to peace and would refuse a reasonable compromise. The war in Vietnam would end, we are convinced, if only our negotiators were imaginative enough to suggest such a compromise. But to put it mildly, we are predisposed to believe that our negotiators are not outstandingly endowed with imagination.

Under the pressure of this feeling, the American government endlessly revised its offers to Hanoi, hoping that concessions, or new formulae, would persuade that government we were "sincere." The only effect of these drafting changes, I am convinced, was to make intransigence more attractive. As an Asian leader once told Johnson, our endless stream of peace offers to Hanoi would appear a sign of weakness to any Asian mind.

I once explained to an old friend who was active in the McCarthy campaign of 1968 that the only issue in the Vietnam war was that we accept the N.L.F. as "the sole legitimate representative of the South Vietnamese people"; we and the South Vietnamese, I reminded him, had long since accepted all the other "peace points" put forward by the spokesmen for Hanoi in both their short and long lists. "But we can't agree to *that*," my friend said with some heat. He continued to support Senator McCarthy, however, without altering the formulae being used in the campaign or ceasing to belabor Johnson for willfully refusing to make peace.

It is elementary American politics that any President in a situation like that of Vietnam would be intensely responsive to the possibility of peace. As a politician, he has nothing to gain from the continuance of war, and everything to lose. I know from my own experience that every plausible opening, and many that were highly implausible, were pursued as effectively as possible in the hectic circumstances of war. Yet the charges persist that Johnson rebuffed several chances for peace and missed several others through clumsiness. It requires fierce and impregnable political principles, or something close to paranoia, to believe that a President, however passionately he is disliked, would in fact miss a reasonable chance for peace. And it takes a vivid gift for fantasy to suppose that any President would indulge his blood lust by plotting secretly to enlarge a war. I never met (or heard of) an official who regarded the campaign in Vietnam with anything but loathing. But the claims go on and on.

A journalist of experience recently reviewed the public statements on Vietnam made during the Kennedy and Johnson administrations. He concluded that "everything is there. Everything was said. There is no basis on the record for the charge of concealment or stealth in the evolution of our policy." I am sure that Truman's record on Korea would meet the same standard.

But many people would not listen.

I believe that this phenomenon—a contest in men's minds between myth and reality—was the main source of what happened to Truman and Johnson. Their fate had more fundamental causes than their own errors and shortcomings. Of course they made mistakes and of course they had shortcomings. But they were opposed by overwhelming forces of feeling and instinct, drawn from the classical view we are all taught to take of the United States in world affairs. Our historical memory sketches a vision of national identity in our minds: Virtuous America, proud and aloof in the wicked world, safe behind two broad oceans, and loyal to what the conventional wisdom regards (wrongly) as the prescriptions of President Washington against entangling alliances. It may take another generation before this tenacious idyll yields to reality, and American opinion fully accepts the twentieth century as a fact—just in time to enter the twenty-first. Even a generation may not be enough if politicians, journalists, and academicians continue to exploit the isolationist strain in the American psyche as a stepping-stone to power.

Nonetheless, the charge is frequently encountered that the government was guilty of concealment, deception, the telling of half-truths, and manipulation in its relation to public opinion. Significantly enough, the charge is confined almost entirely to Vietnam. No such accusation is ever made about Johnson's policy on a dozen other issues, from keeping the troops in Europe to those of trade, monetary policy and nuclear control.

It is often said that these accusations are confirmed by the reports about the *Pentagon Papers* whose publication in 1971 by *The New York Times* and other newspapers occasioned such a storm. Leslie H. Gelb, who directed the study of the Defense Department's documents about Vietnam for the Secretary of Defense, concludes that this is the case, although he also believes that *The New York Times*, and other newspapers, were in error about the chief piece of evidence upon which they relied to establish the claim of "deception."

> I have two serious criticisms of the *Times* stories. First, they should have stated explicitly that President Johnson before the 1964 elections was not part of the general consensus in our government to bomb North Vietnam. Our studies do not show that he was, and indeed depict him as quite resistant to this course. The *Times* headline in this case was particularly misleading. Second, they give a misleading view of CIA findings. While the CIA was arguing that the bombing of the North was having the opposite of the

desired effects, as the *Times* revealed, it was not nearly as pessimistic about the war in the South. Although the full Task Force studies show a much greater complexity in the decision-making processes, the *Times* stories were largely a fair representation.[14]

On the much mooted issue of the credibility of government, Gelb stresses the major effort government officials make "to avoid flat lies. Whether on some occasions they may have failed to live up to their own rigid rule is not the issue that should be confronting us." [15] It has certainly been my experience at all levels of government that officials are painfully conscientious about what they say. They know that their words are part of the official record; they may have to defend them before Congressional committees; and in any event their words go into the archives and become raw material for history. Statements are drafted and redrafted to match the evidence, although it is not always possible or prudent to present all the evidence.

I cannot say whether actual lies have been told under exceptional circumstances. I have never done so, nor have I witnessed the telling of such lies. But that question, as Gelb says, is not a major aspect of the issue—can the people generally trust what government officials tell them?

Gelb's charge is that when public statements about Vietnam, at least, are compared with the content of the Defense Department memoranda he studied, a pattern of "concealment and half-truth" is revealed, founded on "rank paternalism." Our leaders, he believes, suffer from

> the courtly conviction that the American people cannot appreciate the problems and have to be "brought along."
> With the best of motives, I believe our leaders were convinced

[14] "Today's Lessons from the Pentagon Papers," *Life* (September 17, 1971), p. 34. It should be noted that when Gelb refers to "the CIA" view and "the CIA findings" in this passage, he is himself being misleading. The memoranda in question are not sifted, institutional conclusions of the CIA, but memoranda by a panel of representatives of the CIA, the State Department Bureau of Intelligence and Research, and the Defense Intelligence Agency, acting as individuals. (See, e.g., *The New York Times, The Pentagon Papers* (1971), p. 331.)
[15] Id.

they knew best. Issues of diplomacy, war and peace, so the foreign policy community has reasoned, are too subtle and sophisticated for the common man. Besides, it was further reasoned, telling the full story to their own people makes for "complications" with other nations. In their desire to do the best for the nation, our leaders felt they had to protect themselves against public pressures, and in the process they shielded us from the information we needed to make up our own minds.

This paternalism has marked the whole history of U.S. involvement in Vietnam. In the late 1950s, President Eisenhower told us that only the North Vietnamese were violating the Geneva Accords.[16] The whole truth was that we were also breaking those accords ourselves, and specifically that we were behind the rupture of the coalition government in Laos. In the early 1960s, President Kennedy led us down this same road. We were told that the South Vietnamese wanted more American help. That is true. Diem wanted more U.S. arms and money. But what was not told was that Diem did not want Washington to share the powers of his government, which was our condition for more aid. We were told that the Diem coup was a South Vietnamese affair. They did indeed carry it out, but it could not have occurred without our acquiescence and involvement. As Kennedy's press secretary Pierre Salinger has written, Kennedy "was not anxious to admit the existence of a real war . . ." He wanted to keep his options open.

President Johnson followed the same pattern. He, too, sought to minimize the extent of U.S. involvement in order to avoid public pressures either to do more or to do less. He never stopped saying that "we seek no wider war." I am sure he did not "seek" it, but neither did he stop escalating it. Also, as the Pentagon papers show, it was not always the North Vietnamese who escalated first. In early 1965, Johnson Administration officials told us that Saigon wanted us to start sending combat troops. This is true, but it became true after we twisted their arms. President Johnson apparently thought that the only alternatives to what he was doing were to "wave the flag" and risk stirring passions for total victory or to withdraw and face defeat in Vietnam with its worldwide risks, a McCarthyite reaction at home and the end of his Great Society program. So he continued to escalate.

As the war escalated, President Johnson and others invariably began their public statements by insisting that there was "no change in policy." They would go on to describe what were in

[16] As to the propriety of Gelb's usage in referring to the Geneva arrangements as "accords," see pp. 157–161, *infra.*

fact changes. The American people were asked to accept the pretense of perfect consistency.[17]

Are these charges true?

It is true that the United States government, like other governments, does not officially acknowledge secret intelligence operations, although the relevant Congressional committees were regularly briefed on the subject, and the press had detailed stories about them, which were never denied. It would be hard to document the charge that either Congress or the American people were denied information about what the government was trying to do in Laos, for example.

It is, I believe, equally true that none of the other significant facts revealed in the *Pentagon Papers*, and stressed in Gelb's summary, were denied to the public. I have not performed the operation myself, but several journalists I respect,[18] and one of my own students, who has done research on the subject, say they have found every important item in *The New York Times* account of the *Pentagon Papers* in newspaper stories of the time, and that the general pattern revealed by the *Pentagon Papers* is faithfully reflected in statements of high officials, including Johnson's press conferences.

It would be difficult, in my judgment, to find a Senator, a Congressman, or a concerned citizen—to say nothing of a Washington correspondent, or an editorial writer for a metropolitan newspaper—who could honestly claim that he was surprised or shocked at the revelation in the *Pentagon Papers* that earnest officials in the State Department and the Pentagon were alarmed by the course of events in Vietnam; that they were studying every conceivable alternative of policy for the United States under the circumstances, including withdrawal and full-scale war; and that they were divided in their views as to what should be done. It would be equally unlikely, I should suppose, that one could find a citizen

17 Id., p. 35.
18 See, e.g., Richard Harwood, "Few Revelations for Those Who Had Been Listening," Washington *Post*, June 24, 1971, p. A–18, col. 3–5.

or journalist unaware of the fact that every government has a secret service, some more effective than others, and that such services function.

Given the diligence of the press, and the leaking habits of the American government, it would be remarkable—and totally unprecedented—if the situation were different. In my experience, nearly everything a government official receives by way of information or intelligence also appears in the press—sometimes a few days late, but sometimes also a few days early. But the press also contains a great deal of material which does not appear on the official's desk. The only advantage the official has over the newspaper reader is that he has a better basis for distinguishing what is true and what is not true in the newspaper stories—"true," at least, by the standard of what is known to the government. The official can usually tell at a glance who has leaked a given story, and why. And he can normally tell also why a given cliché persists, although all the evidence is against it.

Although the public had all the information, and all the anxieties, revealed in the *Pentagon Papers*, is it nonetheless true that the official version contained in the speeches, statements, and testimony of Johnson, Rusk and McNamara was incomplete and therefore misleading? Official statements should have more weight with public opinion than newspaper speculation, however well informed. Sometimes they do.

It is hard for me to imagine an issue that was more thoroughly ventilated than Vietnam in Congress, in the press, and on every platform of the land; more completely authorized by repeated decisions of Congress and the Presidency; or more dramatically pressed upon the consciousness of the American people by demonstrations and protests of all kinds. Yet over and over again, one hears or sees the allegation that Johnson didn't explain the war to the American people; that he led us into the Vietnam quagmire by stealth; that he dampened and discouraged public debate, and denied the war democratic legitimacy by keeping it invisible.

One can say—and it is surely true—that in the end the speeches of Johnson, Rusk, McNamara and lesser officials on Vietnam no longer stirred the public. Editorials did not complain that Johnson and Rusk were not explaining the war, but that their speeches said "nothing new." "How can we say anything new," Rusk would say, with a grin, "if the situation hasn't changed?" The Mandate of Heaven was slipping away for the Johnson Administration for a number of reasons, as the gap between the administration and public opinion widened. But that phenomenon was not occurring for lack of explanations on the part of Johnson and his troops.

Johnson was often urged to go on television in a rocking chair, talking informally to one or two newspaper men or colleagues. He did it once or twice, and the public response was excellent. People caught a glimpse of him as he is in private talk, or in small groups —vivid, expressive, often eloquent, without any of the stiffness of his usual manner on the podium or on TV. For a number of reasons, he was reluctant to engage in such programs, and hard to persuade. While I advised him to do so, I must admit in retrospect that I don't think such a campaign would have made much difference. The causes for the shift in public mood were too deep.

I believe Gelb comes much closer to the heart of the matter when he writes that during the critical years between 1953 and 1967 or so, by and large we—the general public—"closed our ears to those who did not speak of 'a light at the end of the tunnel.' In 1966, for example, Dean Rusk told the Senate Foreign Relations Committee: 'I would be misleading you if I told you that I thought that I know where, when, and how this matter will be resolved.' " [19] After the Tet offensive, it was equally difficult to get many people to listen to news of more cheerful import.

Of course the presentation of facts about Vietnam—or about any other issue of policy, foreign or otherwise—is a problem in politics and a problem of advocacy. Of course a President has a theory about the course of events, and a policy which he prefers above alternatives. Of course he is aware of the currents affecting public opinion, and seeks to influence opinion, work with it, and gain its support for his own theory about events, and his own preferences of policy. Of course he addresses himself to the pre-

[19] Id., p. 35.

occupations of public opinion, and tries to function within the limits it establishes. Is that the legitimate exercise of the political art, or deception? Leadership or manipulation?

Gelb writes as if the nation uncritically accepted an incomplete and misleading official version of what was happening in Vietnam. Theses of this kind permit critics to dismiss official doctrine out of hand, and save them the inconvenience of reasoned reply. The truth, I believe, is quite different.

American public opinion about foreign policy is far from unsophisticated. And the American attitude toward government is far from deferential. We respect government, but hardly kowtow to it. American opinion generally saw Vietnam, I think, as part of the process of containment, like earlier episodes in Greece, Berlin, and Korea. It heard what the government said, and had many other sources of information as well—the press, letters home from the troops, the reports of returned soldiers, the speeches of Congressmen, and so on.

If public opinion about Vietnam was managed, as Gelb seems to believe, it was the worst job of public opinion management in the history of public relations. I have no doubt that bright young men in the Pentagon thought they were being artful in the selection and presentation of the news. They always do. But the broad lines of public opinion are formed from many sources, and are always beyond the reach of the artful dodgers.

When things began to go badly in Vietnam, after 1963 and 1964, public opinion, like the Congress, supported the large-scale use of ground forces, despite the memory of Korea; equally, it opposed the use of nuclear weapons. It reached this consensus not because its briefing was incomplete on this or that detail, or because its perception of the Vietnam problem was significantly different from that in the minds of government officials. In my experience on the Hill and on the hustings, people outside the executive branch understood the problem exactly as we did. The national decisions of that period were made, I believe, because we are a politically responsible people who basically accept the foreign policy initiated by Truman, and support the decisions of their government. At that time—and to this day—American public opinion believes that the Eisenhower commitment to Vietnam should be made good, but made good in ways, however costly, which minimize the risk of nuclear war. These opinions would have been the same, I am convinced, if the memoranda of John McNaughton and William Bundy had been printed in the papers every morning on the day they were typed to supplement the columns about their ideas which appeared regularly all over the country and the world.

After the military setbacks of 1967 and 1968, the prevailing mood in public opinion, I was told in Congress by doves and hawks alike, was not that we should get out of Vietnam, but that we should "win or get out." I have been assured by Congressmen that this is still the case. Certainly the pattern of elections since 1964, and of Congressional votes on the subject, would bear out this judgment.

What has happened, I should contend, is the crystallization of an intense desire to discover a genuine alternative to the foreign policy the nation has pursued since 1947. In the end, Gelb and other commentators recognize this, rather than the outcry about deception, as the moral of Vietnam.

IV

Man's psychological capacity to ignore facts that would destroy the theories in his mind is not the only factor tending to separate public opinion from the world of reality. More commonplace frailties of human character make an important contribution as well.

During the campaign of 1968, and before, high-minded politicians and journalists said they were convinced that "real" negotiations, leading to "a fair and honorable peace, compatible with our obligations to South Vietnam," could and would be assured by stopping the bombing of North Vietnam, despite the failure of previous bombing halts to achieve any results whatever. At a Washington dinner in 1967 one of our finest senators told me that

Johnson should rely on the American people, who are tough and responsible and will do whatever is necessary to make their word good. But before undertaking such an effort, he said, they want to be sure that every peaceful alternative is tested. All over the world, he continued, we are being promised that a bombing halt now would lead to peace. "I know that you've tried bombing halts before and that nothing has happened. But shouldn't we find out now whether the new approaches are serious?" I asked him what he would do if such a policy failed, or led to another prolonged negotiation, like that of Panmunjom. "We cannot and must not tolerate such a thing," he said. "If that happened, I would make a speech on the floor of the Senate urging a military policy of much greater effort."

"Can I tell my boss that this is a serious proposal on your part?" I asked him.

"Absolutely," he assured me then and later.

When I reported the conversation to Rusk he grinned and remarked that the senator would never go through with it.

Unfortunately, Rusk was right.

Another friend in the Senate complained in 1966 that administration speeches about Vietnam were unconvincing because they talked about protecting the liberty of the South Vietnamese and safeguarding "democracy" there. "Why don't you tell the people we are protecting the balance of power in Asia, and containing China? Everybody understands that."

"You haven't been reading my speeches," I replied. "But I'll see what more can be done."

When he read my next speech, he said, "You're on the right track. But did you have to be so hard?"

Later my friend became a leading advocate of unilateral withdrawal from Vietnam.

In my own thinking about what President Johnson could have done or should have done differently, my mind returns to an aspect of his policy that has not to my knowledge been much discussed as yet—his refusal to appeal to the national feeling over Vietnam. Since my duties did not include the continuing assignments on Vietnam, it took some time after I came to Washington in 1966 before I appreciated the deliberateness of these decisions.

The military element in history has no romantic appeal for Johnson, as it did for Roosevelt, Churchill, and De Gaulle. The campaigns of the past he studies for recreation are political, not military. He has a pronounced distaste for chauvinism. In no area is he more visibly the Populist.

As President, Johnson was acutely aware of the unique military power of the United States. And he feared that it might be difficult to limit the use of that power if national pride were fully aroused about the war in Vietnam. He once remarked that the British had conducted limited military campaigns for centuries along the boundaries of their influence. "We have to get used to the idea," he said. There were no parades to dramatize Vietnam, and no bond drives, even in the period before domestic opposition became intense. In 1968 Johnson and his administration were besieged by congressmen and senators who asked him to wrap the flag around the surtax bill. "Say we're doing it for the boys," they urged, "and we'll have no trouble passing the bill." Johnson would not budge. The battle for the tax increase was fought, and won, as an exercise in monetary policy and political responsibility addressed to the balance of payments and the equilibrium of the monetary system, not to the necessities of war.

I had great sympathy and great respect for the congressmen and senators with whom I spoke about the surtax in 1968. They did their unpleasant duty under difficult circumstances, facing an election that would be dominated, they thought, by hidden currents of unknown magnitude: strong feelings against the war in Vietnam, racial tensions, and anger about student protest in the universities.

Johnson was certain that reason would prevail in the battle for the tax bill, and he and the Secretary of the Treasury, Henry Fowler, finally carried the day after a long and difficult struggle.

However difficult the struggle, Johnson refused to strengthen his hand by stirring the nerve of national pride. He regarded the risks of such a course as excessive.

Thus public feeling about Vietnam was subjected to unequal pressures. The opponents of the war skillfully invoked the powerful magic of our yearning for the past. Johnson would not counter that force with patriotic appeals of comparable emotional impact.

The question I have about this aspect of Johnson's policy is not one of democratic ethics. The essential facts about Soviet and Chinese action in Vietnam, in the Middle East, and elsewhere were not concealed from the American people. But they were not trumpeted out either, or projected in the simplified images of propaganda. Johnson deliberately had the facts presented in the setting of his hopes and efforts for reaching an understanding with the Soviet Union and with China. Over and over again he repeated the chilling theme of his 1966 speech in Arco, Idaho.

> The heart of our concern in the years ahead must be our relationship with the Soviet Union. Both our nations possess unimaginable power; our responsibility to the world is heavier than that ever borne by two nations at any other time in history. Our compelling task is this: to search for every possible area of agreement that might conceivably enlarge, no matter how slightly or how slowly, the prospect for cooperation between the United States and the Soviet Union.

And he realized that one of the most important consequences of the dramatic Cuban crisis in 1962 was the acceleration of the Soviet missile program.

Thus Johnson avoided an atmosphere of anti-Soviet and anti-Chinese hysteria, which could have swept us much closer to general war, despite the rising tide of pressures he faced—pressures quite different from those of the early postwar years, more diverse and sophisticated, more dangerous, and much harder to control. As a result, however, it was possible for large parts of the nation to cling to illusions about the state of world politics. The divisions within the country were therefore deepened and made more intense. The men who had to fight in Vietnam felt isolated and neglected. And many who should have spoken bowed before the storm, or remained silent.

The question that troubles me, in short, is whether there was a way then, and whether there is a way now, to help promote a full acceptance of reality without stirring the nation to a mood of uncontrollable rage, the mood we saw for a moment during the Cuban missile crisis.

I am optimistic enough to believe that if the facts are presented to the American people with the bark on, their response will be as strong, as realistic, and as unhysterical as it was after the seizure of the *Pueblo,* when anger was suppressed in the interest of saving our sailors' lives.

Democratic leaders must of course take public opinion into account. But they are elected to use their best judgment in the light of the circumstances they confront. One of their most vital tasks is to lead opinion and to help shape it—or, if necessary, to go down resisting it. They cannot govern by conforming policy to the latest Gallup poll.

Naturally, Johnson and his chief lieutenants were acutely sensitive to the fact that they were trying to carry out a foreign policy in the midst of a tornado—the tornado of Vietnam. As the Vietnam campaign dragged on, doubt increased, and turned to dissatisfaction, and then to dissent. "Win or get out," men began to say, closing their minds to the risks of escalation or of withdrawal. Slowly, then more rapidly, the tide grew stronger; in some quarters, and especially in the universities, protest became violent as men experimented with the manuals of urban guerrilla warfare. In turn, parents, and the middle-aged middle class more generally, became concerned about a war that was dividing the country so passionately, and, as they thought, provoking such disorder.

As the state of opinion changed, the government redoubled its efforts to explain. But, of course, the harder we tried, the worse the state of opinion about Vietnam became.

The pressure of Vietnam had surprisingly little effect in other areas of foreign policy. Peace was maintained in Europe, and war contained, for the time being at least, in the Middle East. If the storm over Vietnam had not been raging, it might have been possible to prevent the Six Day War,[20] but even that is speculative. The risk of famine in several countries of the Third World was averted

[20] See pp. 260–264, *infra.*

through strenuous national and international action. Important steps toward nuclear agreement were negotiated. NATO was given a political arm and an enlarged political mission. Both international trade and international finance were liberalized through international agreement. The government did not indeed accomplish all it sought to accomplish. But the obstacles it faced were inherent in the intractability of politics, not the fallout from Vietnam.

Johnson was concerned—in all fields—about the risk that the administration might become immured in its ivory towers. At every level, men talked with experts from outside the government to make sure that we were not missing some brilliant idea too obvious for us to notice. Often little that was new came out of such contacts, for the outside expert was rarely able to focus his attention on the issues which the official had no way to escape. Far too often we got Parkinsonian answers: "We never should have gone into Vietnam"; "Our policy in the Middle East should be more even-handed"; "Withdraw from Europe, and let the Germans have nuclear weapons." With some notable exceptions— mainly in the field of monetary and trade policy—these conversations yielded incantations, not genuine advice, and the cold comfort that nothing more tangible was available in the outside world, that we were not in fact prisoners of the ideas which happened to be current within the government.

In the examination of major policy issues, Johnson liked to assign the role of "devil's advocate" to an official, or to a trusted friend not then in government. The devil's advocate for the day would present the case for an unpopular or adverse view, often with great verve, and always with great freedom. But these exercises, too, bracing as they were, rarely revealed a true alternative.

Discussions of this kind were addressed to an unusually full set of documents. Unlike Franklin Roosevelt, Johnson did not insist on short memoranda. On the contrary, he preferred and expected long ones, which, in my experience, he had invariably studied before they were debated in his presence. Those papers, in turn, were the product of a bureaucratic process involving many hours of drafting and redrafting, argument and discussion, and, in many instances, extended consultations as well with key members of Congress and with advisers outside the government.

As the 1968 election approached, the tensions arising from Vietnam became palpable. Among the men outside the government who advised Johnson in 1968—the so-called "elder statesmen" and others—many were primarily concerned about the Democratic party. "It is more important," one of them told the President, "to keep the Republicans out of the White House than to stick to the last comma of Ike's treaty." Johnson's grim and bitter response, as he saw his staunchest supporters drop away, was his announcement of March 31, 1968, taking himself out of the presidential race, so that he could turn the situation over to his successor intact on all fronts. As the author of this section of the *Pentagon Papers* concludes, Johnson's decision "to seek a new strategy and a new road to peace was based upon two major considerations:

> (1) the conviction of his principal civilian advisers, particularly Secretary of Defense Clifford, that the troops requested by General Westmoreland would not make a military victory any more likely; and
> (2) a deeply felt conviction of the need to restore national unity to the American nation." [21]

In the end, then, I conclude that the mistakes that were made during the Johnson Administration were mistakes of judgment, or the consequence of increasing tension between policy and public opinion, not the product of an inadequate or excessively narrow procedure for making decisions, or of an administration staffed only by the victims of bad education in world politics.

I can claim to be the only bureaucrat in American history who went up and down the country explaining to astonished audiences that the main problem of American foreign policy was to resolve a Jungian conflict between our collective unconscious and the facts of life. Perhaps men of different education will be better able to understand the dynamics of world politics than those who

[21] *The New York Times, The Pentagon Papers* (1971), p. 612.

have staffed the State Department, the Pentagon, the White House, and the CIA for the last thirty years. Since those men have come from universities in every part of the country and the world, it is not obvious that a new team, necessarily recruited from the same universities, would have better luck in finding or creating a new set of premises for the foreign policy of the United States.

That is the question to which this book is addressed: Is there in fact an alternative foreign policy, as so many assume? Would there have been true negotiations about Vietnam if we had stopped bombing earlier, or not stopped bombing at all? Were chances for accommodation missed with the Soviet Union, China, or Egypt? Can the United States defend its security by withdrawing its military forces from Europe and Asia, annulling its treaties, and arming to the teeth? or by disarming? Should we consider ourselves bound by the United Nations Charter, when it has been so flagrantly and repeatedly violated by others? Does the United States have any national interest in preventing the use of force in international affairs save to repel invasions, or respond to bombing attacks? If so, how can that interest be defined—is it an interest in the balance of power, or the fate of democratic nations around the world, or of nations linked to us by blood, or religion, or chance?

After all the uproar of the last few years, those questions—essentially intellectual in character—abide.

# 3

## *Eight Premises in Search of a Policy*

PARSING THE LITERATURE about American and Allied foreign policy as closely as lawyers read judicial opinions, I have found it helpful to classify that literature into eight schools, or parties—seven in opposition to the basic ideas of the policy; the eighth in its defense.

Each school is derived from a somewhat different major premise—a different definition of the rightful goal of a foreign policy in general, and of American foreign policy in particular.

Few of those who write about foreign policy make their major premises explicit, and fewer still give reasons for their choice. Major premises usually appear in their writings as self-evident truths, bench marks that are invoked to test policies but are themselves almost never formulated or examined. Sometimes a veritable exegesis is needed to determine the code from which a man's judgments are deduced. In almost every case the writer uses more than one major premise as the source of his conclusions.

The classification outlined in this chapter is therefore no more than a first step toward an analysis of the literature about Western foreign policy, and particularly about American foreign policy. While few books fit exactly into only one of the schools described here, I believe that in combination the eight schools, or parties, cover the entire spectrum of possible positions on the subject and permit one to examine the essential ideas of all the available theses with some clarity, convenience, and precision. In later chapters I set out and comment on the arguments of a number of representative writers in some detail. They supplement the present chapter and should be read with it.

I should add that a reader who plunges into this literature for the purpose of determining the bony structure of the arguments faces some quite particular hazards. The literature is impassioned and polemic. The author may sound like an angry dove, but wind up in his final paragraphs by recommending the policies of deterrence and containment he has been cheerfully ridiculing for three hundred lively pages. The course of an author's reasoning is rarely summarized in a neat syllogism. Sometimes there is so much ritual invective and such colorful fireworks that it becomes nearly impossible to discern what the writer is in fact saying, apart from the fact that he has a low opinion of certain Presidents, Secretaries of State, and other worthies, and is against the sins of "globalism," "anticommunism," "imperialism," "appeasement," or "reaction," as the case may be, and the idea that the United States should be the world's anointed gendarme.

II

The first of the schools, or parties, I should identify among those who write about foreign policy is the school of pacifism, expounding a doctrine for which Americans have always had a special place in their hearts, based in considerable part on the special place of the Quakers in American history. The pacifist contends that war is immoral and that the United States should not engage in it under any circumstances. For all the appeal of his argument to a people that has never wavered from General Sherman's view of war, the pacifist does not explain how one nation can expect to protect its national interests, or indeed to survive unarmed or unprotected, in a world political system that permits others both to arm and to attack and contains several nations that show distinct proclivities in that direction. At best, the pacifist promises, as Tolstoy did, that if one nation disarms, others will be led by shame or public opinion to follow its example. But pacifists never explain why anyone should expect the example of nonviolence to be followed in this notably violent century, or what the democracies could do after disarming if they found that their rivals had not done likewise. Practical men remain unable to make the leap of faith the pacifist doctrine requires. In *The Trouble Makers*, A. J. P. Taylor refuses even to talk about pacifists. They do not qualify as true dissenters and radicals, he argues, because nonresistance is not an alternative policy, but the negation of policy.[1]

The theme of pacifism is more common in the literature about foreign policy than one might suppose. Those who are not pacifists, but oppose a particular war for particular reasons, often invoke or quote those who oppose all war without discrimination. And through an intellectual feat I admire but find difficult to explain, the pacifist argument often approaches its opposite, the argument in behalf of international support for revolution—that is, for perpetual war in a crusade deemed sacred.

The most eloquent and influential pacifists are religious men and often religious leaders. Their views have special resonance in the American culture and considerable political effect. Both Johnson and Rusk were sensitive to the mounting tide of criticism from pacifists during 1967 and 1968 and devoted a good deal of effort to reasoning with them. Their concern reflected both their awareness of the respect for religion that has been so characteristic of American life, and their own involvement in that feeling.

III

The second school is at the other end of the spectrum from that of pacifism—the Doctor Strangelove party of all-out ideological anticommunism. The Strangelovites condemn as appeasement the cautious and limited efforts of the American government and its allies since the war to build a balance of power and to reach

[1] *The Trouble Makers* (1957), Panther ed., 1969, p. 47.

understandings with the Soviet Union and with China. For them the major premise of our foreign policy should be "Écrasez l'infâme." They would be content with nothing less than their own crusade against heresy, and damn the torpedoes.

The Strangelove outlook was deeply antipathetic both to Johnson and to Rusk, who are not ideologues in their approach to foreign policy. Temperamentally they are far more interested in aid to developing countries than in "roll-back," or even in "containment." Their goal was not to reverse Communist revolutions, but to induce Communist regimes to respect certain reciprocal rules of peace. But Johnson was always concerned, as I indicated earlier, about the potential influence of the extreme and simplistic anticommunist strain in American opinion if sufficiently aroused. He worried about its effect both on foreign policy and on civil liberty at home. His overriding goal was to protect national interests without increasing the risk of nuclear war. And he recalled the McCarthy era with loathing.

In nearly thirty years of contact with the men who make and carry out American foreign policy I can recall no responsible American official who said, or hinted, that the goal of American policy should be to "liberate" Russia or China from their Communist rulers. Nonetheless, the thought has a place just below the surface in the American mind and in the minds of other nations. In a situation of turbulence, and of rage at the cumulative and apparently endless frustrations of the Cold War, the opportunity to strike a "decisive" blow would seem tempting to many men who do not otherwise resemble General Curtis LeMay. If we should face another Korea somewhere, or another Vietnam, there would be strong voices to assert that we should stop fighting only on difficult proxy battlefields chosen by our opponents, and wage war directly against the source or sources of our troubles. The brutality of Soviet policy in recent years increases the risk of such a reaction in the West if a future episode should release feelings of anger and frustration now grimly repressed.

The third school in the literature is that of the Communists and their fellow travelers—those who follow the line of one or another of the Communist parties or sects in the world. For them American foreign policy should have no national premise at all. Its goal, they believe, should be devotion to what they consider a Higher Cause. Some are participants in a political movement of revolution based on a version of the Marxist creed and on the political or quasi-military tactics of a particular party or group calling itself Communist. Others are conscious or half-aware followers of such groups, or part of a broader flow of revolutionary opinion and political action, not closely controlled by a Communist party, but generally responsive to its signals and concerns.

There is in every Western country a current of irrational protest, a rallying point for the aggressive instinct, which seeks an outlet in destruction for its own sake. The gospel of purification through fire has ancient roots in millenary creeds, and it has enjoyed an extraordinary revival in recent years.

Commenting on this phenomenon, Professor Noam Chomsky notes that the motives for beneficent social action are sometimes unworthy.

We must recognize these facts, and regret them deeply, but not be paralyzed by this recognition. Anger, outrage, confessions of overwhelming guilt may be good therapy; they can also become a barrier to effective action, which can always be made to seem incommensurable with the enormity of the crime. Nothing is easier than to adopt a new form of self-indulgence, no less debilitating than the old apathy. The danger is substantial. It is hardly a novel insight that confession of guilt can be institutionalized as a technique for evading what must be done. It is even possible to achieve a feeling of satisfaction by contemplating one's evil nature. No less insidious is the cry for "revolution," at a time when not even the germs of new institutions exist, let alone the moral and political consciousness that could lead to a basic modification of social life. If there will be a "revolution" in America today, it will no doubt be a move towards some variety of fascism. We must guard against the kind of revolutionary rhetoric that would have had Karl Marx burn down the British Museum because it was merely part of a repressive society. It would be criminal to overlook the serious flaws and inadequacies in our institutions, or to fail to utilize the substantial degree of freedom that most of us enjoy, within the framework of these flawed institutions, to modify them or even replace them by a better social order. One who pays some attention to history will not be surprised if those who cry most loudly that we must smash and destroy are later found among the administrators of some new system of repression.[2]

Spokesmen for governments and parties of a revolutionary cast try, of course, to identify themselves with this mood of restless, febrile violence, and to use its explosive potential as a political or indeed as a quasi-military force.

The result is a competition in maneuver designed to bring the amorphous and many-sided movement of hatred and outrage under the control of one or another of the rival revolutionary groups or parties.

Those with allegiance to the revolutionary idea range from disciplined activists and their faithful sympathizers to well-meaning idealists and Utopians, who sometimes join in manifestos, demonstrations, or other proposals made by the activists and sometimes decline to do so. Some are engaged in many causes of a political character, others in only a few. In the recent past, many who belong in this grouping have concerned themselves almost exclusively with the problems of the nonindustrialized countries of Asia, Latin America, and Africa, which have also been the primary focus of attention for the Chinese or Cuban Communist parties and those affiliated with them.

While this school shows considerable variety, both in ideas and in methods of action, it has a number of important features that are widely shared. Its members almost invariably find ways of justifying anything done by one of the Communist states, and opposing those moves of American or Allied foreign policy opposed by the Soviet Union, or China, or both. Whatever happens, they tell us, is the fault of the United States, or of the West more

---

[2] *American Power and the New Mandarins* (1967), pp. 17–18.

generally, or the fault of the bankers and industrialists, who, in their view, pull the strings of American and Western power. And as good puritans, much affected by the simplicitudes of Marx, we half believe them.

The books and articles they produce, and their talks on television, rely heavily on pseudo-Marxist arguments. Security, they tell us, is not a problem of political organization, but of economics. The costly Western struggle to achieve an equilibrium in world politics since 1945 can only be explained, they contend, as an imperial search for markets and investment opportunities. This interpretation, they say, accounts even for Korea and Vietnam, where five centuries of naked "imperialism" could not begin to pay the costs of the American security expenditure.

The spokesmen of this school are not numerous, although they are not without influence. They have the advantage of the subliminal prestige of the historic Left in the spirit of all Western and democratic societies. Often they are the same people who in June 1941 discovered overnight that the war against Hitler was a war for freedom, not a mere quarrel among imperialists. Around them cluster larger groups for whom it is psychologically difficult to take positions the True Believers would condemn as "reactionary." Their spokesmen are fashionable and formidable. Few care to challenge them.

v

The fourth party in my classification is that of old-fashioned isolationism. Few people admit directly that they belong to that party. Nonetheless, it has many influential members, men who in effect, but not quite in words, wrap themselves in the togas worn during the last generation by Senators Borah, La Follette and Wheeler and by the elder Senator Henry Cabot Lodge and his friends a generation earlier. These men contend that the United States does not need a foreign policy at all beyond one of icy neutrality. In their view the endless quarrels of a wicked world do not affect our safety and therefore should not concern us. They imagine that we are still living in the relatively stable and open world society of the nineteenth century, and that however far Soviet or Chinese power may extend, Americans will be able to trade and travel freely and pursue their legitimate interests in peace according to the principles of nineteenth-century international law.

It follows, they argue, that the United States should not participate in the vanity and folly of world politics, but should devote all the energies of the nation to its domestic problems. America's main contribution to the stability and progress of the world community, one of these men has said, should be "the example of a model society at home." They pass quickly over the changes in political geography that have occurred since 1914, and they do not explain how we could avoid being drawn into the troubles of the world—as we were in 1917 and 1941—should disorder spread beyond a certain threshold. Only a few contend that we should not have gone to war against Germany in 1917 or 1941, but should have used our "influence" to induce peace without victory. Nor do they tell us who in the modern world could take over the responsibilities for the balance of power on which all depend—responsibilities that Britain and France discharged in the last century—if we refuse to participate in efforts to do so.

To questions of this kind the answer of the isolationists today is that of the spokesmen for the policy of America First in 1940 and 1941: "We shall defend the United States from our own shores when someone starts an invasion."

The fallacy of this view was evident in Wilson's time, and again in 1939, when America discovered that the security of the nation required far more than immunity from invasion. It is doubly evident in the nuclear age, in which international coercion could be made effective by procedures that do not involve invasion.[3]

But the isolationist instinct exists and is gaining strength in the United States and in other countries as a reaction to the burdens the West has carried since 1947. It is a powerful, nostalgic, and inaccessible tide of intense feeling. Its strength was one of John-

[3] See pp. 321–322, *infra*.

son's major preoccupations. He had lived through the battles of the thirties as a young congressman. He had seen Franklin Roosevelt struggle with isolationist resistance through a complex series of acts and statements whose contradictions and inconsistencies faithfully reflected the conflicts within the American mind. He knew both the force of the idea and its danger.

In the United States, in Europe, and in Japan the advocates of this approach to foreign policy rely on an unstated premise: that somehow, without affirmative action on the part of the United States and its allies, the world community will find a pattern of peace—that the conditions of peace will emerge, either through agreement among the United States, China, and the Soviet Union or by the automatic working of benign social forces.

Understanding among the United States, China, and the Soviet Union on minimal and reciprocal rules of public order for world politics is a goal devoutly to be sought by the United States. Indeed, it is the goal the United States has sought through thick and thin since the middle forties. But it is not a policy one can assume has been achieved already or will drop from the heavens without a determined and imaginative diplomatic effort. There is no foundation for the faith in the tendency of the state system to reach equilibrium by itself. That belief is contradicted by the history of the century and the daily pressure of forces working for violent change. We have long since rejected the corresponding theory of automatic equilibrium in the field of economic affairs. There is even less reason for accepting such a view about the nightmare world of international politics.

VI

The fifth and sixth schools in the literature of peace are both non-isolationist, at least in language. They agree in principle that an American return to a policy of isolationism would be dangerous to the national interests of the United States and to the chance for peace. But they do not agree on what the main goal of our foreign policy should be.

One might characterize the spokesmen for the fifth school as believers in the Wilsonian doctrine that the goal of American foreign policy should be not peace, or peace alone, but virtue. Its purpose, they argue, should be something more than the protection of our national interest in the establishment of a peaceful world of autonomous nation-states, each protected against outside interference in its internal affairs. They would regard the foreign policy of the United States as successful only if it resulted in the emergence around the world of states whose internal social and political lives met with their approval. In short, they take Wilson's famous statement that "the world must be made safe for democracy" to mean not simply a world in which American democracy could be safe at home, but a world consisting only of democratic nations.

All members of the fifth school find it difficult to become enthusiastic over the idea of the balance of power. Indeed, for most of them both the phrase and the idea are odious. Nor are they inspired by the notion of peace itself so long as the states system contains members whose internal policies outrage them—Russia or South Africa, as the case may be, or Albania, or Spain, or Haiti. Some preachers of this faith would have us engaged in the world not to support a general system of equilibrium, but only to uphold governments they could characterize as progressive, democratic, and forward-looking. Another group within the same party advances the mirror image of this view as the proper major premise for our foreign policy: that American support should be available only to governments conservative and anticommunist enough to meet with *their* approval.

These men would have us pick allies in world politics the way they decide which teams to root for in professional sports. Some achieve favorable or unfavorable impressions of nations as tourists or as readers of newspapers and novels. It is bizarre, but commonplace, to hear people ready to vote for peace or war because they think a country is "plucky," or "democratic," or "arrogant," or "the underdog," or "in need of a good lesson." These opinions usually rest on scattered and superficial information or on convictions passed down by their grandfathers.

Men of this outlook tend to regard foreign policies addressed to the problem of organizing and curbing the use of power as "immoral"; they speak of foreign policy as "moral" only if it supports and protects foreign governments they deem to be "moral," or people who are related in religion, race, or culture, or share the same history.

Correspondingly, they object when the policy of their nation supports a government they regard as corrupt or wrongly oriented, or a nation of another race or culture. They would not regard a foreign policy as "moral" because its goal is to achieve and maintain a system of peace. Such a definition smacks of "power politics" and is therefore "immoral," by hypothesis, in their scheme of thought.

Both branches of the fifth school, then, would base foreign policy, not on their perception of national interests, but on their particular personal or political enthusiasms. Since the governments of many countries change their political colorations relatively often, such a premise would make continuity in foreign policy impossible. And since socialist revolutions are irreversible, according to the Brezhnev doctrine, the application of the theory would permit us to be "nibbled to death," in Adlai Stevenson's phrase, rather easily.

The members of the school of Wilsonian virtue mistake the cause for the consequence of American involvement in world politics. The goal of a nation's foreign policy is not to help foreign governments some citizens happen to approve, but to protect basic interests in the safety, prosperity, and well-being of the nation itself. It can hardly be contended that the safety and well-being of the United States require the nation to crusade for the conversion of all peoples to faith in the gospel of democracy, or the liberation of all who live under tyrannies. The premise of the fifth school would have had us intervening in the Soviet Union and Eastern Europe, and in many other areas where personal freedom is in peril, ever since World War II. Nonetheless, we feel better and suffer less conflict and guilt when our allies and associates share our social habits and values. Of course the influence of the United States is on the side of progress, democracy, and social action wherever it can be felt, although not many societies are strong enough to sustain the politics of freedom for long, and few indeed adapt their internal policies to suggestions made by the United States.

The strangest myth associated with recent American foreign policy is that the United States invariably supports the status quo, and prefers dictators to the democrats and libertarians of this world, and others who espouse programs of social progress. Since the war the bulk of our economic and military aid has gone to Europe, to Japan, to Iran, to India, and to Pakistan. And we have supported many governments the more "liberal" members of the fifth school would describe as progressive and forward-looking— those headed by Tito, Nehru, Frei, Betancourt, the Shah of Iran, Sukarno, Nkrumah, Nasser, and Ben Bella, to cite a few. During World War II, of course, we helped Stalin's government against Hitler—not because we thought Stalin had become a "liberal" or a "democrat," but because we regarded him as a lesser threat than Hitler to the balance of power. During and after that war we offered the Soviet Union reconstruction loans on most favorable terms, and later invited the Soviet Union and the countries of Eastern Europe to share in the Marshall Plan.

Against this background of experience it is difficult to explain the persistence of the view—which often amounts to an article of faith—that American foreign policy is addicted to the support of those whom the convinced would regard as reactionaries, tyrants, and military dictators.

To worldly idealists like Johnson and Rusk the major premise of the fifth school was attractive, but naïve and irrelevant. The practice of foreign affairs these days requires our Presidents and Secretaries of State to move warily in a realm without heroes, villains, or illusions. Each man with whom they deal—friend, neutral, or adversary—seeks to gain advantages for his nation without incurring risks that could imperil his own position at home. All Johnson's formidable energy was focused on an agenda of issues that seemed critical to the possibility of peace: programs of economic liberalization such as the Kennedy Round of tariff reductions and the reform of the monetary system; the internationalization of aid; the political development of NATO; above all, the quest for agreement with Russia and China. At the same time he had to hold off pressures that threatened to destroy any possibility for creating a system of peace: the withdrawal of troops from Europe; the war in the Middle East; and the apparently endless agony in Vietnam. In confronting these problems, a nice discrimination among governments in terms of their "liberalism" (or "conservatism") did not seem to be the primary issue. For Johnson and Rusk, as for their predecessors, the primary issue was aggression, not virtue.

I do not mean to suggest that they practiced diplomacy coldly or without human feelings. Andreas Papandreou has often said that he owes his life to Johnson. He is right.

The sixth school is that of realpolitik. It is proud of its tough-mindedness. It eschews the major premise of the fifth school as imperialistic. Our foreign policy, as Ronald Steel puts it, should not seek to remake the world in the American image, but only to protect basic national interests.[4] The members of the sixth school consider it absurd to care whether the Ruritanians live under a liberal constitution or an iron-fisted dictator. We should help defend Ruritania, these men would argue, only if it is a country whose resources should be denied to our opponents or whose strategic position or resources are so important to our safety as to justify American protection.

The eloquent spokesmen of the sixth school stress, and stress heavily, that the United States is "overcommitted" and must retreat. But their books and speeches are not clear about how far we

[4] *The End of Alliance* (1964), p. 142.

should retreat in order to stop being overcommitted. Nor do they offer us a clear criterion for deciding what commitments are excessive.

They all agree, for example, that we have a vital national interest in the continued independence and political integrity of Western Europe. Most would add that we and the Europeans have a corresponding security interest in the political independence and territorial integrity of Japan. That interest, manifestly, is to prevent these enormous centers of wealth, skill, and political influence from falling under the control of those who would be our adversaries. Equally, the United States has a security interest in rallying Europe and Japan to full partnership with us in the onerous and expensive tasks of peace.

But some members of the sixth school would confine American programs of security to the protection of a small island of rich white men in Europe, and a few corresponding pockets around the world, and let the rest of the world sink into chaos or slavery. One distinguished critic, a first-rate professor of law, spoke of the campaign in Vietnam as nearly unintelligible, since the United States has suffered no hurt at home comparable to that we have inflicted on North Vietnam, "nor have any allies of ours to whom we have ties of tradition, proximity, culture—and, one might say, race." And a famous senator once argued with Johnson that we had no business being in Vietnam because "they are not our kind of people."

No approach to foreign policy aroused Johnson to comparable passion. "Don't they know," he would ask, "that eighty percent of the people of the world are not white?" But there was a more fundamental reason for his reaction. Arguments of this kind touched the deepest spring of Johnson's nature, his commitment to equality among the races. No one could be much in Johnson's company without feeling the intensity of his zeal in the cause of racial justice.

Other members of the sixth school, who would reject a lily-white foreign policy for the United States as unthinkable, are dubious nonetheless even about defending our interests in the future of the Middle East and the Mediterranean basin, on the flank of Europe, and now gravely threatened by accelerating Soviet incursions. Most of the men of this school would have us bring the troops back from Europe, the Mediterranean, and the Far East. They take these positions without explaining how nuclear deterrence would be credible under such circumstances, and how we could preserve and protect nonnuclear options for dealing with situations of strain. Indeed, many go further. They admit that a general American withdrawal could lead to neutralism or reorientation, both in Europe and in the Far East, but are willing to risk even so drastic a change in the balance of power rather than face the alternative.

VII

Next in this classification I should list a group of men and women who believe that nothing short of "world government" could contain and master the destructive impulses and the habits of violence that have acquired such acceptance and momentum since 1914. In zeal and in policy some members of this school resemble those of the second school, the advocates of an all-out ideological crusade against communism. At the end of the Second World War, for example, Bertrand Russell favored the use of a nuclear threat—and presumably of the nuclear weapon, if necessary—to force the Soviet Union to abandon its politics of expansion and settle down to a course of peaceful cooperation with the rest of the world within the framework of the United Nations Charter. And Senator Fulbright has recently come close to the same position, proposing a new and decisive effort to enforce the Charter absolutely.[5]

Believers in world government are usually dismissed as unworldly idealists, men who misjudge the tenacious grip of the national idea on the minds and behavior patterns of men. And, it is said, they also misjudge the extent to which the world is divided by competing ambitions and ideologies.

[5] "Reflections: In Thrall to Fear," *The New Yorker* (Jan. 8, 1972), p. 41.

When policies of world government, or of the United Nations, are presented as a practical alternative to those being pursued, they are pretense. But the concept should not be ignored as an aspiration for the unstable system of politics and law which has developed so painfully since 1945. It will not do to dismiss this branch of the literature simply as an unworldly philosophy. Of course it is an unworldly philosophy. And there is an unusually large proportion of eccentrics and Utopians in the ranks. But it deserves more consideration than it usually gets. Many great changes in the condition of mankind—the abolition of slavery, for example, and the vindication of women's rights—have been achieved by the zeal and single-mindedness of unworldly, eccentric Utopians.

The process of fission in international society, and the stress of cumulative change, may become so rapid and so bewildering as to make the management of public power almost inconceivably difficult under any alternative set of hypotheses. If one views the history of the last twenty-five years as a race between the forces of fission and those of fusion—between the risks of anarchy and those of monopolar, bipolar or multipolar imperium—the idea of world government takes on a different cast.

Certain trends toward fusion—those in the sphere of monetary and commercial policy, for example, or the cycle of efforts to bring the nuclear weapon under international control—suggest that methods of international collaboration, and indeed of international "government," within patterns that now seem inconceivable, may not be so inconceivable after all. If no other methods can work, then man's instinct for survival, if it still exists, may force us to come together.

These seven schools, each drawn from a different major premise, profess to provide alternative foundations for the foreign policy of the United States as it has developed since 1947. Their implications will be explored in some detail in the next five chapters.

The premise of the eighth school is that foreign policy should be addressed to the protection of national safety, and that it is the national interest of the United States to help achieve an accepted balance of power, which could become the foundation for an accepted system of peace in the world, reaching toward the principles articulated in the Charter of the United Nations as a norm. The limits and dilemmas of that premise will be considered in Chapters 9 and 10 in the light of the examination of its rivals.

# 4

## The Revisionists

BY ANY STANDARD the revisionists belong at one end of the spectrum among those who criticize the ends and means of American and Allied foreign policy since the end of World War II. Most of the members of this group would consider themselves relatively orthodox Marxists in their intellectual formation, although in fact they owe a good deal more to Hobson than to Marx. By one of the ironies of language, it is common to call these men "revisionists" in the literature about foreign policy, though not, of course, in the vocabulary of Marxism.

The revisionist literature derives from books by Gabriel Kolko, Gar Alperovitz and D. F. Fleming, and above all from the fervent and lyrical work of William Appleman Williams. Williams is an old-fashioned Midwestern agrarian radical possessed by a single overpowering idea. Two generations ago men of his cast of mind traced all the world's ills to the sinister manipulations of international bankers or arms manufacturers—"merchants of death"— who, they thought, spun webs of intrigue to draw America into their nefarious and profitable wars. Williams' idée fixe is different. He believes that American foreign policy has been dominated since 1789 by an implacable instinct to expand in order to obtain export markets, without which, in his view, the capitalist system would grind to a halt.

While the books and articles by Kolko, Alperovitz, Carl Oglesby, and men of similar view, hardly march in goose step, they are characterized by a central core of argument that is the foundation (or the assumption) for a major school of writing about recent foreign policy.

This chapter will concentrate on the version of the revisionist argument presented by Carl Oglesby in *Containment and Change*,[1] referring to other writings in the school in order to amplify Oglesby's presentation or to indicate significant variations on some of its themes.

Oglesby's essay is crisp in style and responsive in its reasoning. It has humor, a rare and most welcome quality in the solemn literature of the Cold War. Unlike Chomsky, Oglesby is incapable of ignoring evidence or ideas that do not fit his thesis. His paper is therefore a valuable contribution to a genuine debate, far less obscure in its handling of difficult problems than many other documents in the canon. Moreover, Oglesby does not have much taste for the shrillness and invective which are such notable features of the literature, and is less disposed than some of his confreres to view history as a conspiracy. He does, of course, recite the ritual charges against the bias, arrogance, imperialism, and appetite for power supposed to characterize American foreign policy during the last generation. But he does so briefly, and without enthusiasm. Clearly, he is more interested in the issues than in the game.

II

Oglesby's analysis starts with an arresting proposition.

If the Cold War is really what most Americans consider it to be, then the Cold War is necessary. If it is necessary, then it may very

[1] Oglesby and Richard Shaull (1967). Professor Robert J. Maddox of Pennsylvania State University has studied the methods of some of the revisionist historians, *The New Left and the Origins of the Cold War* (in press, 1972). See also C. S. Maier, "Revisionism and the Interpretation of Cold War Origins," 4 Perspectives in American History 311 (1970).

well be necessary for America to maintain her hold over South Vietnam.[2]

Like many other critics of Allied foreign policy, Oglesby is primarily concerned with Vietnam and the problem of American policy toward China and the developing countries of the Third World. But his approach to Vietnam is quite different from that of most of his cobelligerents. It starts with a subtle analysis of the development of American policy toward the Soviet Union in Europe after the war and traces the application of this experience to the problem of peace in Asia.

Through a series of nearly intuitive moves and countermoves, Oglesby says, the United States and the Soviet Union reached a standstill position in Europe which represents "not a bad vision" —indeed, a "bit of hope." [3] Facing each other as rivals over the devastated Europe of 1945, both the United States and the Soviet Union were understandably afraid, he says—the United States of another long revolutionary convulsion in Europe, directed by the Soviets; the Soviet Union of a threat to the Soviet regime, directed by the West and mounted from Western Europe. But, Oglesby remarks, "the Russian-American war was not fought." [4] Instead a tacit understanding was reached establishing "the territorial lines of the European Cold War." [5]

The theory of Western diplomacy in this process, he says, approximates that laid down by George Kennan's famous article in *Foreign Affairs* in 1947, although it was often expounded in more general terms: No preventive war was necessary; if the West held the line patiently, disallowed recklessness and opportunism, and pushed back where the Russians pushed out, the errors of Communism would reveal themselves, and peace, or at least an acceptable modus vivendi, would emerge in the end.

By 1962 a "strategic power balance" was "undeniable," in Oglesby's phrase, and a pragmatic process of adjustment became

[2] Op. cit., p. 31.
[3] P. 21.
[4] P. 16.
[5] Ibid.

the governing rule of the Cold War viewed as a political process. The mutually qualifying aims of American policy, in Oglesby's formulation, are the avoidance of war and the creation of a stable global society in which liberal values will predominate.

This goal, Oglesby contends, cannot be achieved without effort. It requires the acceptance by both sides of four basic rules:

(1) Global war is an unsatisfactory means for the achievement of global objectives. This rule "*must* be established. But unwise nations may not understand that. So it sometimes becomes essential for the wise nations to produce that commitment among the unwise" by the threat and occasionally the use of military power. "Power plus the credibility of its use equals deterrence, which makes all nations pacifists and creates time and room for diplomatic manoeuvre." [6]

(2) A global truce line must be unambiguously drawn, as the most important of all the rules for a predictable and workable modus vivendi: one must even be prepared to go to war to keep the line intact. Oglesby recognizes Castro's conquest of power in Cuba as an anomaly in this setting, but, he thinks, only an apparent anomaly. Cuba, he says, "will still remain forbidden territory to the major opposition power." [7]

(3) Through the process of defining and securing the truce line the rival powers build up a store of information about each other, develop and habituate themselves to the modus vivendi, and begin to create a communications system, imperfectly at first, and later with more assurance.

(4) Finally, the dividend of this patience is that the common interests so necessary to a more productive relationship will have had time to incubate, and then to prevail.

The model of Soviet-American relations in Europe since 1945, Oglesby contends, suggested the idea that a comparable truce could be realized everywhere:

> Make up your minds to have no big war; draw clearly in the world's good honest dirt a line which you will neither violate nor

[6] Pp. 19–20.
[7] P. 20.

see violated; in the joint superintending of that line, learn a few things about one another, stop dreaming apocalyptic dreams, stop evangelizing the millennium, face the fact that the future is no nation's private property—and so make peace.[8]

The United States looked at Asia "in this wisdom's light," Oglesby says, though only after a period of some turbulence and confusion. But by 1954, he says, "we were copying our European policy in Asia, treaty for treaty, bastion for bastion." [9]

> The first principle of the European wisdom was applied: We shall seek no war with China . . . To prove that we meant what we said, General MacArthur was retired, and the Korean War was cautiously made to disappear. The second principle now had to be established: The truce line had to be fixed. We hold here, they there. No violence must be done to this line; it is the only hope we have that Chinese people decades from now can at last clasp hands with American people.[10]

The line is not unfair, Oglesby says. The United States made no move to protect Tibet or to liberate North Korea or North Vietnam. Chiang Kai-shek remains "penned up." Flexibility about trade, travel, and the exchange of experts is encouraged so long as "the unnegotiable condition of every prospect," the inviolability of the truce line, is respected.

This hypothesis, Oglesby says, makes American policy in Vietnam comprehensible. Its real point is not that China controls Hanoi, but that China should require Hanoi to abide by the basic rules of the Cold War. Oglesby interprets an official speech of George Ball, when he was Undersecretary of State, in the light of this theory. Ball had said:

> "A main focus of the [East-West] struggle has shifted recently from Europe to Asia because the Soviet Union, having grown powerful, has begun to have a stake in the *status quo*. The purpose of the forcible containment of Communist China is to induce a similar change in its outlook . . . This is the issue in Viet-Nam. This is what we are fighting for. This is why we are there." [11]

[8] P. 21.
[9] P. 22.
[10] Ibid.
[11] Pp. 28–29.

Oglesby reads this speech, not unreasonably, as a warning that China "must expand her influence, accept the discipline of the Cold War, and impose that discipline on her Vietnamese friends." [12] I should rephrase the message, I believe more realistically, in this way: Hanoi could not have carried on the war in Indochina without Soviet and Chinese supplies and other assistance. The war should indeed be viewed as an integral part of the process of line-drawing Oglesby describes so vividly. But the rules of the Cold War would in this case require no more, at a minimum, than Chinese abstinence—like the abstinence Stalin finally accepted in Greece—not positive cooperation with us in putting out the fire. Such positive cooperation in putting out fires has been suggested from time to time during the last twenty-five years. Perhaps it really occurred in Korea after the situation there had dragged on long enough to generate a dangerously explosive potential. For different reasons, comparable pressures are now to be expected in the relationship between the United States and China. As these pages are written in the late summer of 1971, it seems reasonable to expect Chinese cooperation in ending the Vietnam war on terms favorable to the United States, in order to obtain American support against the threat of Soviet attack on China from Siberia.

Oglesby infers, quite correctly, that the United States has tried —though without coercion—to induce the Soviet Union to take a more active part in settling the Vietnam war, as it says it did finally in Korea. But without the pressure of credible threats that could be hinted at in the early fifties, but not in the late sixties, American inducements to the Soviet Union (and to China) have so far been unavailing in Vietnam. And the prospect of a rapprochement between China and the United States stirred the Soviet Union to more active support of North Vietnam. As a result, the United States had no real alternative to the slow, bitter, patient course that was followed in Vietnam. As Oglesby points out, the effect of a withdrawal from Vietnam on uncertainty was unacceptably dangerous, for the reasons he gives with clarity and pre-

[12] P. 29.

cision. The political impact of Soviet mobilizations in Siberia and elsewhere may of course produce the realignments in world politics—particularly in Chinese policy—which no lesser pressure was capable of achieving.

Oglesby advances his theory of the Cold War as vastly more rational and realistic than the fudgy explanations frequently put forward by officials. Since I have long expounded the Cold War process in terms strikingly like those Oglesby uses, I can hardly complain of his general thesis. But he is unfair, I think, to some of my former colleagues.

For example, Oglesby argues that it is intellectually insulting to say we are in Vietnam because of the SEATO treaty, since it is obvious that no strong state will hesitate for a moment to violate a treaty that it judges to be harmful to its national interests.[13] But Oglesby's theory of the Cold War turns on the achievement of deterrence by drawing lines and demonstrating one's willingness to use force to insist on those lines as boundaries. Isn't a treaty a solemn and public way to draw a segment of the Oglesby Line? Isn't the existence of a treaty therefore an integral part of the Oglesby Hypothesis, not a less sophisticated alternative to it? And isn't it indispensable for the United States to uphold its treaties, in terms of the Oglesby Rule, in order to maintain the deterrent influence of the Oglesby Line itself?

I should comment also on Oglesby's assumption that strong states ignore treaties at will. It is common to find this assertion made, especially by writers who have never participated in government, and above all by men who advocate more morality in the conduct of politics and flay as "immoral" those who have recently had responsibility for government.

The surest way for a strong state to become a weak one is to evade its commitments.

The fact that France refused to honor its obligations to Israel in 1967 has not helped its diplomacy in the Arab world or elsewhere. On the contrary, the demonstration that a French promise is

[13] Pp. 7–8.

worthless gave the *coup de grâce* to French foreign policy, already weakened by its vacillations and failures thirty years before. The wiser course was that of Churchill before the dilemma of helping Greece during World War II. Britain can afford to lose a battle, he said "but not her honor."

Of course treaties become obsolete when the circumstances in which they originated no longer exist. But unless promises are respected, only force, constantly employed, could safeguard the safety of nations—an alternative to Oglesby's pragmatic vision of the Cold War that would surely reduce international society to Hobbes' vision of man's fate in a Hobbesian state of nature—"nasty, brutish, and short."

Similarly, Oglesby lists and dismisses as naïve, absurd, or dishonest a number of other arguments for the official position on Vietnam—for example, the argument that "if we fail to contain Them here, we shall have to contain Them some place else." [14] This, he says, is always the cry of global empire. In its usual form, it "is primitive, paranoid, and mechanistic." [15] But, he says, the argument conceals a nub of truth: the eternal question whether the conviction that one is fighting for social justice should be considered to justify the international use of force. If one values peace above one's conception of justice, he indicates, the rule is sound.

There is, however, another aspect to Oglesby's comment. The official statements about Vietnam, which he derides, make precisely the point that lies behind his own "rational" theory of the Cold War. The importance of the Oglesby Line in that theory is that if we make it clear at intervals that we are willing to fight for the line, it will become a factor of stability and predictability in world politics. The line is of critical importance, according to Oglesby, precisely because if we fail to insist on respect for it, we shall indeed have to fight Them somewhere else, and more often.

In short, Oglesby's theory turns out to be the same as the offi-

[14] P. 13.
[15] Ibid.

cial version. The Oglesby Doctrine and the Truman Doctrine are identical. Without pausing to discuss each item he raises in debate, let us return to the main thread of his argument.

### III

Thus far Oglesby's argument has advanced three propositions:

( 1 ) If the Cold War is really what most Americans think it is, then it is necessary.

( 2 ) In its most sophisticated version, the Cold War is a way of avoiding war with the Soviet Union or China by respecting interests they define as of particular importance to them, and insisting on their respect for interests we define as of particular importance to us. Through reciprocal adherence to four simple rules a balance of power could be achieved and maintained, and both sides could begin to develop modes of communication and patterns of understanding that should lead to a modus vivendi, and indeed to peace.

( 3 ) This pattern of adjustment developed in Europe and was then applied to Asia, both in Korea and in Vietnam. The Oglesby-Truman theory explains what the earnest and intelligent, if misguided, men who conduct the American government think they have been doing in Vietnam.

The argument against that policy, Oglesby says, must address the issues implicit in his version of the theory and not content itself with the beating of dead horses and with a parade of atrocities:

> The Cold Warrior who sees Asian affairs in this way might be forgiven his exasperation with both China and the American peace movement. He does not need to be reminded of the carnage in Vietnam. Many of his kind have seen it much closer up than the unblooded peaceniks ever will. He is, after all, a man, this Cold War dialectician; he has sons and daughters and he prefers life to death; no one has any right to assume that he is less anguished than the next man by the sight of scorched earth, burnt flesh, and torture. From our observation post outside the Establishment, where we suppose for some reason that the visibility is better, we critics

inform him that his war is not helping the Vietnamese. If he were not gagged by the official pretense that it is, maybe he would reply to us: "Of course. I know that. Do you take me for an idiot?" We inform him that his bombing raids in the countryside and whorehouse abandon in the cities are laying the nation waste, and that this physical and cultural slaughter, by a familiar psychology, is only making more Vietnamese turn Communist. Maybe he wants to say: "What could be more obvious? I struggle with this problem day and night. But why can't you see," he might say to us critics, "that Red China has to yield to the partitioning of Vietnam? Of course that's hard for many Vietnamese to take. But is it really more than history demanded of the Germans, whose society was, after all, mature and a million times more integrated than Vietnam's? And don't we have a perfect precedent in Korea? This tiny sliver of a country that has been partitioned for most of its life—at one time into three parts by the French and before that into hundreds of parts by its warlords—is its present temporary partition really so high a price to pay, if in return for what [sic] we purchase stability in Asia? And if the price of refusing partition is the undermining of that truce line upon which we build all our hopes for an Oriental reconciliation? Be realistic," he says to us idealists; "This is not a perfect world by any measure, and it just so happens that history is all against us. We are doing everything we know how to do to change man's fate by making peace *practical*. We do this not only in the teeth of Red China and these scandalously persistent Vietnamese guerrillas, but here at home we must also fend off you soft-heads who want an impossible peace and those hard-heads yonder who want an unthinkable war." [16]

I have two principal objections to Oglesby's version of American policy since 1947. First, I believe it is too optimistic in its view that the Soviet Union has in fact accepted his rules of crisis management, and that détente and a balance of power in Europe have been achieved and stabilized. As Couve de Murville has recently remarked, "Russian policy in its broad outline has remained set since 1945 . . . it develops in a logical and even inevitable fashion." [17] Russian policy has always been patient, long-sighted, and flexible in finding ways around obstacles without attacking them directly or taking excessive risks. In the Middle East, the Soviet Union is outflanking NATO and trying to render it irrelevant. In

[16] Pp. 23–24.
[17] *Times* (London), March 8, 1971, p. 12.

the Far East, Soviet power, both military and political, flows outward at an astonishing and an accelerating pace, which Western opinion has thus far studiously ignored. While there may have been a strategic balance of forces in 1962, the dynamism of Soviet policy toward science makes the notion of strategic balance for more than a short period of time dubious.

My second objection to Oglesby's version of official policy is that it makes no mention of the United Nations Charter and of the tension in men's minds between the ideas of the Charter and those he expounds.

Oglesby's answer to the theory of American foreign policy during the last twenty-five years consists of three propositions, not necessarily consistent:

(1) The United States, and not Stalinist Russia, is responsible for starting the Cold War.

(2) In any event, the premises that might justify a policy of containing Soviet expansion do not apply to China, which is a peace-loving, isolationist nation, and certainly do not apply in Vietnam, where American policy is genuinely imperialist, dominated by a desire to profit from its control over the economy of South Vietnam.

(3) Then, in an argument altogether distinct from his economic or balance-of-power explanations for American policy, Oglesby contends that American policy is concerned, not with peace or profit, but with ideology, and that its true purpose, at least in the Third World, is to oppose the anti-imperialist revolution of the poor countries. He sees that revolution as an immense and autonomous force, not economic or Utopian in its motivation, but directed simply and exclusively at the destruction of a society deemed evil, and of its leadership. Oglesby identifies himself deeply with this current of feeling. In the end, I believe, this rage to destroy is the true heart of Oglesby's case against American policy, at least as it applies to the Third World. In his view the moral justification for the process of revolt should be deemed to override the goal of peace itself. The Oglesby theory of the Cold War, he concedes, is the only road to international peace. But the

price for peace, to his mind, would be too great. Peace in that sense would allow evil men, institutions, and ideas to survive; therefore, he pleads, we should prefer revolution to peace.

IV

Like most of his fellow revisionists, Oglesby contends that the United States started the Cold War. He ridicules as outmoded orthodoxy the view that Stalin launched the Cold War and that the United States, having nothing to gain from it, did nothing to provoke it. He does, of course, concede that the ideology of Communism has had a part in the self-reinforcing process we call Cold War. Communism, after all, rests on a social theory that, in the name of science, claims that class warfare and war between countries of different social systems are inevitable, and that good Communists should do what they can to advance the cause of proletarian revolution. But the primal guilt for this phase of the conflict, he says, is American.

From the point of view of policy, and from the point of view of historical analysis as well, the argument over who started the Cold War is irrelevant. It is particularly irrelevant if the revisionists are right in portraying the Soviet Union of Stalin's time as a benign and innocent regime, irrevocably committed to the ideal of "socialism in one country," and willing to abandon any trace of an interest in the cause of world revolution in order to cooperate with the West. If the Soviet Union under Stalin had these policies, it is presumably even more pacific today. The moves and countermoves of the Cold War have gone on for twenty-five years at least—since 1917, in fact, in a more general sense. If, for the moment, we accept the revisionist doctrine that Russia has lost its imperial impulse and the Soviet Union its Communist faith, the Cold War would still have a dynamic of its own, rooted in fear. In international affairs, as in family life, the factors that precipitate many prolonged quarrels are shrouded in mystery. Normally they are not so important as the will to bring the conflict to an end. That task involves considerations quite different from the assessment of blame for the first move. The initial cause of a war is often forgotten by the time the parties settle down to making peace. Even when it is not forgotten, the initial cause of a war never controls the process of peacemaking. If Soviet policy under Stalin and his successors really was what the revisionists claim it to have been, there were many Genevas and Camp Davids since 1947 when beleaguered American Presidents would have been happy to gain political prestige at home, and enhance their roles in history, by reaching accommodations with the Soviet Union and China on terms that satisfied the standards of fairness set out by the revisionists. The offers of the Baruch Plan to internationalize nuclear energy, and of the Marshall Plan to assist the Soviet Union and the nations of Eastern Europe were dramatic episodes in a long list of American proposals for general détente. More recently that list includes plan after plan for balanced and mutual force reductions in Europe, including the creation of denuclearized zones, as well as the broader implications of nuclear agreements.

But the whole of the revisionist literature puts great stress on The First Move. To the revisionists the Soviet Union approached the postwar period in a euphoric and Utopian mood, hoping that the wartime collaboration of the Soviet Union and its Western allies would be translated into policies of peaceful collaboration. Kolko comments that in 1943 and 1944 the Soviets "lost contact with reality and believed that co-existence was possible on equitable terms." [18]

To the revisionists the shock above all others that made the Soviets realize that the United States was pursuing a policy of grim hostility was the American "refusal" of a postwar reconstruction loan to the Soviet Union in 1944. Most of the revisionist books and articles stress the episode as one of the critical turning points in the Cold War. All paint a dismal picture of Russia actively seeking a loan, and of American officials delaying and sabo-

[18] Gabriel Kolko, *The Politics of War. The World and United States Foreign Policy, 1943–1945* (1968), p. 337.

taging the project until it died of strangulation.[19] If the United States had pursued a different course during and immediately after the war, these men argue, "it is certain (with the limits of all such hypotheses) that Europe would not be divided today." [20]

To anyone who participated in the making of American foreign policy during and immediately after World War II such arguments are a grotesque fantasy—the complete opposite of the truth.[21] The loan was not "refused." It was made, as soon as the Soviets decided to accept it, in 1945. American officials did not delay or sabotage the project. They pressed the Soviets to accept it with the utmost fervor.

During those years the policy of the United States, fully supported by the chief political and military officials of the government working on Lend-Lease problems—Cordell Hull, Henry Stimson, Henry Morgenthau, Harry Hopkins, Dean Acheson, Edward Stettinius, Jr., John J. McCloy, Adlai Stevenson, Averell Harriman, Oscar Cox, George Ball, and others—was to press with all possible energy to lay the foundation for a relationship of peaceful cooperation with the Soviet Union after the war. In that effort the handling of Lend-Lease arrangements, and the potentialities of a postwar loan under Lend-Lease, were regarded as of central importance.

There was little or no illusion in the government about the nature of Communism, and of the Soviet regime. Few members of

[19] See, e.g., Kolko, op. cit., pp. 337–338; Oglesby, op. cit., pp. 38, 42; William Appleman Williams, *The Tragedy of American Diplomacy* (1959), pp. 151–161, and *American-Russian Relations, 1781–1947* (1952), p. 263; Gar Alperovitz, *Cold War Essays* (1970), p. 42.

[20] David Horowitz, *From Yalta to Vietnam* (1967 ed.), p. 19.

[21] I happen to have been the Lend-Lease desk officer of the State Department for most of the period between 1942 to 1944. In that post I worked directly under Dean Acheson, who was then the Assistant Secretary for Economic Affairs, and for part of the time, after a State Department reorganization, under Charles P. Taft as well. I also had a function and a title within the legal staff of the Office of Lend-Lease Administration. I met almost daily on Lend-Lease matters with colleagues in the Treasury, the Office of Lend-Lease Administration, the Department of Agriculture, and the Army, as well as with political officers of the State Department.

the government suffered from the sentimental fevers of those who thought of Stalin as "Uncle Joe." But that fact gave them a greater sense of concern in seeking to do everything possible to consolidate Soviet-Western cooperation in the postwar period, or at least to prevent a return to the icy atmosphere of the period between the wars. The course of day-to-day relations among the nations allied in a desperate war gave ample evidence of the depth of Soviet suspicions and the abiding character of Soviet inclinations toward expansion. We were fully conscious of the risk that the Soviet Union might follow a difficult, or even a hostile, course in the postwar years. But it was United States policy to minimize that risk, and the effort was pursued with urgency in every possible way. Nobody had forgotten the agreement of 1939 between Hitler and Stalin and all that flowed from it. But we were quick to make excuses for Soviet behavior in that treacherous period and to blame Britain and France for the outcome. And while we found the Soviet Union a difficult ally in the war, here again the American effort was to overcome what we thought might be the causes of such behavior—namely, Soviet doubts about our own motivations.

This policy was sustained and encouraged by a powerful tide in public opinion. Between 1942 and 1945 the Soviet Union was by far our most popular ally. The courage and skill of the Red Army commanded enthusiasm in Congress and in the country. With brutal simplicity, American opinion understood very well indeed that our forces would not have to fight German troops killed on the Eastern front. There was hope everywhere that the fears and suspicions of the period between 1917 and 1941 would be consumed in the fire of war.

There were ominous portents, visible mainly within the government and to those especially interested in Polish or Yugoslav affairs. For example, the Soviets requested medical advice on the problem of treating burns occasioned by fires in tanks. A team of distinguished doctors was assembled and sent posthaste to Tehran. The Soviets changed their minds and refused to allow the doctors into the Soviet Union. There were endless difficulties about cooperation in connection with bombing raids, and, of course, always the bitter, tragic story of Poland.

In retrospect, I view the episode of the proposal for a reconstruction loan as the clearest signal we had at the time that Stalin had made a definite decision at some point in 1944, once it was certain that Hitler was defeated, not to cooperate with the West after the war. Instead, he initiated a policy of expansion that led him later to break the agreements he made with us at Yalta and Potsdam for free elections in Eastern Europe, and to undertake probes in Iran, Greece, Turkey, and, later on, in Yugoslavia. Both Russians and Americans seemed to think that ongoing Soviet dependence on Western reconstruction loans during the postwar period would have been politically and psychologically incompatible with a policy of Soviet expansion—the policy that Stalin planned and initiated during the war in Eastern Europe and Germany, and carried forward thereafter throughout Europe and the Middle East. Stalin was far too realistic to expect even innocent Americans to finance a program of Soviet imperialism.

The project for a postwar reconstruction loan began late in 1943, when Anastas Ivanovich Mikoyan, the Soviet Minister of Foreign Trade, approached Averell Harriman, who was then our ambassador in Moscow, to enquire about the possibility of obtaining more long-range industrial equipment as Lend-Lease during the war, and of making arrangements as soon as possible for American help in the postwar reconstruction of the Soviet Union.[22] We read the telegram reporting their conversation with great hope and set to work at once to prepare a positive reply.

It is often claimed in the revisionist literature that Averell Harriman opposed reconstruction loans to the Soviet Union.[23] On the contrary, he was a zealous and active proponent of such loans from the moment the issue was raised by Mikoyan in 1943. Harriman saw the project from the first "as a factor which should be

---

[22] U.S. Department of State, *Foreign Relations of the United States, 1944*, IV (1966), 1148.

[23] Williams, *The Tragedy of American Diplomacy*, pp. 157–158; D. S. Clemens, *Yalta* (1970), p. 138.

integrated into the fabric of our overall relations rather than dealt with independently in its purely commercial and economic aspects . . . [a matter of high policy on which prompt understanding was] of importance to us . . . as a factor in cementing our relations with the Soviet Union," and good business for the United States as well.[24] In the same period he cabled Hopkins:

> If aid for Russian reconstruction is to be of real value in our overall relations with the Soviet Government as a benefit which they can obtain from us if they play the international game with us in accordance with our standards we must have a well forge[d] instrument to offer them. Vague promises excite Soviet suspicions whereas a precise program offered now to them but kept always within our control to suspend will be of extreme value. Stalin must offer his people quick reconstruction to retain supreme leadership. We on the other hand want Russian business quickly during our period of conversion from war production. I therefore urge that this matter be not left to an interdepartmental committee for study alone but that the subject be energetically pursued in the hope of finding a solution permitting prompt action. I realize of course the political difficulties at home but I hope that the double barrelled advantage of prompt action may offer ammunition for dealing with this aspect.[25]

Hull stressed the same point and the same need for urgency in a memorandum to the President on February 7, 1944.

> You are no doubt aware that Ambassador Harriman has been carrying on informal talks with Soviet officials in a preliminary effort to obtain from them information on the needs of Soviet economy for postwar construction and the best means by which we could be of assistance to them.
>
> This is of such political importance as an indication of our sincere desire to be of assistance to them that it is felt it would be desirable more or less to formalize these preliminary steps. Moreover, the increased Soviet requests for capital goods which cannot easily be justified under Lend-Lease make it imperative to study ways and means of satisfying this demand and making appropriate

[24] U.S. Department of State, op. cit., above, Jan. 9, 1944, p. 1035. See also pp. 1048–1051.

[25] Id., at p. 1053. He urged the same view in a cable to the Secretary of State, pp. 1054–1055.

temporary financial arrangements to assist the Soviets in getting these goods.[26]

In order to speed up the process of preparing such a program and putting it into procurement, Hull suggested the appointment of an interdepartmental committee for the purpose.

Of course, in 1945 and 1946 Harriman urged—and urged wisely—that reconstruction loans were impossible without a basic minimum of political cooperation. But this was apparent to everyone on both sides from the beginning. Harriman had made the same point throughout the war. He believed, as we all did, that American participation in Soviet reconstruction could help tip the balance in Soviet policy toward peace.

The statute book offered only two possible ways to meet Mikoyan's request: a loan financed by the Export-Import Bank, or the hitherto unused "surplus-property disposal" provision of the Lend-Lease Act, authorizing the government to dispose of certain Lend-Lease property on special terms after the end of hostilities. The possibility of using the resources of the Export-Import Bank for the purpose was blocked by 1934 legislation forbidding loans to nations in default on obligations to the American government. After some probing we concluded that there was no feasible way either to obtain a quick modification of that statute—the Johnson Act—or to clear away earlier Soviet defaults. Moreover, the total lending authority of the Export-Import Bank was limited, and the ceiling had virtually been reached. At the time, the bank had no authority to make loans in anything like the amounts being discussed—between $1 billion and $2 billion—and there was no chance of obtaining a change in its statutes or its lending authority on a crash basis.[27] So we turned to the Lend-Lease Act, although ultimate amendment of the Export-Import Bank legislation, and enlargement of its lending authority, was definitely pursued.[28]

The Lend-Lease Act embodied President Roosevelt's ingenious

[26] Id., at p. 1046.
[27] Id., at p. 1047–1048.
[28] Id., at p. 1061.

idea about how to provide war supplies to friendly nations without repeating the disastrous controversy over interallied debts after World War I. The "war debt" argument poisoned world politics for years.[29] Roosevelt foresaw the inevitability of America becoming the chief arsenal of the alliance and put the problem of war supplies on a new footing. If your neighbor is fighting a fire, he said, and needs a hose, of course you lend him yours. After all, quite apart from other considerations, the fire in his house might reach yours. If the hose survives the fire, he gives it back to you. On that basis the Allies should help each other as best they could in prosecuting the war. Thereafter they would reach a settlement with regard to any supplies that had not been destroyed or used up in the course of the war.

The Soviet Lend-Lease program, unlike those for other countries, was based on a fixed schedule of projected supplies and deliveries, called a Protocol. The Soviet Lend-Lease Protocol was prepared with great difficulty once a year. It reflected the Soviet Union's judgment about how best to utilize available shipping space and supplies. It was a document of some thirty foolscap printed pages, setting forth the categories and amounts of supplies and services to be delivered during the year, including military supplies, food, raw materials, industrial plants, and both military and technological training. Subject to rare modifications, the Protocol guided our contracting, allocating, and delivery activities with nearly religious strictness. The Russians were stiff about any changes in its schedules. Their officials had limited authority to agree to modifications, although some changes in procurement and shipping were negotiated. There was, however, no borrowing a cup of sugar over the back fence with them, no swapping of a shipment now for a shipment later, which could easily be arranged with the British, the French, or the Australians. We soon

---

29 Indeed, it is not yet dead. When President de Gaulle became violently unpopular in the United States in 1966 and 1967 the Treasury received thousands of letters suggesting that the United States "collect" the French debt arising from World War I. We used to point out that France still had some claims arising from the American Revolution, which, if paid with interest, would more than offset the American claims of 1917–18.

learned that flexibility of this kind, so helpful in the confusion of trying to supply a dozen theaters of war at once, was beyond the powers of our Soviet colleagues, and we gave up asking.

Under the statute the President had first to find that the defense of a given country was "vital to the defense of the United States." Once this basic finding was made, he could authorize the transfer to the government of that country of goods, services, or information that in his judgment would contribute to the national defense. Since no one could know how long the war would last, the Soviet Lend-Lease Protocols necessarily included major industrial projects as defense plants useful to the prosecution of the war. Their construction could drastically reduce the burden of shipping supplies to the Soviet Union via Murmansk.

In Section 3 (b) the statute provided that the terms and conditions on which a foreign government received aid "shall be those which the President deems satisfactory, and the benefit to the United States may be payment or repayment in kind or property, or any other direct or indirect benefit which the President deems satisfactory." The next section—Section 3 (c) of the Act, on which I primarily relied—provided that after June 30, 1943 (a date later extended to June 30, 1946), or the passage of a concurrent resolution by both houses of the Congress declaring that the President's powers to transfer defense articles and information under the statute were no longer necessary to promote the defense of the United States, the President "shall cease" to exercise his powers to make transfers under the Act, except that until July 1, 1946 (later extended to June 30, 1949), he could make such transfers as might be required to carry out contracts made before July 1, 1943 (later extended to July 1, 1946). That is, the Act specifically contemplated the possibility of transfers for three years after the end of hostilities in order to fulfill surplus disposal contracts entered into before a given day.

Under the authority of Section 3(b) of the Act Roosevelt had already entered into a Lend-Lease Master Agreement with each of the Allies, setting out the principles of mutual assistance that governed the programs and articulating the general approach to be pursued in making the final Lend-Lease settlements after the war. The heart of those agreements was Article VII, which declared that in the final determination of the benefits to be provided the United States in return for Lend-Lease aid,

> the terms and conditions shall be such as not to burden commerce [between the two signatories], but to promote mutually advantageous economic relations between them, and the betterment of world-wide economic relations. To that end, they shall include provision for agreed action [between the signatories], open to participation by all other countries of like mind, directed to the expansion, by appropriate international and domestic measures, of production, employment, and the exchange and consumption of goods, which are the material foundations for the liberty and welfare of all peoples; to the elimination of all forms of discriminatory treatment in international commerce, and the reduction of tariffs and other trade barriers; and in general to the attainment of all the economic objectives [of the Atlantic Charter].

This tremendous mouthful clearly set the course of American policy against any return to the swamps of the war-debt controversy of the twenties. It also sought to commit the Allies against a return to the beggar-thy-neighbor economic policies of the period of autarchy and protectionism between the wars, and to anticipate the policies of full employment and economic liberalism that have characterized Western economic policy since 1945. The economic and political philosophy that produced Article VII has had a creative history since 1943. It led to Bretton Woods, the Havana Charter, GATT, and the Kennedy Round, and its potential is not yet exhausted.

It should also be recalled that Article VII was difficult to negotiate, especially with the British, because of the practice of imperial preference.[30] And it gave rise in Congress to a natural anxiety that Roosevelt—already in his third term—would walk off with all the powers of Congress and remain the imperious master of American politics forever.

Using these ingredients, I drafted a legal theory for meeting Mikoyan's request under the Lend-Lease Act. The basic idea of

[30] See Dean Acheson, *Present at the Creation* (1969), pp. 27–33.

the new agreement would be that as part of the over-all Lend-Lease settlement the United States would contract during the war to sell the Soviet Union after the war those Protocol items that it wanted for postwar use and that were "in the pipeline"—that is, already procured, contracted for, or committed, but undelivered —when the fighting stopped. Since no one could know when the war against the common enemy would end, the Soviet Lend-Lease Protocol necessarily included a considerable number of longer-range items, which would contribute to the war effort and could also be of use to the Soviet economy after the war. Under the proposed Supplemental Lend-Lease Agreement the Soviet Union would obtain these items on a long-term credit, whose interest provision should be slightly above the average of the long- and short-term rates paid by the United States government on its own outstanding debt. With such an agreement on the books, it would be rational to continue to include industrial equipment in the Protocol lists, even though the end of the war in Europe seemed to be approaching. While there had been victories in 1943, and the tide had turned, the Second Front, the landings in Normandy, and the V-bombs were still ahead, and war planning was rightly and necessarily based on the premise of maximum effort until hostilities actually ceased. We thought that the terms of such a supplemental agreement would probably govern the approach to the disposition of delivered lend-lease items that survived the war and that the Soviet Union wished to purchase. Making an agreement of this kind would reduce the pressure to exclude long-term industrial items from the Protocol lists on the legal ground that they could not be justified under the Lend-Lease Act as "defense" items useful in waging war.

The response of the American government to this approach was electric. The administration was eager to reply quickly and affirmatively to the Soviet enquiry, whose political implications were thoroughly understood. Despite the controversial character of its legal theory, my basic memorandum went through the usual bureaucratic gauntlet in record time. I recall one interdepartmental meeting, for example, that started with a short statement of approval by Harry D. White, the chief representative of the Treasury on such questions and a man of fearsome temperament (with whom I happened to be on excellent terms). One of my State Department colleagues, who had missed the import of White's remarks, launched into a lengthy argument designed to overcome the Treasury's institutional attitude of dubiety, at this stage of the war, about nearly all forms of expenditure and Harry White's quite special distaste for anything that looked as if we were being "soft" to Britain or France. I got up, went round the table, and whispered in his ear, "Shut up, Harry has said 'yes.' If you go on, he may change his mind." My colleague quickly terminated his eloquent speech.

The project duly went to the President with the support of all the departments and agencies involved in the Lend-Lease program. The President promptly approved.

The document also included the suggestion that the United States use Section 3 (c) of the Lend-Lease Act as the legal basis for initial reconstruction loans to our Western allies until Congress and the President could develop a more comprehensive basis for reconstruction programs. When the plan was explained to the relevant House and Senate committees, the prevailing reaction was one of hearty approval, with an undertone of resentment about the proposal to make similar contracts with the Western allies. Of course we should help the Russians, these congressmen said. But why do we have to help the others? "The Russians are killing more Germans," several congressmen remarked.

While the Congressional committees did not object, or object much, to the use of Section 3 (c) of the Lend-Lease Act as the foundation for surplus disposal agreements to sell off items contracted for under Lend-Lease programs and undelivered at the end of hostilities, they became more and more concerned lest the section become the basis for relief and reconstruction programs not yet authorized. Spokesmen for the Executive branch gave firm assurances to this effect, which were reiterated in an amendment to the Lend-Lease Act in 1944. Loans under Section 3 (c) of the Lend-Lease Act were in fact made to several Western allies as the first postwar reconstruction loans.

The administration was constantly struggling with the sensitivity of Congressional opinion about the possibility that Roosevelt would use the Lend-Lease Act to establish postwar commercial, monetary, or reconstruction policies without Congressional authorization, or make Lend-Lease transfers for political purposes rather than those of the war. As the war approached its end, Congressional concern on this point became more acute. The congressmen could not see how to distinguish surplus-disposal loans from reconstruction loans; and they were far from convinced that the administration would draw such a line to their satisfaction. The exchanges on the subject became more and more agitated in the hearings on the renewal of the Lend-Lease Act in 1944 and 1945, despite the more and more categorical assurances of administration witnesses on the subject. Indeed, in 1945 Senator Taft led a movement in the Senate that would have required all Lend-Lease shipments to stop the instant hostilities ceased. It was defeated, on a tie vote, only by the vote of the Vice-President.[31] These battles undoubtedly influenced President Truman's controversial ending of Lend-Lease shipments in 1945—a decision he later regretted.[32]

Early in 1944 the proposal for a supplemental Lend-Lease agreement under Section 3 (c) of the Lend-Lease Act was made to the Soviet government, and a draft text was submitted in May. An atmosphere of hope, of urgency, and of optimism prevailed in the United States government. While all other negotiations with regard to Lend-Lease agreements were centered in Washington, Ambassador Harriman pressed hard to be allowed to conduct these particular discussions in Moscow, where he could deal directly with senior Ministers capable of making or obtaining deci-

[31] See G. C. Herring, Jr., "Lend-Lease to Russia and the Origins of the Cold War, 1944-1945," 56 *Journal of American History* (1969), 93, 102-104.
[32] Harry S Truman, *Memoirs*, I (1955), 227-229. See Herring, op. cit., at pp. 108-109.

sions. The Soviet government accepted the draft text as the basis for negotiations and settled down to a process of probing which at first seemed no more than its usual suspicious procedure of hard bargaining. Questions were asked and answered in lengthy telegrams. Straining to be forthcoming, the Americans agreed to many changes in the draft text agreement.

We were acutely conscious of the risk that Russian popularity in Congress and in public opinion might vanish when the euphoria of great military victories gave way to difficult political bickering over the future of Poland and like problems. Eager to establish a solid basis for political cooperation between the two countries after the war, we urged speed on the Russians all through the spring and summer of 1944—the summer of the Second Front and the high tide of Soviet-Allied relations. The State Department's compilation of documents records several such episodes. There were others.

After the Bretton Woods conference a Soviet representative, M. S. Stepanov, pursued the talks in Washington. At least ten lengthy meetings were held in the State Department alone during July and August 1944, with Acheson presiding. Those talks went into every aspect of the complex American document, exploring its terms with care and spirit, and with exasperating tediousness as well. A revised text was given to the Soviets in September. The American government thought a signing was imminent. Disagreement had been narrowed to trivial details without evident significance. As late as October 1944, in a formal note, the Soviet government, "considering entirely timely the raising by the Government of the United States of America of the question of a long term credit in connection with certain deliveries of industrial equipment from the United States," said it had "the intention of offering its proposal on this question in the near future." [33]

On November 6, 1944, a Soviet representative called on Acheson and in a chilling interview conducted in the third person ("the Soviet representative requests the Secretary") asked

[33] U.S. Department of State, *Foreign Relations of the United States, 1944,* IV, (1966), 1150–51.

whether Stepanov had "negotiated" or "asked questions" about the American proposals. With visions of the poor man against a wall somewhere for exceeding his instructions, Acheson assured the Soviet representative that his colleague had made enquiries and not commitments. The Soviet caller, General L. G. Rudenko, chairman of the Soviet Purchasing Commission, delivered to Acheson a letter from Stepanov. In that letter Stepanov called attention to a misunderstanding as to whether he and Acheson had "agreed" on one aspect of the proposed Lend-Lease agreement. He continued:

> As to the contents of the draft agreement and the appendices thereto, sent to me, I have to point out that the draft contains several provisions unacceptable to the Soviet Union, for instance the limited date of placing orders, the amount of discount when determining the prices, as well as the amount of percentage rate, regarding which no agreement was reached during the negotiations between us.[34]

Acheson's reply went well beyond the text of Stepanov's letter:

> I wish to assure you that in regard to the question of Appendix no. 1, there was no misunderstanding between us since this specific question was not discussed in detail in Washington. In this connection, we fully understand that the Soviet authorities in Moscow after giving further and careful consideration to Appendix no. 1 desire to propose amendments to the schedule contained in that Appendix. We will be pleased to receive the further views of the Soviet Government in regard to this matter.
>
> In connection with the other questions raised in your letter, we completely understood that the final draft submitted to you contained certain provisions to which your instructions did not permit you to agree. You will recall, in this regard, that in presenting the final draft to you, we explained that it represents on the points at issue the final position of the United States Government. Moreover, you will recall that in working out the details of the final draft it was explained that because of definite legal limitations we were not in a position to make any further changes in the proposed agreement on several of the specific points which you raised during the discussions.
>
> It is our sincere hope that the Soviet authorities after giving

[34] U.S. Department of State, *Foreign Relations of the United States, 1944*, IV, (1966), 1152.

careful consideration to the proposals made will authorize the conclusion of the agreement as contained in the final draft submitted to you, with such modifications as may be mutually agreed upon in Appendix no. 1.[35]

American solicitude for Stepanov's fate is echoed later, when a memorandum carefully notes that Mr. Stepanov had "registered his non-concurrence" to certain features of the plan embodied in the September draft.[36]

The Soviet reply promised in its note of October 31 was delivered on January 3, 1945, immediately before the Yalta Conference. Molotov handed Harriman an aide-mémoire starting with this memorable thought: "Having in mind the repeated statements of American public figures concerning the desirability of receiving extensive large Soviet orders for the post-war and transition period, the Soviet government considers it possible to place orders on the basis of long term credits to the amount of six billion dollars." This figure, the note explained, would include orders for locomotives, railroad cars, rails, trucks, and industrial equipment placed under Lend-Lease, but not delivered before the end of the war. The credit period would be thirty years, and the interest rate 2-¼ percent.

Harriman said that he would of course take up the note with our government. He reminded Molotov that as yet the United States had statutory authority only to deal with that part of Molotov's proposal referring to the Lend-Lease Act, and "that, as he knew, we had been trying for months to come to an agreement with the Soviet Government with respect to financing those requests which we had received from them for industrial equipment under the fourth protocol." He also pointed out that the interest rate offered in the American "final" document, in September, was 2-⅜ percent, not 2-¼ percent. He stressed that while the non-Lend-Lease part of Molotov's plan would require study and new legislation, he considered "the moment entirely favorable for ar-

[35] Id., pp. 1152–53.
[36] U.S. Department of State, *Foreign Relations of the United States, The Conferences at Malta and Yalta, 1945* (1955), p. 317—hereafter referred to as Yalta Papers.

riving at a final agreement about the Lend-Lease orders for the war period and for the opening of preliminary discussions on the question of credits after the war."

Molotov agreed that the Lend-Lease aspects of his proposal should be settled now, and said he was instructing Gromyko to do so in Washington, but he thought the remainder of the question should also be given consideration. "The future development of Soviet American relations [he said] must have certain vistas (prospectus) before it and must rest on a solid economic basis. The question of the Lend-Lease credit under the fourth protocol was only a small part of the question now before us." [37]

There is no record, or recollection, of Gromyko having carried out Molotov's instructions in Washington.

Harriman urged the government to ignore the Soviets' strange behavior, which he interpreted as Armenian bargaining tactics. He pressed for a positive response, provided Soviet political behavior was tolerable.

> It is of course my very strong and earnest opinion [Harriman wrote] that the question of the credit should be tied into our overall diplomatic relations with the Soviet Union and at an appropriate time the Russians should be given to understand that our willingness to cooperate wholeheartedly with them in their vast reconstruction problems will depend upon their behavior in international matters.[38]

At that moment a crosscurrent was introduced by the American Treasury. On January 1, 1945, Henry Morgenthau wrote to the President advising him that the Treasury had been thinking about a reconstruction loan to the Soviet Union far more ambitious than the Lend-Lease project. Morgenthau said that Harriman was strongly in favor of the loan and that if the idea interested the President he would like to discuss it with the President and the Secretary of State. On January 10 Morgenthau sent Roosevelt a plan for a $10 billion loan to the Soviet Union, at 2 percent interest, to be paid over thirty-five years. On January 17, at a meeting in Stettinius' office, Morgenthau took still another

[37] Yalta Papers, pp. 310–312.
[38] Yalta Papers, p. 313.

new tack. The delay in the Lend-Lease negotiation was deplorable, and he blamed it entirely on the State Department's addiction to "bargaining and bickering" and its failure to make a "clearcut very favorable proposal which would be considered by the Soviet Government as a concrete gesture of our goodwill." [39] The Treasury had been reviewing the entire question and had concluded that we should make new proposals for the agreement under Section 3 (c) of the Lend-Lease Act, which would offer the Soviet Union approximately the same amount of credit, but without interest. On the other hand, we should reject their proposal for a discount from cost prices.

Even in the chaste prose of official memoranda of conversation, Acheson's reply to this suggestion blisters. After noting that the delays in the Lend-Lease negotiations had been entirely on the Soviet side, he recalled that the idea of an interest-free loan for reconstruction purposes had been suggested the year before, when the Three-C project was being drafted. "This suggestion had, at that time, been vetoed by representatives of the Treasury Department who stated that we could not offer such long-term credits at a lower rate of interest than that which the United States Government itself had to pay in order to borrow money." Acheson then reviewed the history of the enterprise, "emphasizing the extremely liberal terms offered in the final agreement . . . which, however, the Soviet government has not seen fit as yet to accept." [40]

Shortly afterward the Treasury withdrew its support for the idea of an interest-free loan, and the President decided not to "press" the loan project further until he met with Stalin at Yalta in a few days.[41]

In the corridors, or over cocktails at Yalta, Harriman asked Molotov what had happened to the project. "Oh, yes," Molotov said, "we'll be glad to help you avoid a post-war depression by taking an interest-free loan." Harriman then suggested to Molo-

[39] Yalta Papers, p. 320.
[40] Yalta Papers, pp. 320–321.
[41] Yalta Papers, p. 323.

tov that Stalin raise the subject with Roosevelt; it was not done.

Stettinius also raised the matter with Molotov during a luncheon meeting at Yalta. The Soviet government expected to receive reparations from Germany, Molotov said, "and hoped that the United States would furnish the Soviet Union with long term credits." Stettinius said he was ready to discuss the problem of long-term credits at any time—at Yalta, or thereafter in Moscow, or in Washington.[42] Again, there was no Soviet response.

On March 10, 1945, after several inconclusive American attempts to obtain Soviet acceptance of the plan, the Soviet government requested that all reference to the possibility of a supplemental Lend-Lease agreement under Section 3 (c) of the Act, covering industrial equipment and materials, be omitted from the Fourth Protocol, since the Soviet government now counted on a solution to the financial problem along the lines of the aide-mémoire of January 3.[43] This was a mysterious suggestion, to say the least, since the proposal of January 3rd expressly contemplated that the supplemental Lend-Lease agreement would be signed. The United States accepted the Soviet decision as confirming its view that the Soviet government "has rejected the United States 3-C proposals." [44] It went forward with the Fourth Protocol nonetheless, and continued to explore alternative possibilities for postwar reconstruction loans, keeping in mind the injunctions of Congress, and the assurances given to Congress, that the Lend-Lease Act would not be used as an independent source of authority to make reconstruction loans beyond its surplus-disposal potentialities.

The matter of postwar loans to the Soviet Union was pursued after Yalta, under Lend-Lease, UNRRA, and the revised statutes of the Export-Import Bank. While Stalin told some visiting congressmen in September that the United States had suggested no talks or discussions with reference to the Soviet request of Janu-

[42] Yalta Papers, p. 610.
[43] U.S. Department of State, *Foreign Relations of the United States, 1945,* V (1967), 986–987. See also pp. 968–984.
[44] Id., at p. 981, 988–1005.

ary 3, there had in fact been several conversations on various aspects of the problem, and at least two letters from Harriman inviting proposals from the Soviet Union for loans under the Export-Import Bank's new statute.[45]

An agreement providing for the purchase by the Soviet Union of Lend-Lease supplies in inventory or under contract in the United States was in fact made on October 15, 1945, covering approximately $400 million of such supplies, on terms substantially the same as those proposed in the original offer under Section 3 (c) of the Act, which would have covered a great deal more than that amount if it had been accepted in 1944.[46]

The last record of any discussion of the possibility of an Export-Import Bank loan in the amount of $1 billion was a conversation between General Rudenko and Leo T. Crowley on August 28, 1945.[47] The United States indicated that it would wish to link further credit negotiations to the negotiations for a Lend-Lease settlement, covering the value of Lend-Lease supplies that survived the war. Such a settlement has not yet been made. As late as February 1946 the United States was still urging the Soviet Union to agree to negotiations that would lead to a settlement of all outstanding economic issues between the two governments, including the question of the credit requested in August, 1945.

Thus the famous episode of American postwar reconstruction loans for the Soviet Union ended with a whimper, not a bang. The Soviets avoided a situation of ongoing long-term dependence on American loans for their reconstruction. But they obtained substantial American aid nonetheless through UNRRA and through the Lend-Lease surplus-disposal contract of October 15, 1945. They could almost certainly have obtained a loan of $1 billion or more through the Export-Import Bank had they been willing, like other Lend-Lease recipients, to supply the United States with an inventory of Lend-Lease supplies and equipment that sur-

[45] U.S. Department of State, *Foreign Relations of the United States, 1945*, V (1967), p. 1039.
[46] Id., at pp. 1031–44.
[47] Id., at pp. 1034–42.

vived the war and had postwar utility. All the anxieties on both sides about the political implications of an ongoing credit were shown to be illusory. The one statement about the affair that cannot be made is that the United States rejected, refused, or delayed dealing affirmatively and substantively with Soviet loan requests.

At some time during 1944 or early 1945 Soviet policy clearly changed. Whether that change was irreversible can never be known. Perhaps the loan was rejected at that time only because Stalin thought that UNRRA assistance, German reparations, and the economic exploitation of Eastern Europe were a cheaper, more flexible, and politically less restrictive way to recovery. Certainly the Soviet government occasionally raised the question of credits later on, but never seriously pursued it. The Soviets knew also that postwar conflicts over Poland, Iran, Greece, Turkey, and the countries of Eastern Europe had created a political atmosphere in the United States and Europe completely different from that of 1943 and 1944, one that made special legislation for the purpose problematical, to say the least.

But American policy was persistent, despite these obstacles. The offer of the Marshall Plan in 1947 was made to the Soviet Union and the countries of Eastern Europe, as well as to those of the West. Poland and Czechoslovakia hastily accepted, but were forced later publicly to withdraw their acceptances. I believe that if the Soviet Union had accepted the Marshall Plan offer, the sophisticated and realistic American appreciation of the importance to the United States of peace with the Soviet Union would have dominated all contrary currents, and that the necessary legislation would have been passed.

Oglesby says that the Marshall Plan offer to the Soviet Union and the countries of Eastern Europe, made "out of complex and no doubt defensible motives, . . . came too late. In Stalin's view, to accept it then would have been the same as to accept the economic and ultimately the political hegemony of the United States in Eurasia." [48]

I can find no substance in Oglesby's argument that the Marshall

[48] Op. cit., p. 44.

Plan offer came "too late." If the minimal political conditions for a large-scale American reconstruction loan to the Soviet Union implied American "hegemony" to Stalin in 1947, he must have reached the same conclusion three years earlier. The problem had not changed. Nor had American policy.

Williams, too, contends that by postponing postwar issues when, as he thinks, they were first raised in 1942, "the United States failed to formulate a policy in response until the opportunity to negotiate a firm understanding on both sides had been lost." [49] Williams imagines that in the darkest hours of the war, when the main preoccupation of the Allied governments was to prevent defeat and to mobilize the forces of victory, the United States, Britain, and the Soviet Union could have drawn up realistic postwar plans for Eastern Europe and other regions and given the Soviet Union assurances about postwar loans. His hypothesis is a fantasy. No one knew then how, or where, or when the war would end, nor indeed whether it could be won. To trace the fatal parting of the ways between the Soviet Union and the West to the failure of the American government to respond in 1942 to impalpable hints, which Williams magnifies into diplomatic démarches, would make nonsense of a great deal of subsequent history, including the reconstruction loan project to which Oglesby, Kolko, Alperovitz, and Horowitz attach so much importance.

If there was an opportunity for an understanding in 1942 or 1943, as Williams suggests, why was it lost by 1944, 1945, 1946, or 1947? The answer, Kolko and Williams seem to believe, is that dependence on an American loan, with its implicit and explicit conditions of peaceful cooperation, would have denied the Soviets a free hand, politically and militarily, in Eastern Europe and else-

---

[49] *American-Russian Relations, 1781–1947*, p. 263. James MacGregor Burns, in *Roosevelt: The Soldier of Freedom, 1940–1945* (1971) suggests that the Allies' failure to invade France in 1942 led Stalin to resume the Cold War. An invasion of France was unthinkable in 1942, and dubious in 1943, without the training period of North Africa and Italy both for British and for American troops. Burns's hypothesis does less than justice to Stalin's principles, and to his sense of reality.

where. Kolko puts it more elegantly. The Lend-Lease reconstruction loans, or like loans, would have amounted to "neo-colonialism," and required the reintegration of the Soviet economy into capitalism.[50]

This may have been Stalin's view. If so, it was a conclusion he reached in 1944 or early 1945 at the latest; if that was his conclusion then, the revisionists can hardly argue at the same time that the United States government refused the Soviet Union a postwar reconstruction loan under the Lend-Lease Act, or delayed or sabotaged those negotiations, or later ones, or in some other way missed an opportunity to reach an understanding with the Soviet Union that might have prevented the Cold War. Both propositions cannot be true.

Professor Hans J. Morgenthau's hypothesis is more plausible, although he puts the date of Stalin's decision earlier. "From 1943 onward," he says, "with Soviet victory over Germany assured, the main purpose of Soviet foreign policy changed from security to territorial expansion." [51] The difficulty with this argument is that it is hard to reconcile with Mikoyan's request for the loan in the first place and the laborious negotiations to which that request gave rise.

The concentration of the revisionists on the issue of the reconstruction loan is misleading and myopic. The relationship between the Soviet Union and its Western allies during and after World War II is a complex affair of many strands, some new, some old. The experience of war was a prodigious one, shaking patterns that had prevailed since 1917. Was there a moment when peaceful cooperation between the Soviet Union and the West might have been achieved? No one will ever know, and glib assertions that an opportunity for peaceful coexistence was missed for this or that reason are meaningless save as exercises in self-deception. The serious and dedicated men who direct the Communist governments and parties of the world always understood

---

[50] Kolko, *The Politics of War*, op. cit. supra, p. 338; Williams, *The Tragedy of American Diplomacy*, p. 155.
[51] *A New Foreign Policy for the United States* (1969), p. 59.

the yearning of public and governmental opinion in the West for accommodation. Their only problem, during the war and thereafter, was whether the minimal conceivable price for that accommodation was more than they wanted to pay.

Above all, the search for a "mistake" in Allied policy that led the Soviets to decide, once and for all, to pursue policies of expansion rather than cooperation after the war ignores the deep and sincere convictions of those who govern the Soviet Union and lead the Communist parties of the world. These men had been schooled for many years in the view that they were indeed engaged in a Cold War with capitalism—a Cold War explained by Lenin as inevitable, and one they were bound by the dialectic of history to fight and win. Many of these men had found the wartime policies of collaboration with Britain and the United States repugnant, and indeed heretical. To continue such policies into the postwar period—to forgo opportunities for spreading the gospel in the bitter and disorganized societies of Europe and other continents—would have seemed to many as an abdication of their proudest and most urgent responsibilities. Debates on this theme had preoccupied communist theorists and practitioners for generations, and preoccupy them still.

This aspect of the revisionist literature ignores another fundamental aspect of the Cold War as a phenomenon of history: the optimism and naïveté of much of American opinion about foreign affairs. While the government, by and large, harbored no illusions on the subject, American opinion believed that wartime collaboration with Russia would lead to postwar cooperation as well. Even the government hesitated to act on the evidence for several years after the war, swallowing even Kalyn in its hope.

I vividly recall a conversation on these themes one spring evening in 1944 with my colorful boss of that period, Dean Acheson. He was, of course, one of the ablest and most engaging men of his time, wise, brave, and capable of large views, and at the same time whimsical, indiscreet and occasionally outrageous. He was an authentically great man, and a delightful, if sometimes formidable companion.

Our talk started as we walked up Pennsylvania Avenue from the old State-War-Navy Building, where the State Department then functioned in Victorian splendor, toward his home in Georgetown, where we planned to finish the day with a drink.

"Here we are," I remarked, "on the street where Sherman paraded his army in their rags at the end of the Civil War, skinny, fierce, tough, carrying chickens on their bayonets. We're building an army like that. It's taken nearly five years. If we're not careful, it will vanish overnight.

"What are the Russians up to? The picture in Eastern Europe looks awful. We can't even get them to take the reconstruction loan they asked for. Should we consider telling them a few home truths while we still have some military power?"

Acheson had the capacity to change moods instantly—to become entirely serious when he should, even though he had been telling stories or joking a moment before. Now he became very serious indeed. We explored the implications of the question as we walked, later as we had a drink, and at intervals for several days thereafter. We concluded that any such approach was inconceivable and wrong. The Russians were allies whose contribution to the war was appreciated and respected. There was a vague but pervasive feeling that however wrong their methods were, they were identified with the ideal of social justice. The regard for them in Congress and in the country was high and warm. It was probable that after the war the Soviets would pursue the policies of hostility we could see so clearly foreshadowed already. But the finest qualities of the American character required that we give the Russians the benefit of the doubt at this stage. We couldn't turn on allies at the end of a war and tell them to open up "or else." Before that point came, if it ever did, we should have to "exhaust the administrative remedies"—try every conceivable alternative first.

I have often thought of that conversation. Could the Western allies have followed such a course, as Bertrand Russell urged them to do early in the postwar period? Should they have done so in the name of the greatest good for the greatest number?

I reach the same conclusion in retrospect that Acheson and I did then—that we are not, and should not become, a people capable of such behavior.

It does not follow, of course, that we should have waited as long as we did to counter the menace of Soviet policy. The shape and content of world politics would have been altogether different if we had insisted in 1945 on the fulfillment of the agreements of Yalta and Potsdam calling for free elections in Eastern Europe, or prevented the take-over of Czechoslovakia in 1948.

What was clear about Soviet-Allied relations in 1944 was that a cumulative process of thrust and counterthrust had started, or had been renewed. That process has continued at an accelerating pace ever since. It may have originated in false or inaccurate perceptions by each side of the other's purposes. But it has acquired a momentum independent of such "causes." The historian's problem is to portray the process as best he can; the problem of policy for every American President is to bring it to an end.

The portrayals of Soviet-American relations between 1941 and 1950 in the revisionist literature are partial and polemic. They are concerned only to "prove" that the Cold War was our fault. They rarely mention the offer of the Baruch Plan for the international control of nuclear energy, American acquiescence in the Soviet conquest of Eastern Europe, or events of comparable import. And they strain to explain away or to justify the successive Soviet acts of hostility, expansion, and bad faith. Those episodes were alarm bells and had a cumulative effect. First, they weakened the wartime atmosphere of optimism and hope about the future of Soviet-Western relations. Then they aroused in the West a mood of fear and anxiety, which gradually became more intense and later crystallized into the conviction that the outward thrust of Soviet (and then of Chinese) power had to be contained. Above all, they portray American policy as grimly determined to precipitate a war, and they never catch either the climate of American opinion or the strength of America's desire for peace. That phenomenon is a force that can always be counted on. When Johnson met Kosygin at Glassboro in 1967, after twenty hard years of Cold War, his rating in the Gallup poll shot up to new highs. Nixon enjoyed the same response to his project of a trip to China.

In short, like Mrs. Clemens trying to shame Mark Twain by repeating his bad language, the revisionists have the words but not the music.

v

In attempting to explain the revisionist image of American behavior toward the Soviet Union during and after the war, Oglesby, like most men of his outlook, falls back on an economic theory that came into the Marxist literature through John Hobson and Lenin rather than from Marx himself. Following the poetic version developed by William Appleman Williams, he argues that the United States created the Cold War out of its own deep expansionist ethos. "A prairie wind blew the Yankee clipper through the Pacific." The capitalist system will collapse, in his opinion, unless it constantly finds new foreign markets to exploit.

> There is nothing more common in our economic mentality, nothing more constant in our foreign policy, than this conviction that the basic problem of the American business system is domestically undistributable wealth, and that the basic solution to that problem, its essential and only anodyne, lies in our penetration of foreign markets—most especially the markets of those lands which we now think of as the underdeveloped . . . countries.[52]

Oglesby quotes with relish a number of particularly foolish speeches by distinguished senators, businessmen, and public officials who have shared his economic fallacies over the years.[53]

His teacher, Williams, argues that the leaders of thought in the great agricultural areas of the United States first understood the need for markets in less developed countries and pushed the nation on its "imperialist" course.[54] This hypothesis doubtless explains why the senators from Midwestern agricultural states, such

[52] Op. cit., pp. 65–66.
[53] See, e.g., pp. 50–55, 61–67.
[54] *The Roots of the Modern American Empire* (1969).

as Borah, Norris, La Follette, Nye, Wheeler, and Shipstead, have typically been such devout internationalists over the years.

Generations of economists have exploded this doctrine without weakening its hold on public opinion.[55] Everyday experience contradicts it. Between 1945 and 1950, and again after Korea, the United States accomplished successful transitions from a wartime to a peacetime economy without benefit of the Soviet or the Chinese market. Regional and technological shifts of resources within the economy demonstrate the ease with which even very large transfers can be handled. Guided by methods of planning developed during the last generation, capitalist societies have achieved impressive facility in organizing the shift of resources from one use to another without disturbing over-all equilibrium. Compared to the gigantic movements represented by the development, for example, of the American chemical industry or the Pacific Coast economy of the United States, the transfers that would be involved in increasing or reducing agricultural production in response to the opening or closing of market opportunities in India or Vietnam are trivial. Monetary and fiscal policy, for all the errors committed in their names, are proving reasonably adequate tools of capitalist planning. The capitalist world has had many economic troubles since 1945. But it has avoided a recurrence of the great depression of the thirties, or anything like it.

Yet men like Oglesby—and he is by no means alone—keep repeating with fervent sincerity the absurd thesis that capitalist economies will collapse unless they somehow subsidize the dumping of their "surpluses" abroad, especially to the nonindustrialized countries, with which we have hardly any trade at all.

There is no innate and implacable tendency in capitalism to generate "surpluses" that have to be dumped abroad. Modern full-employment capitalist economies are poor, not affluent, in terms of the private and public demands made upon them. There is never enough output to satisfy the demands for housing, for roads, for schools, for plants, for public services, for goods, for

[55] I did my best on the subject in *Planning for Freedom* (1959), Chap. 6, and pp. 49–60.

offices, for cars, which in all capitalist countries press upon the available supply of labor, of savings, and above all of managerial skill and organization and of entrepreneurship. This is why taxes and interest rates are so high today compared with those of the thirties, and why there is everywhere a shortage of skilled labor and of other skills. And this is why it is so difficult to find money, entrepreneurship, and management to organize economic activity in many of the nonindustrialized countries of the world.

I do not, of course, mean to suggest that foreign trade and investment are not important or economically useful activities when they reflect the benefits of the principle of comparative advantage. But a glance at the statistics confirms what is in any event obvious—that except for raw materials, the bulk of world trade, like the bulk of the commerce within a country, consists of specialized exchanges among the advanced and industrialized nations, not between the industrialized and the less industrialized nations.

The problem is summed up in the answer I once got when I tried to press a banker to make a helpful loan to an underdeveloped country. "Let's assume," he said, "that all these memoranda about the project are correct. Can you give me a good reason why I should make this loan, and then travel frequently to an uncomfortable place, face the risks of devaluation and nationalization, and probably have to give bribes, which is something I hate, when I can make so much money at home, or in Europe, or in Australia?" If there were a grain of truth in Oglesby's thesis, it would be easy to get aid appropriation from Congress and to find capital funds for the less developed countries. The truth is quite the contrary. Aid appropriations are difficult to obtain and are most grudgingly given. Church groups, not big business, help to persuade Congress to make them. In the end, the motivation for such legislation is human decency, not concern for the survival of the capitalist system. If the economy needs the spur of a budget deficit, Congress and business opinion have learned, it can come as well from a slum-clearance program, or from a tax cut, as from unrequited exports to Ruritania.

To Oglesby, however, such realities do not exist. The motivation for the Cold War is plunder. The United States wants peace, to be sure, but only

> a certain kind of peace, one which seems to have very little to do with letting good neighbors alone or with democracy or progress . . . For us, peace finally exists when the world is finally safe for American businessmen to carry on their business everywhere, on terms as favorable as they can be made, in settings managed preferably by native middle-class governments, but if need be by oligarchic and repressive ones, by the old foreign grads of Fort Bragg, or if the panic hits in a pivotal place, by our own Marines . . .
>
> The West wants a world that is integrated and (in Max Weber's sense) rationalized in terms of the stability of resources, labor, production, distribution and markets. As the leader of the West, America wants that integrated rationalized world to run under the management of her own business people. Others do not. They have acquired powers of resistance in the East. Therefore there is an East-West struggle, in our time called the Cold War.[56]

The argument for peace through achieving and maintaining a balance of power, which Oglesby developed so carefully in the first part of his essay, turns out, he says, simply to be a mask for free-world imperialism. The goal of United States foreign policy is not the security of peace for its own sake, he says, but peace as the key to commercial advantage. He has some difficulty fitting South Vietnam and South Korea into his thesis, for manifestly American commercial and investment interests in those countries will never approach the costs incurred in preventing them from being overrun. But, he argues, there is no paradox after all. South Vietnam is "potentially" an important economic unit, which could become a significant trading partner of the United States. And it could play a significant part as well in forming a reasonably stable political community in Asia which would not be dominated by China and in which all the nations of the Pacific, including China, could participate independently. This is indeed the goal of United States policy in Asia. But Oglesby's attempt to explain a strategic and political problem as an economic one fails: Japan doesn't need trade with South Vietnam, any more than it

[56] *Supra*, note 1, pp. 70–71.

needs trade with North Korea or Burma, in order to make it possible to avoid becoming totally dependent on China.[57]

It is certainly true that the future orientation of Japanese policy and of Chinese policy are and will remain major strategic concerns of the United States, and that the American interest in the Pacific basin would most surely be protected by the development of patterns of regional cooperation in which all the nations of the area could share. Because Oglesby feels bound to describe the problem in mechanically economic categories, he almost misses the political and strategic point. But because he is an incurable intellectual, he cannot quite force himself to do so completely.

The key question for the whole region—and for areas far beyond the Pacific—is how China is to be modernized. By investment capital squeezed from the Chinese people alone? By borrowings from many countries, or from a few? Through relatively open policies of trade and education, such as those which have worked so well in Japan? By other means? What is at stake for the United States in this series of questions is far more important than potential future exports to Vietnam, comparable, say, to our exports to Greece. Our national concern is not primarily economic—although it is hardly a disgrace for a government to safeguard the economic well-being of its people—but psycho-social. The heart of our national interest in the area is to minimize the risk of war by preventing the emergence of hegemonial configurations of power in the region. Such patterns of power could once more arouse fears that would degenerate into panic, and therefore make possible the outbreak of war to prevent what is perceived as the prospect of domination.

VI

Oglesby's argument about imperialism as the cause of the Cold War leads him to what I believe is the essence of his book: the advocacy of revolution, at least in the Third World, as a good in

[57] Op. cit., pp. 128–129.

itself. He turns to this theme from his exercise in economics with almost visible relief, as if he recognized the perfunctory and unsatisfactory character of his economic proofs.

There is a contradiction in the structure of Oglesby's argument. The revolutionary impulse, he says, is in part the product of the failure of the United States to have set effective programs of economic growth into motion in many nonindustrialized nations.[58] But he also says that the motives of such revolutions, which he believes we should not oppose and perhaps should even encourage, have nothing to do with social and political improvement, but express the drives of aggression.

The first element in his argument is stated in this form:

> The United States has shown in Europe that it knows how to reconstruct bombed-out capitalist economies. But it has not shown in the Third World that it can develop Western-style political economies: in pre-industrial countries where there is no capitalist class structure, no entrepreneurial tradition, no skilled urbanized work force, and no internalized commitment to capitalist lifestyles, the arrival of the American corporatist is in fact a disaster. Preoccupied with the extraction of resources for export and the immediate exploitation of all opportunities without regard to the damage this does to others, our business statesmanship may justly claim to have excited the underdeveloped world's growing revolutionary demands. But it is nothing but double talk for this same statesmanship to pretend that it assents to those demands—the demands for unobstructed opportunity to develop the natural wealth of the nation, for time and freedom to cultivate a national economic style, for exemption from the Cold War, for political independence.[59]

It is commonplace to find the assertion that American companies operating in less developed countries have enormous internal power there. My years in the State Department have convinced me that the exact opposite is the case. The companies live in fear and trembling. Their concessions are broken, their taxes increased, their prices renegotiated, or their properties confiscated, and they say "Thank you," and kowtow meekly, to boot. The

[58] Op. cit., p. 106.
[59] Ibid.

United States government never dreams of sending the gun boats to protect them, and generally ignores episodes of this kind once a mild note of protest has been filed. When Peru nationalized the property of an American oil company, in breach of an international arbitral award and without compensation, the Nixon Administration managed even to ignore the Hickenlooper Amendment, which specifically provides that all American aid should be cut off in such cases.

Many of the developing nations, of course, scrupulously respect the rules of international law and of their own laws governing foreign investments. And despite Oglesby's sweeping statement, many of them have successfully achieved programs of economic development and high rates of economic growth. Sometimes the United States and other foreign nations or international institutions have helped in such programs. Sometimes they have been entirely indigenous. In all cases, however, the primary effort has been national. And in all the cases that I have studied, the development plan has relied heavily, if not exclusively, on massive supplies of foreign entrepreneurship. Indeed, it is nearly inconceivable for most underdeveloped nations to achieve economic progress without foreign businessmen and capital. As Oglesby points out, they simply do not possess an adequate supply of men trained to perform the function. The formation of such groups is necessarily one of the central tasks of their planning effort, whether organized by government or by the market alone.

Having asserted the conventional claim that the United States is responsible for the failure of many development programs in the Third World, Oglesby reaches the final theme of his argument, which he expounds with passion and eloquence.

The dominant purpose of American foreign policy, he argues, is not to oppose aggression, but the independence of the Third World. The doctrine of the "open door," so characteristic of the American approach to foreign policy, requires the United States to fight "the anti-imperialist social revolution of the poor."

There is, he says, an international communist movement.

This theory of the International Communist Conspiracy is not the hysterical old maid that many leftists seem to think it is. It has had an intimate affair with reality and it has some history on its mind when it speaks. There *is* a revolution which *is* international—one only has to count the perturbations and look at the map to see as much. In some less than technical sense, this revolution *is* "communistic," if by that we mean that it will probably not produce capitalist economies, that it will probably create autarkic and controlled economies, authoritarian central governments, programs of forced-march wealth accumulation, and the forcible dismantling of rich elites. And if not by any means melodramatically conspiratorial, the several national liberation movements, in their early stages especially, *do* make an effort to coordinate themselves; they do so, pathetically unadept, because they consider their enemy to be internationally coordinated himself—a view which is entirely correct. And to the extent to which this revolution aims at terminating the masterdom of the rich, an aim which automatically implicates America, the revolution *does* aim itself at America—it aims itself, rather, at an America which most Americans have forgotten about: Rockefeller, Englehard, U.S.A. There is just no use being deluded about that. But what is added on for pure political effect is that ugly edge of clandestinity, pointless and merciless ambition, that cloud of diabolism which has nothing to do with the sustaining force of the revolution itself. And what is *subtracted* from the reality—much more important—is the *source* of the ferment, the *cause* of the anger, the supreme question of the *justice* of rebellion. What this theory gives us is a portrait whose outlines are not unreal, but whose colors have been changed from human blacks and browns and yellows into devil's red, and whose background has been entirely erased. Thus, the theory wildly disorganizes and mismanages the very real history that allows it to survive. And if it lies within the power of an idea to pervert a nation's generosity and curse its children, then the widespread American acceptance of this view of revolution may forecast a bitter future for us all.[60]

Why have so many turned to revolutionary violence in the developing world and not only in the developing world? Oglesby's answer owes more to Freud than to Marx. He urges the release, and indeed the worship, of the impulse to destroy what is hated. Men seek the redress of their grievances through political action, and through demonstrations, which are in fact "prayers." [61] When

[60] Op. cit., pp. 132–133.
[61] Op. cit., p. 144.

such procedures do not produce the result they deem just, their yearning turns to despair.

Sometimes mass-based secular prayer has resulted in change. But more often it has only shown the victim-petitioners that the problem is graver and change harder to get than they had imagined. The bad sheriffs turn out to be everywhere; indeed, there seems to be no other kind. It turns out that the king is on their side, that the state's administrative and coercive-punitive machinery exists precisely to serve the landlords. It turns out that the powerful know perfectly well who their victims are and why there should be victims, and that they have no intention of changing anything. This recognition is momentous, no doubt the spiritual low point of the emergent revolutionary's education. He finds that the enemy is not a few men but a whole system whose agents saturate the society, occupying and fiercely protecting its control centers. He is diverted by a most realistic despair.

But this despair contains within itself the omen of that final shattering reconstitution of the spirit which will prepare the malcontent, the fighter, the wino, the criminal for the shift to insurgency, rebellion, revolution. He had entertained certain hopes about the powerful: They can tell justice from injustice, they support the first, they are open to change. He is now instructed that these hopes are whimsical. At the heart of his despair lies the new certainty that there will be no change which he does not produce by himself.[62]

Once a man has accepted this conclusion, however irrationally by the standards of others, his goal becomes not change, but destruction. "The fundamental revolutionary motive," Oglesby writes, "is not to construct a Paradise but to destroy an Inferno." [63]

"What do you want?" asked the worried, perhaps intimidated master. "What can I give you?" he inquires, hoping to have found in this rebel a responsible, realistic person, a man of the world like himself. But the rebel does not fail to see the real meaning of this word *give*. Therefore he answers, "I cannot be purchased." The answer is meant mainly to break off the conference. But at one level, it is a completely substantive comment, not at all just a bolt of pride. It informs the master that he no longer exists, not even in part.

At another level, however, this answer is nothing but an eva-

---

[62] Op. cit., p. 145.
[63] Op. cit., p. 147.

sion. The master seems to have solicited the rebel's views of the revolutionized, good society. The rebel would be embarrassed to confess the truth: that he has no such views. Industry? Agriculture? Foreign trade? It is not such matters that drive and preoccupy him. The victorious future is at the moment any society in which certain individuals no longer have power, no longer exist. The rebel fights for something that will not be like *this*. He cannot answer the question about the future because that is not his question. It is not the future that is victimizing him. It is the present. It is not an anticipated Utopia which moves him to risk his life. It is pain. "Turn it over," he cries, because he can no longer bear it as it is. The revolutionary is not *by type* a Lenin, a Mao, a Castro, least of all a Brezhnev. He is neither an economist nor a politician nor a social philosopher. He may become these; ultimately he must. But his motivating vision of change is at root a vision of something absent—not something that *will* be there, but of something that will be there *no longer*. His good future world is elementally described by its empty spaces: a missing landlord, a missing mine owner, a missing sheriff. Who or what will replace landlord, owner, sheriff? Never mind, says the revolutionary, glancing over his shoulder. Something better. If he is thereupon warned that this undefined "something" may turn out to make things worse than ever, his response is a plain one: "Then we should have to continue the revolution." [64]

"It cannot be too much emphasized," Oglesby concludes, "that the interest in developing other social forms, however acute it will become, follows, *does not precede*, the soul-basic explosion against injustice which is the one redemption of the damned." [65]

Oglesby's paean to the spirit of revolt follows the path of Freud's *Civilization and Its Discontents* and *Group Psychology and the Analysis of the Ego*. The rebel is totally possessed by his predicament and by his rage. Except for rebellion, there is nothing. He is swept on by a "psychic flood," through which he affirms that life is death.[66]

It is hard to imagine a more vivid confirmation of Freud's analysis, nor a more compelling portrayal of what Freud called the struggle between civilization and the death wish—between the

[64] Op. cit., pp. 146–147.
[65] Op. cit., pp. 147–148, italics in original.
[66] P. 154.

forces of love and those of death.[67] The impulse to destroy, Freud argued, is basic and universal in man. So is the mysterious force of love, which leads man to build families, gardens, cities, and nations, and to reach out for universal brotherhood. To become a civilization, Freud contended, a society must employ all its resources of law and magic to restrain, and indeed to repress, the impulses that Oglesby glorifies. Freud knew that social groups, ruled by their unconscious, were capable of feats of violence that involved each member in expressing primitive and regressive exaggerations of hatred. The individual, however civilized, can easily be submerged in such general waves of contagious emotion.

In the name of civilization Freud urged that the influence of law and custom, of tradition, of institutions, of symbols, of taboos, of rewards, and of prestige all be used by society to strengthen the forces of love, the only possible source of progress, and to curb those of death.

In the name of revolt against injustice Oglesby exalts death, and would sweep civilization away.

A sense of identification with the revolutionary impulse at home and abroad, and especially in the Third World, comes in the end to dominate Oglesby's book. He is simply overwhelmed by the mysticism of revolution. His preliminary analysis of the problem of peace as a problem of power is forgotten. He finishes with an exordium that does not mention the issue. Indeed, he does not even say what foreign policy he thinks the United States should pursue with regard to Europe, Canada, Japan, or a number of other advanced countries. His economic argument disappears as completely as his essay in geopolitics. Having argued that economic interests determine foreign policy, his feelings are completely absorbed by the tragic drama of some of the countries of the Third World, where American economic interests are trivial, except for oil and ores, compared with its trade with and investment in Canada, Europe, and Japan.

There are ironies as well as contradictions in the revisionist argument, even in the hands of a candid and sophisticated writer

[67] See Chapter 9.

like Oglesby. The pseudo-Marxist doctrine of imperialism to which he must be loyal interferes with his perception of reality. He portrays the United States government as endowed with supernatural powers. In his view the United States will crack the whip and land the Marines at the whim of the United Fruit Company, or its equivalent, anywhere in the world. Nothing could be further from the truth. The fact is that the writ of the United States doesn't run very well in Mississippi, and it doesn't run at all in the Third World. But Oglesby's ideology prevents him from seeing that the social convulsions of some countries of the Third World arise from their own failures of social organization and leadership, not those of the United States.

His doctrine prevents him from seeing an even deeper and more tragic irony as well. When the revolution prevails, when the British, or French, or Dutch go home, when the fighting dies down and the music stops—what then? Then the new nation, proud of its independence, faces the necessity for social organization, for bureaucracy, for entrepreneurship, and for education, if its political independence is to be matched by economic progress. Then economics and technology have their revenge. So does the Protestant ethic. If Oglesby had taken even a casual look at the statistics on the subject, he would have noticed a striking fact: the nations of the Third World that have made most economic and social progress are those that have utilized the energies of the market and the motivations of private business, not those that followed one or another of the totalitarian models.

# 5

## *The Foreign Policy of*
## *Noam Chomsky*

No RECENT WRITINGS about foreign affairs have been received with more enthusiasm than the passionate essays of Noam Chomsky. Chomsky's scathing attacks on the hypocrisy and unctuousness of official dogmas, and on the good faith of those charged with responsibility for government, gladden many hearts.

Professor Chomsky's papers do not fall neatly into any one of the categories set out in Chapter 3. The search for Chomsky's major premise is a bracing intellectual exercise. I am not at all confident, after considerable effort, that I can define the touchstone in terms of which he determines the morality and legitimacy of American foreign policy.

Chomsky describes himself as a libertarian socialist, and his arguments have some Marxist or neo-Marxist themes. But most of the men whose views are considered in Chapter 4 would think Chomsky suffers from anarchist or other Left deviationism and from an occasional indulgence in nationalism. The dubious orthodoxy of his Marxism apart, Chomsky also identifies himself with the American liberal isolationists, and particularly with Randolph

Bourne, who opposed American entry into the First World War in 1917. Like members of the fifth school, his emotional reaction to potential opponents seems to have a considerable effect on his judgments about war and peace; at times, but not always, he appears to reach opinions about security on grounds of political sympathy rather than of national safety. For example, he supports the rightness of American participation in the war against Hitler's Germany, but not against Wilhelm's. While he is vehemently anti-Stalinist, he does not question the rightness or the extent of American cooperation with Stalin in World War II. In addition, Chomsky's papers have pacifist elements, and a burning commitment to the idea of revolution, or at least to his own particular vision of revolution, as a good in itself—indeed, as nearly the highest ideal to which modern man can devote himself.

Chomsky's writings derive from moral indignation of a fundamental cast. A sense of outrage about the war in Vietnam precipitated his entry into the lists, but he is attacking much more than American participation in the Indochinese conflict. His target is the emergence of the United States as an "imperialist" power. That development started, he contends, at the turn of the century. It was accelerated by American participation in the First World War, to which he frequently refers as an error. While he nowhere criticizes America's role in the Second World War as such, the evolution of the United States as an "imperial" power was given renewed momentum, in his view, by many of the policies it adopted after the Second World War, and perhaps by the entire cycle of America's postwar policies—although on this point his analysis is obscure. He does not comment, for example, on the justification for NATO, or for the security treaties with Japan, Australia, and New Zealand.

That the American position in Vietnam is a moral "obscenity," Chomsky says, is no longer debatable.[1] He equates American policy in Vietnam with the Italian attack on Abyssinia and the Russian invasion of Hungary in 1956. His objection to the American

[1] *American Power and the New Mandarins* (1969), Pantheon ed., 1969, p. 9. Further citations to Chomsky's writings in Chapter 5 refer to this book.

role in Vietnam is not its cost, or the fact that it has taken so long, or that it may fail in its objective, or that it has had a bad press in Europe, or is divisive at home, but that it was wrong in the first place, and that every day the war continues is a crime equal to that of the Nazis. Fervently invoking the cause of truth, he calls for "intellectual sanity" and a complete change of outlook toward foreign policy, based on an intellectual analysis of the nature of the problem of peace, not in Vietnam alone, but in the entire world.

II

Since he believes that the disease stems from intellectual error, it follows that the cure for it must also be intellectual. It is natural for him to begin with an attack on the intellectuals whose mistakes, in his view, have permitted the idea of American imperialism to impose itself on American opinion. These intellectuals— the New Mandarins—are, he argues, above all the "liberal" scholars and publicists who since 1917 have made themselves the servants of and apologists for the American military interest ("the war machine," in his vocabulary). They are, he says, a meritocratic elite, seduced by the charm of proximity to power. They gain proximity to power, he believes, by praising the plans of the military. They may also be seduced by their professional interest in the problems offered to them for study. Thus at least three of the seven essays reprinted in *American Power and the New Mandarins* are devoted to the problem of intellectual integrity. At times Chomsky seems to believe that a "value-free" science of social policy is possible and desirable; at others he asserts the need for a more limited concept of intellectual objectivity, in the sense of scrupulous and disciplined scholarly criticism, rooted in independence and in the traditional values of democracy.

Of these preliminary papers the most comprehensive is "Objectivity and Liberal Scholarship," which delineates the major tenets of his creed.

The moral and intellectual realm from which Chomsky's values

147

derive is that of anarchism. He sees the revival of anarchist thinking in the New Left as the most promising development of recent
years. "If this development can solidify," he writes, "it offers
some real hope that the present American crisis will not become
an American and world catastrophe." [2] Mikhail Bakunin and Rosa
Luxemburg are among his heroes, especially for what he describes
as their connection with the "left-wing critique of Leninist
élitism," which he thinks could well be applied to the machinery
of the modern welfare state.[3] His attack on the American Mandarins and on the threat of their ideology to a decent intellectual
life focuses not only on some of the literature that defends American policy in Asia but on Gabriel Jackson's book *The Spanish
Republic and the Civil War: 1931–1939,* to which he devotes the
bulk of "Objectivity and Liberal Scholarship."

The first part of the paper—in which he purports to answer a
number of political scientists writing about peace in Asia—fairly
represents his method. It consists of a series of brief quotations
from their articles, which Chomsky regards as sufficient in themselves to demonstrate the absurdity of the views they espouse and
"the widespread abandonment of civilized norms" among "liberal" intellectuals "closely identified with American imperial
goals." [4] Occasionally he adds by way of rebuttal a few counter-
quotations from sources whose judgment he trusts—that is, from
books or articles by Kolko, Alperovitz and other revisionists.

But he writes about Jackson's book and the Spanish Civil War
with much greater care and with deep concern for the Spanish
Civil War as an event of importance, as indeed it was, in the history of modern revolutionary politics. Praising Jackson's book as
a superior exercise in scholarship, he condemns it for not giving
enough emphasis to the anarchist revolution of 1936 in northern
Spain, which Communist-led forces of the Spanish Republic
finally crushed in May 1937.

Chomsky describes the revolutionary events of 1936 in north-

[2] P. 19.
[3] Pp. 72–73.
[4] P. 72.

ern Spain—a revolution within a revolution—as a spontaneous and Utopian uprising of the masses, a creative and purifying social event of the kind for which he yearns, characterized by personal freedom, the dissolution of oppressive institutions, and the dawning of true socialism. The repression of these tendencies by Communist influence demonstrated again, Chomsky finds, that the Soviet Union is a right-wing enemy of the "people's revolution," believing only in cast-iron dictatorship ruled by a rigid bureaucracy. Chomsky criticizes Jackson for believing that one of the Soviet Union's motives for intervening in Spain was to advance the cause of worldwide revolution and to identify itself with the revolutionary tendency in world politics. For Chomsky, apparently, the word "revolution" should be restricted in its denotation, and the leaders of the Soviet Union not allowed to use the word or to give it a definition of their own. Jackson's treatment of the theme, Chomsky believes, demonstrates that "a deep bias against social revolution and a commitment to the values and social order of liberal bourgeois democracy has [sic] led the author to misrepresent crucial events and to overlook major historical currents." [5]

### III

The exposition of Chomsky's political ideals as the source of his theory about foreign policy is carried a step further in his basic paper, "The Revolutionary Pacifism of A. J. Muste: On the Backgrounds of the Pacific War," the most nearly systematic piece of work in his book.

The essay was written as a tribute to the distinguished American radical leader, A. J. Muste, whose revolutionary pacifism, Chomsky believes, "was, and is, a profoundly important doctrine, both in the political analysis and the moral conviction that it expresses." [6]

But Chomsky cannot accept Muste's revolutionary pacifism

[5] P. 124.
[6] P. 159.

either as an absolute moral commitment or in terms of Muste's psychological justification for it—the principle that "like produces like, kindness provokes kindness," so that nonviolence would appeal to "the essential humanity of the enemy." This view Chomsky finds unpersuasive. "It is very difficult," he says, "to retain a faith in the 'essential humanity' of the S.S. trooper or the commissar or the racist blinded with hate and fear, or, for that matter, the insensate victim of a lifetime of anti-Communist indoctrination." [7]

Chomsky undertakes to test Muste's doctrine by considering the moral rightness of the American reaction to what he describes as Japanese "aggressiveness" in 1941 "under the circumstances of the anti-fascist war," which he calls "the most severe of tests," far more difficult than demonstrating the moral evil of the war in Vietnam. His analysis leads him to pose three questions as critical: (1) Should America have followed alternative diplomatic approaches toward Japan before Pearl Harbor? (2) Should the United States have gone to war at all after Pearl Harbor? (3) Should the United States have fought back as hard as it did and used the atom bomb and other heavy bombing raids at the end of the war?

After more than forty pages of effort Chomsky finds that he cannot answer these three questions, even the first and the third. "When I began working on this article," he writes, "I was not at all sure [that Muste's doctrine could survive the test]. I still feel quite ambivalent about the matter." [8] While the alternative approach Muste proposed appeals to Chomsky as "both eminently realistic and highly moral" when compared either with the diplomacy Roosevelt and Hull actually pursued or with the compromises and accommodations proposed by Grew, he cannot bring himself to rule out "the claim that the United States simply acted in legitimate self-defense," nor indeed to say more for Muste's argument, which he characterizes as debatable, than to regret that it was so remote from American consciousness at the time. If

[7] P. 162.
[8] P 59.

such a radical critique had been given more attention, he suggests, it might have helped to prevent Hiroshima and Nagasaki.[9]

What was Muste's alternative policy which in his view the United States should have pursued after Pearl Harbor?

In 1941, Muste argued, the Allies controlled the bulk of the world's surface and resources and confronted a group of discontented nations—Germany, Italy, Hungary, and Japan—that possessed far fewer resources, but were determined to alter the situation in their own favor, even at the risk of war. If the war came, he thought, America and her allies would win, but after victory America would be forced by plausible arguments of fear and safety to follow the path of world domination; it would become accustomed to reliance on war and violence, and its soul would be stained with evil. The alternative, Muste contended, was a serious attempt at peaceful reconciliation, with no attempt to fasten sole war guilt on any nation; assurance to all peoples of equitable access to markets and essential materials; armament reduction; massive economic rehabilitation; and moves toward international federation.[10]

In response to this statement of the theme, Chomsky reviews the history of Japanese-American relations in the thirties, and that of Japan's attack on China, and its occupation of French Indochina, a strategic move that Chomsky views as threatening both to China and to the Dutch East Indies.

Chomsky sympathizes with many of Japan's grievances. And he condemns the United States for what he regards as the hypocrisy of its response to Japanese moves that were no worse, he thinks, than many made in the past by Britain and the United States. But he cannot defend Japan's use of force to extend its New Order in Asia or its attack on Pearl Harbor. While he criticizes many features of American diplomacy and suggests that more conciliatory approaches (such as those urged by Ambassador Joseph Grew)

---

[9] Pp. 207–208. This ambivalence, however, does not deter him from calling attention to "the horrifying reality" that the United States "has laid waste a helpless Asian country" three times in a generation (p. 4).

[10] Pp. 164–165.

might well have averted the attack on Pearl Harbor, he never commits himself to the policy of conciliating ("appeasing") Japan favored by Grew and others at the time and since; instead, he contents himself with ridiculing a number of writers for their self-righteous defense of American and Japanese policy. He identifies himself with those in Japan who criticized the Japanese policy of imperial expansion in fundamental ways.[11] But he also refers to the Second World War as an antifascist war, which, in his value system, seems enough to justify it. In the end, the problem he set for himself paralyzes him. He confesses that he cannot answer the questions with which he starts.

IV

Perhaps one explanation for the extraordinary dénouement of Chomsky's basic paper is that its analysis is conducted at several levels, which are not sharply distinguished.

He quotes a sentence of Muste to explain the implications of revolutionary nonviolence as a principle of action: "In a world built on violence, one must be a revolutionary before one can be a pacifist."[12] To Chomsky, if not to Muste, this principle seems to justify some use of violence, at least in the service of his own concept of revolution. In his discussion of the Spanish Civil War, for example, he seems to approve whatever violence was involved in the anarchist revolution of 1936; he condemns the violence of the Spanish government in suppressing the anarchist revolution; and he does not comment, save perhaps by implication, on the justification for the use of violence by General Franco in furthering the cause of his revolution, or by the Spanish Republic in resisting it.

But before the challenge of Pearl Harbor he cannot bring himself to deny the national premise. In Chomsky's system, it would seem, the United States had a moral right to use force in defending itself against the attack by imperialist Japan, allied to Hitler

[11] Pp. 184–185.
[12] P. 160.

152

and Mussolini. If that is true, Japan was wrong, in Chomsky's terms, however real its grievances, in using force to improve its lot. According to Chomsky, any nation has a right to defend itself against attack simply because it is a nation, even though the fighting has nothing to do with the cause of revolution, in Chomsky's sense or in any other; and correspondingly, it seems reasonable to suppose, Chomsky would say that nations are bound not to use force against other nations, even to achieve goals Chomsky would regard as just, and even when the attacker is a revolutionary nation in Chomsky's sense and the victim a reactionary or even fascist one.[13]

What theory—that is, what set of consistent propositions—can be distilled from Chomsky's book as the source of this judgment?

Chomsky sheds no light on the answer he would give to this question. Nor does his presentation permit us to infer what other rights a nation possesses, in his view, by reason of its membership in the society of nations, even if it does not meet his standards of revolutionary anarchism.

Manifestly, inarticulate premises govern the analysis of his essay. If he concludes that Japan breached a rule of right conduct by attacking Pearl Harbor, he must believe that the nature of international society, and the necessity for agreed conditions of cooperation among the nations living within it, should be deemed to give rise to certain limits on the sovereign freedom of each nation to use military force—even against nations whose social systems Chomsky abhors. If this is the line of his thought, it follows that other nations have the right, if not the duty, to take steps (beyond those of pure self-defense against armed assault) to minimize the risk of like events in the future—for example, by entering into security arrangements of deterrence designed to ensure the enforcement of rules whose legitimacy Chomsky assumes, or takes for granted.

[13] The latter point may be beyond Chomsky's theory. In such a conflict he might justify the use of force in the service of revolution—or at least of his kind of revolution. He does, however, condemn the Soviet attack on Hungary of 1956.

Chomsky does not discuss the problem of peace as such—that is, the problem of organizing international society as a political community. His treatment of Pearl Harbor shows that he would admit certain international rights, even for nations like the United States, whose internal policies he disapproves. At several points he remarks in passing that of course the rich and satisfied powers favor the peace of the status quo, in which they have what he regards as an exploitative stake. But I have been unable to discover from his essays whether he believes that the United States as a nation has a right he would regard as legitimate to decide on a course of action—support of NATO, for example—designed to protect the national interest as the majority conceive it, at least if such a course is adopted and carried out by constitutional methods of decision-making and in ways consistent with international law.

v

Chomsky approaches the burning question of Vietnam in the context of this intellectual universe. Unhappily, his treatment of the issues in the Vietnam conflict provides the reader with few additional clues to the theory of foreign policy he would substitute for what he regards as the imperialist policy the United States has pursued since 1898.

He starts his basic paper on Vietnam, "The Logic of Withdrawal," with an intriguing statement suggesting that here, at least, he may answer some of the questions posed or implied in the introductory chapters of his book.

> International affairs can be complex, a matter of irreconcilable interests, each with a claim to legitimacy, and conflicting principles, none of which can be lightly abandoned. The current Middle East crisis is a typical, painful example. American interference in the affairs of Vietnam is one of the rare exceptions to this general rule. The simple fact is that there is no legitimate interest or principle to justify the use of American military force in Vietnam.
> Since 1954 there has been one fundamental issue in Vietnam: whether the uncertainty and conflict left unresolved at Geneva

will be settled at a local level, by indigenous forces, or raised to an international level and settled through great power involvement.[14]

Chomsky's analysis of the war in Vietnam is built around three basic themes. First, the contest is a civil war, internal to the Vietnamese nation, so that American assistance to the government in Saigon is intervention in the internal affairs of a nation and thus a violation of international law as codified in the Charter of the United Nations. Being illegal, it is therefore also immoral. Second, American intervention has gone far beyond the point of military assistance to a friendly government and involves the use of American influence to select men favored for rule and to impose American ideas about social and political organization on another people—ideas about democracy, capitalism, corruption, economic planning, land reform, urban development, and so on. This aspect of American policy is naked imperialism and no more justified than the imperialism of Japan in Manchuria, or of Hitler, Mussolini, and Stalin on many occasions. Finally, the contest itself has been conducted with a ferocity and on a scale that are in themselves barbarous. No end, he suggests, could justify the use of such means.

We should be alarmed, Chomsky writes, when the government for whose policies each citizen bears personal responsibility acts in ways that

> tear to shreds the delicate fabric of international law and disregard our treaty commitments and constitutional processes. Granting the inadequacies and frequent injustices of international law and the institutions set up to give it substance, there is still much truth in the conclusion of the Lawyers Committee on American Policy in Vietnam: ". . . the tragedy in Vietnam reveals that the rules of law, when so flagrantly disregarded, have a way of reasserting the calm wisdom underlying their creation. If international law had been followed, both Vietnam and the American people would have been spared what Secretary General U Thant has described as 'one of the most barbarous wars in history.' " [15]

I for one fully agree with the general thesis embodied in this statement, that there is wisdom in the pattern of international law.

[14] P. 22.
[15] Pp. 240–241.

But I do not agree with the application Chomsky makes of it to the war in Vietnam. I conclude, on the contrary, that however debatable the wisdom and prudence of America's course in Vietnam may be, there can be no serious debate about its legality, from the point of view either of international law or of the law of the American constitution. American action in Vietnam fulfills the obligations of the nation both under the Charter of the United Nations and under the SEATO treaty (whose bearing on the problem Chomsky does not mention), and has been carried out—save for exceptional deviations—in full conformity to international law and the procedures of our own constitutional law regarding the use of military force.

Since Chomsky's case starts with the thesis that American policy in Vietnam is illegal, the argument should be reviewed in some detail.

The heart of Chomsky's case about the legality of American action in Vietnam is a premise to which he refers only obliquely as a collateral issue.

> It is curious, incidentally, that today only the United States and the "Communists" insist that South Vietnam is a separate and independent entity. The Saigon authorities maintain, in article 1 of the new constitution, that "Vietnam [not South Vietnam] is a territorially indivisible, unified, and independent republic," of which they claim to be the rulers; article 107 of the constitution specifies that article 1 cannot be amended. Hence in their view, even if Ho Chi Minh were to have sent his entire army to South Vietnam, he would not have been guilty of "aggression," but only of insurrection and subversion.[16]

It is quite true that the constitution of South Vietnam, like those of Korea and West Germany, seeks formally to keep alive the concept of a unified nation. That is also the underlying Arab view of the Arab-Israeli conflict—that with the end of the British mandate the nation of Palestine emerged within its boundaries, and the battles of Arabs and Israelis since are simply a form of civil war, internal to that nation.

But that was not the premise accepted at Geneva in 1954, at

16 P. 243.

least for a transition period of indeterminate duration. The arrangements made at Geneva in 1954 frame Chomsky's argument. Indeed, like most other critics of American policy, he relies on them almost exclusively as the source of the international commands the United States, in his view, has failed to carry out. In this respect Chomsky differs from Gabriel Kolko, a historian of Chomsky's general political outlook, who concludes that "it is quite erroneous to suggest that the United States was ready to recognize the outcome of a Conference and negotiated settlement it had bitterly opposed at every phase." [17]

Chomsky finds more concreteness and less ambiguity in the Geneva arrangements than most other students of the conference, which dealt with Korea as well as Indochina, and was dominated in its Indochinese phase by the disaster at Dien Bien Phu and France's desperate concern for a cease-fire.[18] The conference resulted in a cease-fire agreement between France and the Vietminh, and in a declaration, which was not signed by any of the delegations and was approved orally by only four of the nine participating governments. The United States, in a separate statement, dissociated itself from the declaration, although it said it would not use force to disturb the settlement. The government of South Vietnam formally protested against some of its terms.

The famous "Declaration" of the Geneva Conference, therefore, has only a most tenuous authority. It is no more than advice offered by four nations to a number of others, which indicated, then and later, that they had no intention of accepting it.

The Geneva Conference was held, of course, at a critical moment in the laborious and dangerous process of ending the fighting that threatened many areas of the Far East in the aftermath of the Second World War—Korea, Formosa, French Indochina, Malaya, the Philippines, the Dutch East Indies, Burma, and India. It was linked as well to the tortuous processes of European politics —the fate of the European Defense Community, the role of Ger-

[17] *The Roots of American Foreign Policy* (1969), p. 108.
[18] Robert F. Randle's excellent and conscientious analysis, *Geneva 1954* (1969), is the best available study of the conference and its outcome.

many in Europe, and other difficult and vital problems affecting the relations of Britain, France, and the United States. The fragile cease-fire in Korea had just been reached. President Eisenhower had declared that it would be "a fraud" to settle the war in Korea without also ending the wars in Indochina and Malaya.[19] The government of France was imperiled by the strains of the contest in Indochina. The Soviets and the Chinese were concerned about American reluctance to concur in a political settlement for Indochina that would result in the creation of a new Communist state in that country, and about the threats of American military action which accompanied the expressions of that reluctance. In that important if debatable book *Khrushchev Remembers*, Khrushchev is quoted as saying that he and his colleagues "gasped with surprise and pleasure" on hearing the French proposal to divide Vietnam at the 17th parallel, which was the absolute maximum they would have claimed as an opening gambit in the negotiation.[20] In fact, both the Soviet and the Chinese representatives made concessions that facilitated the limited agreements of Geneva.[21]

The Geneva arrangements of 1954 did bring hostilities in Indochina to an end, at least for a time, pursuant to the cease-fire agreement and a vaguer plan outlined in the Declaration and somewhat ambiguously "approved" by France, Great Britain, the Soviet Union, and China. The Vietminh and the authorities in South Vietnam acquiesced in the program of the Declaration unwillingly, without formally agreeing to it.

So far as Chomsky's argument is concerned, the critical provision of the Geneva arrangement—particularly, of course, the cease-fire and the regrouping of military forces—was that it gave "international blessing to the independence of Laos and Cambodia and establish[ed] two political entities in Vietnam." [22] The Vietminh was to withdraw its forces from Laos and Cambodia and

[19] State Department Bulletin, April 27, 1953, p. 601.

[20] Strobe Talbott, ed., *Khrushchev Remembers* (London, 1971), pp. 482–483.

[21] Chester L. Cooper, *The Lost Crusade: America in Vietnam* (1970), pp. 75–101; Randle, op. cit., pp. 200–203, 346–348, Chap. 23.

[22] Cooper, op. cit., p. 98.

from the area south of the 17th parallel in Vietnam. For Laos and Cambodia this amounted to the recognition of the existing governments as the sole legal authorities. For Vietnam the agreement meant that in the northern zone Ho Chi Minh's Democratic Republic of Vietnam became the de facto government, while in the southern zone Emperor Bao Dai's state of Vietnam was expected to consolidate its authority. It was then in the final stages of attaining full independence from France and was soon to become a republic.

Paragraph 7 of the Final Declaration provided for the possibility that the provisional regimes in North and South Vietnam could be united as a single state, if the people of both states decided to do so through free elections under the supervision of an International Control Commission consisting of Canada, Poland, and India. But it was also clear that for the time being the two parts of Vietnam were to be separate states, as was the case in Germany and Korea. The interplay of tension among China, the Soviet Union, and the Western allies at that point of time—in the aftermath of Korea, with crises in Greece, Turkey, and Berlin barely resolved, and war still raging in Malaya and the Philippines —permitted no other outcome. As Cooper says,

> the American and both Vietnamese delegations [at Geneva in 1954] had a prescience that the "withdrawal zones" would take on much greater significance as political zones, but the pressures to reach agreement were such that their reservations were ignored or swept away. If the other major powers at the Conference, the British, French, Soviet and Chinese Communists, thought very much about the ultimate implications of splitting Vietnam at the 17th parallel, they probably chalked up Vietnam, with Korea and Germany, as another "divided country" which, sooner or later (probably much later), would somehow be unified.[23]

To underline the implications of this policy, provision was made to allow individuals to migrate from one area to the other in the expectation of a division of the country, which might well last for a considerable time and result in regimes of different social character. Nearly a million people moved from North Vietnam to

[23] Ibid., p. 100; Randle, op. cit., pp. 429, 445–446.

South Vietnam under this arrangement. The regimes in Saigon and Hanoi became "governments" in every practical sense, exercising the normal authority of governments, although they were not universally recognized as such for purposes of diplomacy.

In both parts of Vietnam efforts of great vigor were pursued to consolidate the authority of the new regimes. Chomsky contends that American support for this process in South Vietnam somehow constituted a "violation" of the Geneva "agreements." The contention can hardly be serious. Chomsky never argues, for example, that Ho Chi Minh's campaign to establish party control in North Vietnam, and Soviet or Chinese support for Ho's effort, violated the Geneva accords in letter or in spirit. On the contrary, the development of separate and independent regimes, both in North and in South Vietnam, was exactly what the Geneva Conference contemplated.

The United States made certain basic positions explicit in 1954. While we were not a party to the Geneva arrangements, we were far from indifferent to their content. It was extremely clear at the time that there were some outcomes at Geneva we would not accept.[24] Our posture was a powerful factor in inducing the compromise that was achieved. Further, we stated that we should view any renewal of aggression in violation of the Geneva cease-fire with grave concern, as seriously threatening international peace and security. And we took the same stand on the reunification of South and North Vietnam that we took in regard to Germany and Korea, which are also nations divided against their will by the circumstances of the Cold War. Our policy was that in Vietnam, as in Germany and Korea, we should continue to favor unity by peaceful means and ultimately through free elections under United Nations supervision (that is, *not* under I.C.C. supervision), but that reunification through the use of force was inadmissible. Since neither the United States nor South Vietnam had signed the Geneva cease-fire or the Declaration, we took the position at an early date that we were not bound by the date of 1956

24 Randle, op. cit., pp. 556–557.

proposed in paragraph 7 of the Declaration for the referendum on reunification.[25]

Conditions in 1955 and 1956 were hardly favorable to the possibility of free elections under international supervision in North Vietnam. Ho Chi Minh was in the midst of a "land reform" program designed to consolidate his political power. At least 50,000 peasants had been executed under that program, with perhaps twice as many detained in prisons and forced-labor camps. As Chester Cooper remarks, "if Ho would have permitted the kind of elections in the North that were envisaged in the Geneva Agreement, he would have been the first Communist in history ready to accept the results of a free election." [26] Senator John F. Kennedy asked at the time "that the United States never give its approval to the early nationwide elections called for by the Geneva Agreement of 1954 . . . neither the United States nor Free Vietnam is ever going to be a party to an election obviously stacked and subverted in advance." [27]

Since the referendum provisions of the Geneva accords could not be carried out as scheduled, the government of South Vietnam announced its unwillingness to participate in such an election in 1956. The Soviet Union and Great Britain, as cochairmen of the Geneva Conference, did not object.

The controversy over the propriety of these decisions often suggests that the failure to hold a referendum on reunifying Vietnam in 1956 somehow justifies the use of force by North Vietnam to gain control of South Vietnam. This is not the case. Such an argument proves too much. It would license the unification of Germany and Korea by force. Both these countries were promised reunification through free elections which have not been held. One could hardly contend that the use of force to unify these divided countries comes within the scope of Article 51 of

[25] Randle, op. cit., pp. 343–344.
[26] Cooper, op. cit., pp. 158–159. See also pp. 149–151.
[27] "America's Stake in Vietnam," in American Friends of Vietnam, *A Symposium on America's Stake in Vietnam* (1956), p. 13.

the United Nations Charter as self-defense or as assistance to a government exercising its "inherent" right of self-defense. But Article 51 is the only exception to the flat rule of Article 2, Section 4, of the Charter, prohibiting the use of force as an instrument of national policy. However broadly one should interpret Article 51, in the light of its history and the purposes of the Charter as a whole, it cannot stretch so far. And that is exactly what the Security Council decided in 1950, when it held that the attempt by North Korea to unite that nation by force, on the ground that the nation had been wrongfully denied reunification by political means, violated the Charter; that South Korea could legally resist the attack in the name of Article 51; and that other nations were privileged—and indeed obliged—to assist South Korea in its efforts at self-defense.

After 1954 or 1955 there were in fact and in law two Vietnamese states, as there are two German and Korean states in fact and in law. While these states are not universally accorded diplomatic recognition, neither are they outlaws and pariahs in international society. They must be considered to have the normal protections of international law, including those embodied in Article 2 of the United Nations Charter. They are not fair game for any would-be conqueror. There is something indescribably bizarre in hearing the same speaker, in different parts of the same speech, say that the United States must accept the division of Germany into two states as a *fait accompli*, and that it must also accept the natural and inherent right of North Vietnam and North Korea to unify those nations by force.

Chomsky's paper on Pearl Harbor can rest on no other theory. Chomsky's analysis seems to conclude that Japan was wrong to attack Pearl Harbor, despite the existence of many grievances he regards as legitimate; Chomsky also seems to conclude that the United States was right to fight back after Pearl Harbor. If there are two Vietnamese states, two German states, and two Korean states—and there are—it follows from the theorems applied in Chomsky's essay that North Korea was wrong to attack South Korea in 1950; that North Vietnam was wrong to attack South

Vietnam (or if one prefers, to assist an indigenous revolt within South Vietnam), starting in the 1950s; and that either German state would be wrong if it should use force to attack the other. It follows further that the state attacked in each such case would be right, in terms of Chomsky's analysis, to fight back, and that it would be equally right for friendly states to assist its efforts at self-defense.

Thus the war in South Vietnam cannot be considered a civil war, internal to the "state" of Vietnam. No such state exists.

Nor is Chomsky's argument improved if one assumes—as he often does—that the attack on South Vietnam is not a campaign that has been organized and directed by Hanoi from the beginning, but an insurrection within South Vietnam, assisted by North Vietnam as an "ally." [28] From the point of view of international law the distinction is immaterial. Assistance to a rebellion within a state is just as much an act of war against that state as an open invasion. The rule is basic to the idea of international law and to the position of states within the international system.[29] It was a problem that preoccupied President Lincoln nearly every day of his term of office. And it has had a good deal of subsequent history—during the Spanish Civil War of the 1930s, for example, when Germany and Italy helped the revolutionaries; and during the Greek Civil War of the forties, when the revolutionaries were assisted by the Soviet Union through Greece's Communist neighbors.

But in the perspective of international law, to which Chomsky often refers with approval as his standard for judgment, the problem of Vietnam must include the South East Asia Collective Defense Treaty, generally known as SEATO, as well as the Geneva arrangements. Chomsky never mentions SEATO. In that treaty, negotiated and ratified shortly after the Geneva Conference, the United States, Australia, France, New Zealand, Pakistan, the Philippines, Thailand, and the United Kingdom became guarantors against direct and indirect aggression not only for the three non-

[28] Chomsky, op. cit., p. 243.
[29] See pp. 35–36, above.

Communist successor states of French Indochina, but for Southeast Asia as a whole.

In the preamble to the treaty the signatories declared their sense of unity publicly and formally, as notice to "any potential aggressor" in the area. In Article II they undertook, "separately and jointly," to "maintain and develop their individual and collective capacity to resist armed attack and to prevent and counter subversive activities directed from without against their territorial integrity and political stability." The first paragraph of Article IV provides that "*each* party recognizes that aggression by means of armed attack in the treaty area against any of the Parties" (or against states or territories designated in the protocol to the treaty, which lists Laos, Cambodia, and what is now South Vietnam, if they choose to be protected) "would endanger its own peace and safety, and agrees that *it will* in that event act to meet the common danger in accordance with its constitutional processes" (italics added). In contrast to the individual and categorical obligation of paragraph 1, paragraph 2 provides that if threats to the peace other than armed attacks arise, "the Parties shall consult immediately in order to agree on the measures which should be taken for the common defense." [30]

While SEATO has had a checkered history as an international organization, the treaty did put the United States directly into the Southeast Asian picture. As Chester Cooper points out, "It was a commitment, albeit one considerably less robust than was originally conceived, to involve the United States in the security and economic development of the countries in that area—a part of the world which until 1954 had been pretty much left to the British and the French." [31]

The United States government has squarely based its policy in Vietnam on the SEATO treaty, as well as on South Vietnam's

[30] See Randle, op. cit., pp. 539–541, on the formal relation between SEATO and the Geneva arrangements. In Randle's view the treaty was the culmination of Dulles' strategy for cushioning and containing the effects of French defeat in Indochina, which could not have been prevented as a practical matter.

[31] Cooper, op. cit., p. 114.

inherent right of self-defense and on our right under the Charter of the United Nations to assist South Vietnam in that defense. For example, President Eisenhower noted in a formal statement in 1957 that South Vietnam is covered by the treaty and said "that aggression or subversion threatening the political independence of the Republic of Vietnam would be considered as endangering peace and stability" within the meaning of that document.[32] The theme has been sounded in official speeches and statements ever since. Both Congress and four Presidents have reiterated the conclusion that North Vietnam's participation in the war constitutes "armed attack" within the meaning of Article IV of the treaty.

The commitment of SEATO was later reiterated, so far as the United States is concerned, in the Tonkin Gulf Resolution of the Congress, passed in 1964. That Resolution—since a matter of considerable controversy—says:

> The United States regards as vital to its national interest and to world peace the maintenance of international peace and security in southeast Asia. Consonant with the Constitution of the United States and the Charter of the United Nations and in accordance with its obligations under the Southeast Asia Collective Defense Treaty, the United States is, therefore, prepared, as the President determines, to take all necessary steps, including the use of armed force, to assist any member or protocol state of the Southeast Asia Collective Defense Treaty requesting assistance in defense of its freedom.

Senator Fulbright explained that the passage of this Resolution fulfilled the language of the SEATO treaty requiring each nation to carry out its obligations under the treaty through its own constitutional processes. Whether Congressional action of this kind is necessary under the American Constitution, or whether the President can properly act alone in carrying out treaty obligations, as President Truman did in Korea, remains a matter for debate. There can be no question, however, that the United States speaks with a stronger voice when the President and Congress act together, as they did in Vietnam.

[32] State Department Bulletin, May 27, 1957, pp. 851–852. See also State Department Bulletin, April 27, 1959, pp. 579–583.

The vote of the Congress on the Tonkin Gulf Resolution has another dimension in American constitutional law and politics. President Truman missed his opportunity to obtain a Congressional resolution of support for his action in Korea,[33] although such a resolution was offered at one point by Senator Taft. As a result, the United States fought in Korea under the United Nations Charter, which is a treaty of the United States, and under the President's inherent constitutional powers in carrying out the treaty obligation. During the Korean war, there was no Congressional action comparable to the passage of the Tonkin Gulf Resolution, and other Congressional actions in support of the war.

The legal posture of American intervention in Korea stirred up a constitutional storm. There was concern at the apparent authority of the Security Council, an international body sitting in New York, to take a vote that would bind the United States to go to war—concern about sovereignty, and concern, too, about the seemingly unlimited powers of the President in relation to those of the Congress. There was, of course, repeated Congressional support for various aspects of the Korean war, and for the war itself, through appropriations statutes and otherwise. But after the war became unpopular it was often called "Truman's War."

It is frequently claimed—and Chomsky's language suggests that he agrees with the charge—that United States action both in Korea and in Vietnam was illegal as a matter of American constitutional law because Congress had not in either case passed a joint resolution called a declaration of war.

Theses of this kind have no support in the language or the history of the Constitution. The United States, like every other sovereign nation, has full authority under international law to use force both when a state of war has been "declared," and the international law of war invoked, and under many circumstances in times of peace as well. The categories of the Constitution delineating the powers of the nation as a sovereign member of the society of nations are addressed to the rubrics of international law. In international law, states are entitled to use force against other

---

[33] Dean Acheson, *Present at the Creation* (1969), pp. 413–415.

states pursuant to formal declarations of war, which fully invoke the Law of War, or, without such formality, as a means of self-help in times of peace. The use of limited force in time of peace is confined to obtaining redress against acts or policies of other nations which are deemed to violate international law, and for which amends have proved unobtainable by political means. A solemn declaration of war signals maximum hostility, including invasion and perhaps the political destruction of one's opponent. The use of limited force in time of peace has different political implications. It focuses attention only on the provocation—i.e., Pancho Villa's raids in the United States during Wilson's administration, or North Vietnam's activities in South Vietnam during the long Indochinese War. Politically, such uses of limited force convey an intention simply to eliminate an offense, and to confine the military effort to means reasonably proportionate to the end sought. Different words are used to describe different forms of self-help—retorsion, reprisal, pacific embargoes or blockades, limited intervention to protect nationals, humanitarian intervention to restore order in situations of massacre, natural disaster, or extreme civil disturbance. They are all subsumed under the notion of an inherent and sovereign right of self-defense, which has been re-enacted as Article 51 of the United Nations Charter.

The presidency was one of the two great inventions of the Constitution—the other being judicial review. The weakness of the executive under the Articles of Confederation was one of the major reasons for holding the Constitutional Convention of 1787. The founding fathers sought to make possible a President who would have enough power to discharge the executive task, both at home and abroad, but not enough to become a tyrant or a king.

The Constitution provides that the President is the repository of "the executive power" of the United States, that he is Commander in Chief of the armed forces, and that he is under a duty to see to it that the laws be faithfully executed. It also provides that treaties enacted under the authority of the United States are the supreme law of the land. Congress, on the other hand, possesses "all legislative powers . . . granted" by the Constitution itself, including the power to raise and support the armed forces and "to declare war, grant letters of Marque and Reprisal, and make rules concerning captures on land and water."

During the first two decades of our history under the Constitution of 1789—a period of acute international turbulence—the respective authority of Congress and of the President with regard to the use of the armed forces was a matter of active controversy. Several issues of principle were settled, not only by the pattern of practice but by decisions of the Supreme Court as well. The system of ideas that emerged from this period has a special weight, since it was produced by the generation of men who had drafted and enacted the Constitution. The rules that embody their experience have controlled constitutional usage and doctrine ever since.

Among those rules several are of particular importance to Chomsky's thesis. The President has wide powers in the field of foreign relations, which he can exercise without Congressional authority even when diplomacy comes near to war, notably the power to issue a declaration of neutrality. The Louisiana Purchase of 1803 was of course the most far-reaching exercise of the President's independent power over foreign relations, and of the treaty power, in our entire history. The President, too, can use the armed forces at his discretion, and without Congressional authority, in a number of situations where international law would recognize the propriety of the use of force during a time of peace—reprisals against guerrillas operating from Spanish Florida, for example; the collection of debts; the suppression of piracy; and other instances of the use of force in time of peace going well beyond that of replying to armed attack, the example Madison had given in the debates over the Constitution to illustrate the kind of independent military powers the President possessed.[34]

[34] J. G. Rogers, *World Policing and the Constitution* (1945); W. T. Revely III, "Presidential War-Making: Constitutional Prerogative or Usurpation?," 55 *Va. L. Rev.* 1243 (1969); R. A. Falk, ed., *The Vietnam War and International Law* (1968), Vol. II (1969); J. N. Moore and J. L. Underwood, with collaboration of M. S. McDougal, *The Lawfulness of United States Assistance to the Republic of Vietnam* (Pamphlet edition, 1966), reprinted in 112 Cong. Rec. 15, 519, 15,553–15,567 (1967), 5 Dusquesne L. Rev. 235 (1967). My own views on the law of the subject are developed in detail

President Washington put down the Whisky Rebellion in Pennsylvania even though that state had not requested federal assistance which Article IV of the Constitution suggests as a condition precedent for federal action of the kind.

While the campaign to take Florida from Spain is perhaps the most extreme instance of Presidential independence in the history of the war power, the most pertinent of the historical episodes for present purposes was the limited war with France—"John Adams' Undeclared War"—which arose out of French raids on American shipping. Congress passed a series of acts authorizing limited maritime warfare with France. Those statutes did not declare a state of war to exist in the sense of international law. Such declarations have far-reaching consequences, both in international and domestic law, authorizing all kinds of activities otherwise illegal or of doubtful legality, from censorship and blockade to the internment of enemy aliens.

The legality of these dispositions by the Congress and the President came before the courts in a series of cases concerned with the legality of captures at sea and the disposition of prize money. A number of these cases reached the Supreme Court, which decided that the provision of the Constitution regarding declarations of war was not exclusive, but that Congress could authorize hostilities in more restricted ways if it wished to do so.

> Congress is empowered to declare a general war [Justice Chase said], or Congress may wage a limited war; limited in place, in objects and in time. If a general war is declared, its extent and operations are only restricted and regulated by the *jus belli*, forming a part of the law of nations; but if a partial war is waged, its extent and operation depend upon our municipal law.

The hostilities with France, the Justice declared, were "a limited, partial war," in which Congress had not made France our general enemy; "but this only proves the circumspection and prudence of the legislature." [35] In a later case dealing with the same subject Chief Justice Marshall noted with approval that neither side had

---

in "Great Cases Make Bad Law: The War Powers Act," 50 Texas L. Rev. 833 (May, 1972).

[35] Bas v. Tingy, 4 Dall 37, 43–45 (U.S. 1800).

ventured to claim that hostilities could only be authorized by a declaration of war.[36]

These early cases also sharply defended the civil control of the military, and held an officer liable, despite authorization from the President, when the President had authorized him to commit an act not covered by statute.[37]

The constitutional boundaries sketched by this early experience have remained the guidelines of practice ever since. The United States has used its armed forces abroad at least 150 times since 1789. Formal declarations of war have been issued on only five occasions. In about one-fifth of the remaining cases Congress authorized the use of force by the President through legislation which did not involve a declaration of war. In the rest, including some extended campaigns, the President acted on his own authority.

Of course the nation faces foreign-policy problems today altogether different from those it faced in 1800, or indeed in 1900. And of course Congress should play an active and responsible part in the formation of foreign policy. I am no friend of unlimited presidential discretion to decide when the nation should go to war.

The circumstances of modern world politics, however, require Presidents to act quickly, and often alone. That fact does not preclude the possibility of effective democratic policy-making in the field of foreign relations. Congress may be able to act effectively both before and after moments of crisis or potential crisis. It may join the President in seeking to deter crises by publicly defining national policy in advance through the sanctioning of treaties or other legislative declarations. This was a practice that Eisenhower and Dulles used a great deal, both in Asia and in the Mediterranean. Equally, Congress may participate in policy-making after the event through legislative authorization of sustained combat, either by means of declarations of war or through legislative procedures having more restricted legal and political consequences.

36 Talbot v. Seeman, 1 Cranch 1, 28–29 (U.S. 1801).
37 Little v. Barreme, 2 Cranch 170 (U.S. 1804) (per Marshall, C. J.).

Both forms of Congressional action are of equal constitutional legitimacy.

For present purposes it is enough to point out that through the Senate's action in ratifying the SEATO treaty, and Congress' action in passing the Tonkin Gulf Resolution, and several other pieces of legislation, Congress and the President had acted together, both in giving advance notice of American policy toward Vietnam and in reaffirming that policy after hostilities began, and then increased in intensity. So far as the constitutional proprieties are concerned, the American involvement in Vietnam occurred through a procedure that is a model for democratic decision-making. There is no basis for the charge that the American course of action in Vietnam violates the internal law of the United States or arrogates power to the President at the expense of Congress. In this regard the constitutional practice with regard to Vietnam was more punctilious than that used in Korea.

So much for Chomsky's argument that American assistance to South Vietnam violates international law and the internal law of the United States—the foundation for his charge that America's course in that conflict has been a moral obscenity. Many courts by now have passed upon the constitutionality of the war in Vietnam. All have given the same answer—that whether the United States acts or does not act under the SEATO treaty; whether it decides to help or not to help a friendly government in measures of self-defense against a rebellion aided, or instigated and organized from abroad; whether the President and Congress "declare" war, or choose the less risky course of limited war—all these, the courts have said, are matters within the discretion entrusted to the President and to Congress under the Constitution, and therefore "political" questions beyond the control of the courts. But when the courts decide that the way in which the political arms of government exercise such discretion is a "political" question, they are not abstaining from a decision on its legality. On the contrary, they are deciding that the choices made—wise or unwise—were within the zone of discretion entrusted to the political branches of government, and are therefore legal.

Occasionally Chomsky seems to proceed on another footing, recognizing the separate identity of the two Vietnamese states. For example, he quotes Secretary of Defense McNamara, who said that the United States is fighting in Vietnam "to preserve the principle that political change must not be brought by externally directed violence and military force." [38]

In McNamara's view, Chomsky says, it is

> perfectly legitimate for "externally directed violence and military force" to be employed to guarantee political stability—that is, when it is the United States that exercises this force. In fact, he goes still further. We even have the right to use our military force to carry out social and political change. Thus the pacification program, which is under American military control, "involves nothing less than the restructuring of Vietnamese society" [according to Secretary McNamara, but, Chomsky says] it is in his view, a legitimate, in fact laudable program. Thus the principle we are fighting to preserve is not the principle of nonintervention by military force in the affairs of other nations. Rather it is the principle that the United States, and the United States alone, may intervene in the internal affairs of other nations to guarantee political stability and even to restructure their society.

In any event, Chomsky says, North Vietnamese aid to the Viet Cong forces in South Vietnam is less in volume than American aid to South Vietnam—a point whose relevance to the legal issue he is trying to make I cannot understand.

> But [he continues] North Vietnamese interference has been in support of social change of a sort that we define as illegitimate, whereas ours is in support of stability (or occasionally, restructuring) that we have determined to be quite proper. To be concise, we are fighting in Vietnam in fulfillment of our role as international judge and executioner—nothing less.[39]

In its primary application Chomsky's argument fails for the reason indicated earlier, namely, the clear distinction in international law between external assistance to a state and external assistance to rebels against a state—the legal distinction in the Spanish case dur-

[38] Chomsky, op. cit., p. 247.
[39] Pp. 247–248.

ing the thirties between aid to the government of Spain and aid to Franco.

But Chomsky also examines the American position in Vietnam in the light of another principle.

"Why," he asks, "do we have this right" to help South Vietnam resist the North Vietnamese attack? "The answer," he says, "has been given by many statesmen and scholars: It is in our national interest."

Chomsky's sentence omits a critical step in the reasoning of the "statesmen and scholars" to whom he refers. The United States has a legal right to assist South Vietnam under the Charter of the United Nations, because South Vietnam was defending itself against armed attack by North Vietnam; *and* it decided that it was in the national interest to exercise that right. The "statesmen and scholars" to whom Chomsky refers may have been mistaken in their answer to his question. But it can hardly be said they were violating international law. There are many situations in which it might be contended that the national interest of the United States would be served by military intervention (in Cuba, for example), but where such intervention would not be legally permissible. No effective intervention has occurred.

But beyond the legal issue Chomsky ridicules the notion that the United States has a national interest in safeguarding the territorial integrity and political independence of South Vietnam or other small states in Southeast Asia, and perhaps in the Third World altogether. He dismisses concern about the possible expansion of China as a myth, and policies for "containing" China or stabilizing the area around China as rhetoric designed to conceal programs of naked imperialism, intended to suppress revolutionary movements of social change and to maintain capitalist governments in power in Southeast Asia—governments that could bring the region into the orbit of the American economy. He nowhere mentions the consequences of possible American withdrawal in South Vietnam on the political future of Southeast Asia, Korea, or Japan, or indeed upon the deterrent power of American commitments in the Middle East or in Europe.[40] Nor does he examine the possibility that the national security interest of the United States is to help establish an international order of independent states, save to dismiss it as a self-righteous assumption that American policy is "benevolent."

Other writers develop these aspects of the case against American foreign policy as "counterrevolutionary" and "imperialistic" more fully than Chomsky. One aspect of that phase of the debate was taken up in Chapter 4; another will be considered in Chapter 8, where the problem of security policy toward the Third World will be reviewed as a whole.

VI

Chomsky promises his readers that he will outline an American foreign policy that could assure the legitimate security interests of the nation without involving it in "imperialism." In view of his robust criticism of the failure of others to be candid, realistic, coherent, systematic, and intellectually honest, it is hardly unfair to expect him to present his theories in ways that meet his own commendable standards.

The challenge to those who favor American withdrawal from Vietnam, he writes, "is to create the understanding that we have no right to set any conditions at all on a political settlement in Vietnam; that American military force must be withdrawn from Vietnam, and from the other simmering Vietnams throughout the world; that American power and resources and technical skills must be used to build and not to repress or to 'contain' or to destroy." [41]

What does Chomsky mean by "other simmering Vietnams"?

One should no doubt take seriously the insistence of administration spokesmen that one purpose of the present violence is to prove that wars of national liberation cannot succeed; to demonstrate, that is, in the clearest and most explicit terms that any revo-

[40] See Chomsky's comment on the Middle East, quoted on p. 154, above.
[41] P. 275.

lutionary movement that we—unilaterally, as in Vietnam—designate as illegitimate will face the most efficient and ruthless machinery that can be developed by modern technology . . .

It is easy to be carried away by the sheer horror of what the daily press reveals and to lose sight of the fact that this is merely the brutal exterior of a deeper crime, of commitment to a social order that guarantees endless suffering and humiliation and denial of elementary human rights. It is tragic that the United States should have become, in Toynbee's words, "the leader of a world-wide anti-revolutionary movement in defense of vested interests." For American intellectuals and for the schools there is no more vital issue than this indescribable tragedy.[42]

At this stage we can put to one side Chomsky's failure to perceive that American policy has been directed since 1947 at deterring and resisting aggression, not revolution—save perhaps in the singular case of Guatemala; that it has done nothing to prevent recent changes of social policy in Peru, Bolivia, and Chile; that it offered aid on a large scale during and after World War II to the Soviet Union and the countries of Eastern Europe, and to Castro, Nasser, Ben Bella, Nkrumah, and Sukarno at the beginning of their regimes; that at critical moments it indicated its support for Tito's far-from-capitalist regime in Yugoslavia, and has developed helpful patterns of cooperation with Communist Romania; and that it has made repeated offers of large-scale aid to North Vietnam if that country would desist from trying to conquer South Vietnam, Laos, and Cambodia.

Chomsky's argument seems to derive from a different premise altogether—a belief that "revolution" is so sacred a cause in terms of human happiness that where "revolution" is involved, the United States and its allies should suspend or abandon their laborious efforts to fulfill the principles of the United Nations Charter against the use of force as an instrument of national policy. Chomsky nowhere explains how this conviction can be squared with his repeated invocation of the rules of international law as a sure guide for American foreign policy. Nor does he tell us how to determine which movements claiming the mantle of "revolution" should be allowed to spread their creed with the sword, and

[42] Pp. 312–313.

which deterred or resisted in the name of international law. When he speaks of American commitment to a social order "that guarantees endless suffering and humiliation and denial of elementary human rights," he presumably refers to capitalism. Does he mean the modern and democratic welfare-state capitalism of the United States, Western Europe, and Japan, of Australia, New Zealand, Canada, Chile, Mexico, Israel, and other countries? It is hard for me to understand how these social systems can be characterized as guaranteeing "endless suffering and humiliation and denial of elementary human rights." For all their imperfections they are certainly far superior to any known alternatives, past or present, both in assuring economic and social progress and in protecting freedom. Furthermore, Chomsky frequently excoriates the social order of the Soviet Union and indicates that "while sympathizing with China's problems, one may still react with dismay, perhaps even outrage, to the authoritarian and repressive character of the Chinese state, as one may have varying reactions to the society that is developing" in China.[43] While I have found no direct references in his book to the quality of life in North Vietnam and North Korea, I suspect that he would similarly dissociate himself from seeming to approve those societies as embodying his own ideal of "libertarian socialism."

From what principles of foreign policy do Chomsky's conclusions derive? If we can isolate Chomsky's axioms, what deductions can we make from them about the systematic and nonimperialist foreign policy he would substitute for that of the United States since 1947?

Chomsky refers in his book to four modern wars—the Civil War of 1936–39 in Spain; Japan's program of expansion in the thirties and forties; the war in Vietnam; and the crisis in the Middle East. He believes the United States was right to use force against Japan after Pearl Harbor. What did he think the United States should have done about Spain when the democratic Spanish Republic was overthrown by a revolution assisted by Germany and Italy? The American record, he says, is "hardly one to inspire

[43] P. 267.

pride." [44] The United States, he comments, purported to be neutral in Spain, but in fact there were some breaches of neutrality, at least by private American companies, that favored both the government and the revolutionary force of General Franco. But Chomsky does not indicate what kind of American policy toward Spain would have "inspired pride" in terms of his ideas about foreign policy. I can find little or no trace in his book of the policies he thinks the United States should pursue in Europe or the Middle East; in southern Asia, Arabia, or Iran; or toward modern Japan. The passage quoted on p. 154 would seem to indicate that in some areas, even in the Third World, he would support security programs of deterrence or of resistance to aggression.

> If it is the responsibility of the intellectual to insist upon the truth [he writes in a discussion of Vietnam], it is also his duty to see events in their historical perspective. Thus one must applaud the insistence of the Secretary of State on the importance of historical analogies, the Munich analogy, for example. As Munich showed, a powerful and aggressive nation with a fanatic belief in its manifest destiny will regard each victory, each extension of its power and authority, as a prelude to the next step. The matter was very well put by Adlai Stevenson, when he spoke of "the old, old route whereby expansive powers push at more and more doors, believing they will open, until, at the ultimate door, resistance is unavoidable and major war breaks out." Herein lies the danger of appeasement, as the Chinese tirelessly point out to the Soviet Union, which they claim is playing Chamberlain to our Hitler in Vietnam. [45]

How does this thesis apply, in Chomsky's judgment, to American policy in Europe and the Middle East? In 1946, he says, there was a Russian attempt to impose by force a pro-Soviet government in northern Azerbaijan that would grant the Soviet Union access to Iranian oil. [46] This was rebuffed, he thinks, by superior Anglo-American force. The "bland assumption" that the Western allies had a right to rebuff the Soviet probe, he writes, "is most

[44] P. 121.
[45] Pp. 352–353.
[46] P. 328.

revealing of deep-seated attitudes towards the conduct of foreign affairs." [47]

But how would Chomsky have had the United States react to similar probes in Greece and in Berlin and to the installation of Soviet-controlled regimes in Eastern Europe? His only answer to questions of this kind is to assure his readers that if more conciliatory policies had been pursued—and especially if we had been willing to contemplate the neutralization of Germany—the Cold War in Europe would "probably" have been avoided.[48] Optimistic prophecies of this kind were reviewed at greater length in Chapter 4.

In the end, therefore, Chomsky fails to articulate even the outlines of the alternative foreign policy, based on an alternative conception of the national interest, that he promised in his introduction. True, he tells us we should avoid the "simmering Vietnams" of world politics. But he doesn't tell us how to distinguish them from situations of aggression where presumably his respect for international law, and his sense of history, would require a defensive response. Nor does he consider the contention that a stable balance of power, based on reciprocally accepted rules of restraint, is the necessary if not the sufficient condition for peace in a world community of nation-states.

[47] P. 329.
[48] See, i.e., p. 328, n. 13.

# 6

## *Senator Fulbright's Universe*

FEW MODERN BOOKS on foreign policy have been so influential as Senator J. William Fulbright's classic lectures, *The Arrogance of Power*.[1] To find a work of comparable impact on American opinion one has to go back to Mahan.

Fulbright approaches foreign policy as a challenge to the American spirit. In dealing with other nations, he says, we must choose between two Americas,

> the America of Lincoln and Adlai Stevenson, [and] . . . the America of Teddy Roosevelt and the modern superpatriots. One is generous and humane, the other narrowly egotistical; one is self-critical, the other self-righteous; one is sensible, the other romantic; one is good-humored, the other solemn; one is enquiring, the other pontificating; one is moderate, the other filled with passionate intensity; one is judicious and the other arrogant in the use of great power.[2]

Identifying himself with Lincoln and Adlai Stevenson, Fulbright invokes the desirability of a tolerant atmosphere "in which unorthodox ideas would arouse interest rather than anger, reflection rather than emotion. As likely as not, new proposals carefully ex-

[1] The lectures were delivered at Johns Hopkins University in 1966 and published in the same year.
[2] Op. cit., p. 245.

179

amined would be found wanting and old policies judged sound; what is wanted is not change itself but the capacity for change." [3]

Senator Fulbright's book is dazzling in many perspectives as an artifact of American intellectual history. But our concern here is with the Senator's view of what foreign policy is for and what the goals and methods of American foreign policy should be. I shall therefore concentrate on that facet of his thought.

As is already obvious, Fulbright has a healthy taste for the joys of combat. He praises civility, but often flays those with whom he disagrees. Thus we should put to one side a number of familiar charges against American foreign policy which Fulbright makes effectively and with polemic relish. He devotes a good many vivid pages to our supposed affinity for dictators and reactionaries. And he often lambastes the government for indulging in the "globalism" of an "anti-communist crusade."

The first of these charges is canvassed elsewhere.[4] It is hard to discover a factual predicate for the second, the charge of a global anticommunist crusade. In the period before the development of the Soviet nuclear weapon the main events in what Fulbright calls "the anti-communist crusade" were the offer of the Baruch Plan to internationalize nuclear weapons and science; the offer of reconstruction loans to the Soviet Union and the countries of Eastern Europe through the Marshall Plan and earlier programs; and our tacit acquiescence in the Soviet conquest of Eastern Europe, which in our view violated the agreements made at Yalta and Potsdam. The Western nations began to resist Soviet expansion systematically only in 1947, when at last we most reluctantly decided that the promises of Yalta and Potsdam would not be kept and that Soviet power threatened Turkey, Greece, and Berlin, and indeed Western Europe as a whole. It was the Czech coup of 1948, against the background of earlier threats to Greece and Turkey, and the warning of Truman's speech in March 1947 that led to the passage of the Vandenberg Resolution and then to NATO and some rearmament. The same kind of threat produced

[3] Op. cit., pp. 32–33.
[4] See p. 90, above.

the same kind of response later on when we stepped in to help South Korea and Communist Yugoslavia retain their independence. These were all policies that Senator Fulbright approved at the time and approves still. They do not bespeak a "crusade" against communism, but an effort to maintain the most sensitive of all borders, what Duncan Hall has called "the international frontier," where the interests of the great powers conflict and where, above all, stable compromises must be sought in order to make a balance of power—and therefore peace—possible.[5]

As for "globalism," the attempt to give more concrete substance to the charge is equally mystifying. In the days of our atomic monopoly the United States never threatened the Soviet Union, or pressed it to undo the revolution, or even to open its regime. Nor did we undertake seriously to drive Soviet power from Eastern Europe, by nuclear threats or otherwise. The world is always full of troubles that the United States has no thought of taking unto itself. Coups d'état occur on an average of twice a month. The United States has taken an active interest in only five or six of the fifty-five or fifty-seven situations of armed conflict in the world during the last twenty-five years.[6] The criteria actually used for deciding which conflicts affect our national interests are a far cry from those of a universal policeman who rushes whenever he hears the gong.

When one gets beyond the purely polemical side of Fulbright's book one finds an argument without structure. Fulbright makes no attempt to set out the principles that in his view should govern the activities of the nation abroad. As a result the reader must fall back on do-it-yourself. Bringing together bits of evidence about the senator's views found here and there in the interstices of his

[5] *Mandates, Dependencies and Trusteeship* (1948), Chap. 1. The theme is developed further in his remarkable book *Commonwealth, a History of the British Commonwealth of Nations* (1971), pp. 396–414, 567.

[6] L. P. Bloomfield and A. C. Liess, in their *Controlling Small Wars* (1969), count 54 episodes of war or the threat of war having international ramifications and involving or seeming to involve small powers and local conflicts in the first instance. There have been others since their book was finished. And they omit episodes such as the Berlin airlift and the Cuban missile crisis, where great powers were directly involved on both sides.

book, we must formulate the key propositions of Fulbright's theory for him.

Fulbright does not take one theory of foreign policy as his major premise and stick to it consistently. On the contrary, he slips from premise to premise, using at least four, and perhaps five, of the propositions listed in Chapter 3 as the basis for his exposition. His book is heavily laced with strong pacifist sentiment and includes many quotations about the horror of war. He often asserts as a criticism that American foreign policy has failed because it hasn't produced democracy everywhere our influence has been felt. Over and over again he urges that we should cut back or abandon overseas efforts in favor of social improvement at home.[7] He claims that we are involved far beyond the limits of "our proper concerns," but nowhere tells us how to define those proper concerns. He recognizes, for instance, that the destruction of German and Japanese power as a result of the war, and the rise of Russia and China, created a situation that required our response;[8] he contends that our security is endangered by aggression, not communism,[9] and supports what we did in Europe, in Korea, and elsewhere to arrest the expansion of Soviet and Chinese influence. He concedes that as a nation the United States has "vital interests" and responsibilities that should not be neglected.[10] But his argument becomes gossamer as one attempts to apply it to concrete problems of choice and use it as a guideline to determine when we should act and when we should remain passive before changes in the map of world politics brought about by force.

The dominant theme of Fulbright's book is Decline and Fall. Like an Old Testament prophet, he stands before his people warning them that their sins—and above all the sin of pride—will bring doom upon them.

America is now at that historical point at which a great nation is in danger of losing its perspective on what exactly is within the realm of its power and what is beyond it. Other great nations,

[7] E.g., op. cit., pp. 20–21, 134–135, 255.
[8] Op. cit., pp. 77, 108–109, 185, 211–212.
[9] Op. cit., p. 81.
[10] Op. cit., p. 217.

reaching this critical juncture, have aspired to too much, and by overextension of effort have declined and then fallen.[11]

Fulbright does not fear that America may be tempted to seek world conquest. But he does fear "that she may be drifting into commitments which, though generous and benevolent in intent, are so far-reaching as to exceed even America's great capacities." Thus he prays "that America will escape those fatal temptations of power which have ruined other great nations and will instead confine herself to doing only that good in the world which she *can* do, both by direct effort and by the force of her own example." [12] Power, he thunders, has a dangerous attraction for mankind, especially when it is in the hands of men who exemplify, not the mildness of democratic humanism, but the hard crusading intolerance of puritanism. Power leads men to become arrogant and self-righteous, to confuse force with virtue, and to conclude that they have God's favor because they are mighty in battle.

Every American—and most especially Americans of the puritan temperament—must say "Amen" to Fulbright's sermon. None would deny the moral force of his warning, nor disparage his hope for peace. The problem with his epistle is not its wisdom, but its meaning. Is the issue really to determine what goals of American policy are "generous and benevolent," or which ones are in the national interest? Fulbright's choice of words reveals an ambiguity, or confusion, which runs through his book. Should American foreign policy be directed to the protection of national interests, or is it a kind of national philanthropy, a commendable activity for a rich country, but one which can be cut back when we can no longer comfortably afford to do "so much good" in the world? Is it beyond America's power to protect its national interests? If so, which ones, and why?

## II

Perhaps the best evidence about how Fulbright would answer these questions is to be found in his treatment of the hostilities in

[11] P. 3.
[12] P. 4.

Korea and Vietnam. Fulbright defends our support of South Korea, but opposes our assistance to South Vietnam. He attempts to distinguish the cases at two points in his book.

Korea [he writes] is another example (e.g. of how poor we are at spreading the gospel of democracy). We went to war in 1950 to defend South Korea against the Russian-inspired aggression of North Korea. I think that American intervention was justified and necessary: we were defending a country that clearly wanted to be defended, whose army was willing to fight and fought well, and whose government, though dictatorial, was patriotic and commanded the support of the people. Throughout the war, however, the United States emphasized as one of its war aims the survival of the Republic of Korea as a "free society," something which it was not then and is not now. We lost 33,629 American lives in that war and have since spent $5.61 billion on direct military and economic aid and a great deal more on indirect aid to South Korea. The country, nonetheless, remained until recently in a condition of virtual economic stagnation and political instability. Only now is economic progress being made, but the truly surprising fact is that having fought a war for three years to defend the freedom of South Korea, most Americans quickly lost interest in the state of the ward for whom they had sacrificed so much. It is doubtful that more than a handful of Americans now know or care whether South Korea is a "free society."

We are now engaged in a war to "defend freedom" in South Vietnam. Unlike the Republic of Korea, South Vietnam has an army which fights without notable success and a weak, dictatorial government which does not command the loyalty of the South Vietnamese people. The official war aims of the United States government, as I understand them, are to defeat what is regarded as North Vietnamese aggression, to demonstrate the futility of what the Communists call "wars of national liberation," and to create conditions under which the South Vietnamese people will be able freely to determine their own future. . . .

What I do question is the ability of the United States or any other Western nation to go into a small, alien, undeveloped Asian nation and create stability where there is chaos, the will to fight where there is defeatism, democracy where there is no tradition of it, and honest government where corruption is almost a way of life.[13]

At a later stage in his argument Senator Fulbright returns to the problem:

[13] Op. cit., pp. 14–15.

The Korean war was fought under the auspices of the United Nations for an ultimately limited purpose. The United States provided most of the forces from the outside, but a great many other members of the United Nations sent troops and the United Nations itself took part in the direction of the war. After the abandonment of the disastrous attempt to occupy North Korea, which brought hundreds of thousands of Chinese soldiers into the conflict, the war was fought for the limited purpose of repelling a clear act of aggression which had been incited by Stalinist Russia.

In Vietnam the United States is fighting virtually alone and for vague purposes in a war which is not an international conflict but an insurrection in one part of a divided country supported by the other part. Aside from the token forces provided by Australia and New Zealand for their own political purposes, the only other outside force in Vietnam besides the large American army is a Korean force of forty thousand men heavily subsidized by the United States. Except for peace proposals offered by the Secretary-General, the United Nations plays no part in the war and is generally ignored by the belligerents; indeed, many members of the United Nations are extremely critical of the American involvement in Vietnam, and it is most unlikely that if a vote were taken, the United States could muster a majority in the General Assembly in support of its policy. As for the SEATO Treaty, three of its seven members provide no active support for the American military effort, and at least one, France, is extremely critical of American policy.[14]

It is significant that Senator Fulbright nowhere discusses the strategic interest of the United States in either country from the point of view of the defense of Japan or Southeast Asia or the implications for the balance of power of their possible take-over.

But let us examine the reasons Senator Fulbright does give for supporting our course in Korea, and opposing it in Vietnam.

First, is there a difference between Korea and Vietnam in terms of the character of the governments and societies involved? And if so, do these differences affect or define our national interest in the security of the two areas? Is it in our national interest, as Senator Fulbright suggests elsewhere, to restrain the undue expansion of Soviet and Chinese power, or to help only strong and worthy governments already capable of resisting aggression?

In the first years of the Korean war the South Koreans were

[14] Pp. 109-110.

bitterly criticized in the United States on precisely the grounds advanced by Senator Fulbright as a criticism of our involvement in Vietnam: corruption, military ineffectiveness, and unrepresentative government, which was not supported, it was claimed, by the people of the country. The economic dynamism, the relative unity, and the military strength of South Korea came about as a consequence of victory in the war, and of the American presence. They developed slowly. There is no self-evident reason why the gifted people of South Vietnam could not do as well as the Koreans if they had the same opportunity to develop in relative safety.

But what relevance do these issues have if the purpose of our intervention, both in Korea and in South Vietnam, was to help preserve a balance of power by preventing aggression supported by one of the large Communist powers—if our goal, that is, was to defeat one form of aggression and thus to deter others? Despite Senator Fulbright's strictures on our weakness in spreading the gospel of democracy, he concedes that we did not go into Korea or into Vietnam as democratic missionaries, but to defeat an aggression deemed important to our security interests. I presume that he would support the statement issued at the conclusion of the talks between President Nixon and Prime Minister Sato in 1969 that "the security of the Republic of Korea is essential to Japan's own security"—and therefore to ours, in view of our deep interest in maintaining a close and cooperative association with Japan. From his book or his speeches, however, it is impossible to determine whether he regards South Vietnam as a "vital" security interest of the United States, a "significant" one, or a minor one, worth some effort but not too much, or as a country where we have no security interests at all. He nowhere discusses the reasons that led President Eisenhower and the Senate to make the commitments of 1954 and 1955, and President Johnson and the Congress to make the commitments of 1964 and 1965, or the effect of American withdrawal now on the policies of Japan and the nations of Southeast Asia or on China and the Soviet Union.

What of the other reasons Senator Fulbright advances to distinguish Korea from South Vietnam?

There is no substance to his distinction between the Korean hostilities as an international war and those in Vietnam as an insurrection or a civil war.[15] Both Korea and Vietnam are nations divided against their will by the circumstances of the Cold War, as Germany is. All three were promised their unity through elections. Those elections have not occurred. Instead, separate political entities have come into being, states, whether recognized or not, but surely legitimate political bodies within the international community, explicitly protected by the United Nations Charter. In Korea, the attempt of North Korea to unify the nation by force was open and visible. It was condemned by the United Nations (during the period of Communist boycott), and the resistance of South Korea was justified as legitimate self-defense. In Vietnam the effort took the guise of North Vietnamese assistance to an "insurrection" in South Vietnam. But in international law this is a distinction without a difference. It is an act of war for one country to assist (or, *a fortiori*, to incite or to organize) an insurrection in another. Surely Senator Fulbright would not apply his reasoning to condone East Germany's support for an insurrection in West Germany, or vice versa, although Germany is at least as much a nation as Vietnam, and like Vietnam, Germany was assured political unity through internationally supervised elections.

Fulbright seems at one point to find an explanation, if not quite a justification, for Hanoi's attack on South Vietnam in the history of the Geneva understandings of 1954, and especially in the failure to hold a referendum in 1956 on the unification of North and South Vietnam.[16] There are serious difficulties in such a conten-

[15] Op. cit., p. 51. He takes his analogy to a rhetorical extreme when he asks what the North Vietnamese are doing in trying to conquer South Vietnam "that is different from what the American North did to the American South a hundred years ago, with results that few of my fellow Southerners now regret" (p. 107).

[16] Pp. 116–117.

tion.[17] The most conclusive is that Korea, too, was promised its unity through free elections which were never held. In that case Fulbright regarded the use of force to unify the country as impermissible, even though national unity could not then be obtained by peaceful means. In the name of the United Nations Charter, he fully backed the international effort to prevent the conquest of South Korea. The Charter makes only one exception—that of self-defense under Article 51—to its prohibition against the use of force as an instrument of national policy. In the Korean case the Security Council and the General Assembly ruled that the North Koreans were not entitled, under Article 51 or otherwise, to unify the Korean nation by force even if the failure to unify the nation by political means was wrongful.

Both in Korea and in Vietnam, then, force was used in an effort to unify a nation divided into two political entities—two countries, in effect, at least for the time being. And both Korea and Vietnam are divided nations that happen to lie along the most sensitive frontier in the world, that between the realms of the two social systems. The two cases cannot be distinguished on this ground either.

It is equally hard to see how Fulbright's reference to the United Nations defines his view as to the primary purpose of American foreign policy. In the case of Korea it was possible to organize international resistance to aggression under the banner of the United Nations because the Communist nations were boycotting the Security Council and the General Assembly at the time. In the case of Vietnam the United States has succeeded in getting Vietnam on the agenda of the Security Council, but no further. The Security Council was not designed to function as a peace-keeping agency when great powers disagree. But the problems of peace, of national interests, and of enforcing the Charter are the same when the great powers agree and when they disagree.

Senator Fulbright also remarks that three of the seven signatories of the SEATO treaty are not providing forces for the war in Vietnam. Again it is difficult to perceive the bearing of his

[17] See pp. 155–172, above.

comment on his attempt to distinguish Korea from Vietnam or to help define the national interests of the United States. In Korea the United States acted under a United Nations vote, but not under a security treaty of the United States. I should have supposed that the case for United States intervention was stronger, not weaker, because of the existence of the SEATO treaty.

The SEATO treaty was part of the effort following World War II to end a wave of hostilities that involved Korea, Indochina, and Malaysia, among other countries. These prolonged hostilities threatened to engulf the whole region and the two superpowers as well.

Since the SEATO treaty was made, Britain and France have largely withdrawn from the Far East, and the problem is beyond the prudent reach of Pakistan, which is directly vulnerable to Chinese pressure. It would be hard to imagine French forces returning to Vietnam under any circumstances. These facts do not alter the obligations of the remaining signatories, or their right to take action under the treaty, as they have.[18]

Fulbright's idea is more general and more powerfully supported in opinion. It is part of the surviving mystique of the League of Nations era that "collective security" is somehow more righteous than security achieved by the efforts of a nation acting alone. This proposition is frequently taken by Fulbright to be self-evident. "Unilateral" is a pejorative adjective in his vocabulary, "collective security" a phrase of favorable denotation. The issue is much deeper. The moral quality of an act cannot be determined by so simple a test. The criteria for reaching such decisions range more widely and are far more complex.

At another point in his book Senator Fulbright remarks that perhaps the strongest argument in favor of our course in Vietnam is that withdrawal now would weaken the deterrent power of American commitments in Asia and elsewhere in the world.[19] In this the senator is quite correct. We are acting in Vietnam—and this was not the case in Korea—under President Eisenhower's

[18] See pp. 163–165, above.
[19] P. 128.

189

SEATO treaty and under repeated Congressional mandates, including a joint resolution of the Congress. An abandonment of South Vietnam now would present the makers of American foreign policy with problems completely different from those involved in our decision to undertake the campaign in the first place.

But Fulbright does not pause to examine this issue at any length. In 1970 Senator Fulbright suggested the use of an American guarantee to consolidate a peace agreement in the Middle East. Comparable guarantees by France, Great Britain, and the United States were ineffective to prevent the Six Day War in 1967. The American controversy over Vietnam has already gravely weakened the deterrent influence of America's word. If the United States walked out of Vietnam, what credence would any party attach to a new treaty?

Senator Fulbright is too sophisticated to embrace the common contentions that the war in Vietnam is "illegal" or "immoral."

He knows the constitutional history of the war power in the United States too well even to suggest that a formal declaration of war is necessary before the President may order the armed forces into action, especially where treaty obligations are being upheld and where the President's actions have been supported by a joint resolution of the Congress.

Equally, the senator avoids even the suggestion that our course in Vietnam is "immoral." He knows that this charge is simple to assert, but difficult to sustain. One can make a strong case against the war in Vietnam as imprudent; excessively expensive, considering the interests at stake; unwise; badly conducted; and cruel. But unless all war is immoral, it is not easy to claim that it is immoral for the United States to uphold its treaties, or to help a nation resist aggression, even at great cost.

We are left, then, with Richard Rovere's conclusion, after a much fuller analysis than Fulbright's—that from the point of view of international politics and of the American interest, there is no significant difference between the attack on South Korea and the attack on South Vietnam. With memorable intellectual honesty, Mr. Rovere concludes his article by saying that he was in favor of what we did in Korea and is against our course in Vietnam, but that he cannot explain why.[20]

Fulbright's analysis of the American policy toward Korea and Vietnam does not, then, fit any one hypothesis about the foreign policy he would have the United States follow. I have had no more success in inferring a guiding principle from the rest of *The Arrogance of Power*, his other writings, his speeches, and the pattern of the actions he has supported and opposed. I have found it impossible to formulate a theory of foreign policy generally consistent with the positions Fulbright has taken. His standards for judgment vary. At times he seems to be saying that the United States should concentrate exclusively, or almost exclusively, on building a model society at home. At other points he urges American support for the promotion of democracy abroad, though not to the point where our foreign policy would become a "global" crusade against all forms of tyranny. "An excessive preoccupation with foreign relations over a long period of time," he writes, "is more than a manifestation of arrogance; it is a drain on the power that gave rise to it, because it diverts a nation from the sources of its strength, which are in its domestic life." [21] Perhaps so, although his statement does not do full justice to the complex and many-sided impact war has had on social systems throughout history. Nations and societies have indeed been destroyed by war, even by wars they have won. The tragedy of Athens dissected by Thucydides is perhaps the most luminous episode in this cycle. The history of Europe since 1914, which has not thus far had its Thucydides, is surely another. Some wars, however—the Crusades, for example—have had quite different social consequences.

But my problem with Fulbright's last-quoted sentence is deeper. What does he mean by "excessive"? If the purpose of foreign policy is to safeguard the important interests of a nation,

[20] "Half Out of Our Tree," *The New Yorker*, October 28, 1967, p. 60, at pp. 98–100.
[21] Op. cit., p. 20.

and if the nation is living through a time of turbulence and violence that seems to threaten those interests—"vital" interests and interests that are important but less than "vital"—how does one decide how much preoccupation with foreign relations is appropriate and how much is excessive? For considerable stretches in his book Fulbright seems to assume that foreign affairs is an optional, nearly irrational activity, alien to the main business of American society. In a characteristic passage he says, "It seems to me unnatural and unhealthy for a nation to be engaged in global crusades for some principle or ideal while neglecting the needs of its own people." But in the next sentence he qualifies his thesis sharply. "It should be very clear that what is called for is not a wholesale renunciation by the United States of its global responsibilities. This would be impossible even if it were desirable." [22] But Fulbright does not tell us clearly how he would distinguish "global crusades for some principle or ideal" from "global responsibilities" and national interests.

As one tunnels through the successive layers of Fulbright's prose, each derived from a different major premise and sounding in turn pacifist, isolationist, or Wilsonian, one does find an ultimate layer built of quite different materials. Despite the tone and emphasis of his book, a number of key passages indicate that in Fulbright's opinion the United States does have some security interests in the structure and substance of world politics, and that foreign policy is not entirely a matter of being "good," or doing "generous and benevolent" deeds, or pursuing "some principle or ideal." These judgments stem from a theory that is nearly inarticulate in his book and seems to be almost grudgingly included, namely, a sketchy echo of classical balance-of-power doctrine that would have sounded familiar to Metternich and Castlereagh —for whom, indeed, the senator has some words of praise.[23]

Perhaps the most substantial evidence to support this line of speculation about what Fulbright really thinks is his approval of the American and Allied response to the situation resulting from

[22] Op. cit., pp. 134–135.
[23] Op. cit., pp. 183–184, p. 255.

the destruction of German and Japanese power in World War II; his discussion of possible Vietnam solutions, at least in 1966, when *The Arrogance of Power* was published; and his recent statements about what American policy should be in the Middle East.

Formally, Fulbright invokes Wilson's remark as a text, "not a balance of power, but a community of power; not organized rivalries, but an organized common peace."[24] In fact, however, he reaches decisive conclusions based on quite different ideas.

> The cold war of the last twenty years was spawned by the total victory of 1945. The total destruction of German and Japanese power created a vacuum which was soon enough filled, quickly and eagerly by Russia and belatedly and reluctantly by America . . . It was the total defeat of Germany that resulted in her division, and that division, the product of total victory, became the paramount issue in a new, great, and still unresolved conflict.[25]

It was necessary, in his view, for the United States to take measures in and near Europe to contain the expansion of Soviet power. And Eastern and Western Europe cannot hope to come together by weakening the link between Western Europe and the United States. "Much of the hope for an improvement of relations leading to the ultimate reunification of Europe derives from the approximate balance of power between the two sides. Were Western Europe to be detached from America, an imbalance would come into existence, one which might tempt the Russians once again with the possibility of dominating Western Europe."[26]

Perhaps it is cruel to examine Fulbright's book so carefully. It was written, after all, in 1966. Its prescriptions about the possibility of bringing the two halves of Europe together make melancholy reading today. To Fulbright's mind Communism is being weakened by nationalism and is being humanized.

> The possibility for a degree of reconciliation in East-West relations derives in large part from enormously important changes which have been taking place within the Communist world. Communism has ceased to be the monolith it seemed to be in Stalin's

[24] Op. cit., p. 157.
[25] Op. cit., p. 185. See also pp. 77, 109, 186–188, 217–219.
[26] Op. cit., p. 211.

time; its practice is increasingly being nationalized to fit the conditions of particular countries. What is more important, the communism of Eastern Europe and the Soviet Union is slowly but steadily being humanized.[27]

Trade, cultural relations, and partnership with the West in great constructive enterprises would lead to a decline in ideology. The reconciliation of East and West, he said, is primarily a psychological problem, to be solved by putting hostile groups into relations of interdependence. And when Khrushchev made his "unfortunate" remark "We will bury you," Fulbright is "inclined to think" he was talking about peaceful competition in the production of goods and services and in efforts to raise popular living standards, not military threats.[28]

Similarly, there is a substratum of power politics in Fulbright's treatment of Vietnam, China, and the Cuban missile crisis, despite the prevailing atmosphere of another outlook. As we have seen, he still supports the decision to fight in Korea and Kennedy's handling of the Cuban missile crisis. And in his proposals for winding up the Vietnam war, at least in 1966, he urges that we make significant and magnanimous concessions to the Viet Cong as an act of "common sense" in a tragic situation, but warns that we should not engage in a disorderly withdrawal or abandon South Vietnam to the Viet Cong.[29]

Fulbright considers a general settlement of neutrality and accommodation for Southeast Asia the only way to achieve a stable balance of power there and avoid endless friction between the United States and China.[30] To that end, Fulbright presented an eight-point plan for local and general peace in the area. All the items in Fulbright's plan for peace in Asia are proposals that had already been tried and repeatedly rejected. If North Vietnam should be so unreasonable as to reject these proposals once again, Fulbright concludes, the United States should consolidate its positions and plan to remain indefinitely. "The United States, as the

[27] Op. cit., pp. 201–202.
[28] Op. cit., pp. 202–204.
[29] Op. cit., pp. 182, 199.
[30] Op. cit., pp. 185–200.

nation with principal, though not exclusive, responsibility for peace and stability, cannot accept defeat or a disorderly withdrawal from South Vietnam." [31]

Here again the advantage of hindsight after five bitter years reveals that Fulbright's analysis rests on wishful thinking.

A considerable part of Fulbright's book is given over to the problem of economic development in the Third World and its bearing on the problem of peace. He urges that aid for the countries of the Third World be organized on a multilateral basis, through international agencies, so as to avoid political and military involvement in their troubles. And he seems to share the fashionable but entirely erroneous fear that "the task of modernization is too large and socially disruptive to be accomplished by democratic methods." [32] The chief lesson of experience with the development process all over the world is that planning for growth cannot hope to succeed without making maximal use of the market mechanism and of market incentives. No other path mobilizes a comparable mass of energy and entrepreneurship. This factor has been critical to progress in such countries as Malaysia, Mexico, Iran, Tunisia, Formosa, India, and the Ivory Coast, when compared to the record of many others, from China and Cuba to Egypt, Syria, and the Sudan, which have experimented with dictatorial methods, and have thus far made little use of the potential energies and incentives of the market.

Fulbright's conclusion leads him to urge that we not worry about the ideology of Third World governments or intervene to oppose "revolution." He sees Vietnam as a purely ideological affair. We are left, he says, "with two essential reasons for our involvement in Vietnam: the view of communism as an evil philosophy and the view of ourselves as God's avenging angels, whose sacred duty it is to combat evil philosophies." [33]

In this regard he contrasts our action in Vietnam with our course in Europe—which he approves as an entirely nonideologi-

[31] Op. cit., p. 196.
[32] Op. cit., p. 70.
[33] Op. cit., p. 107.

cal effort to contain Soviet power—and with that in protecting South Korea against "aggression" supported by the Soviet Union. But an extension of Soviet power in Western Europe would have transformed West European society. And the "aggression" in Korea was carried out in the name of a revolution that would have swept away the regime in South Korea.

How would Fulbright have us tell which forms of international support for revolutions in the Third World the United States should oppose, by force if necessary, and which it should ignore or applaud as inevitable spray on the tides of history? I can find no trace of an answer to the question in *The Arrogance of Power*.

The puzzle of Fulbright's reasoning is not resolved by his important speech on the Middle East in 1970. There, too, as in Korea and Vietnam, a war of "national liberation" in behalf of the Palestinians has been proclaimed. There, too, Soviet power is expanding, directly and through proxies. And in this case, too, Fulbright answers all the key questions both with a "yes" and a "no." The claim of an American interest in the exasperating quarrels of the region has been exaggerated and exploited, he says. The growing Soviet presence in the area is a consequence of American mistakes, and is not of central importance in any event. On the other hand, the potentialities of the situation, once exaggeration has been eliminated, genuinely do threaten American interests with transformations that would be irrevocable if they occurred, and therefore require an American response.[34]

Perhaps the ultimate significance of Fulbright's book is that it so faithfully mirrors unresolved conflicts of reason and instinct as to the springs of action. Its influence measures the extent to which Fulbright's readers share his conflicts. What the book reveals, above all its other lessons, is that action in response to the perception of threat is so automatic, and so deeply rooted, as to be nearly beyond the reach of reason.

[34] *Cong. Record*, Aug. 24, 1970, pp. 14022–39, esp. at pp. 14036–37.

# 7

# *Realpolitik*

By INVOKING nearly archeological methods one can discover in Fulbright's book and speeches the shadowy outline of a theory of foreign policy perhaps more fundamental to his outlook than the other theories woven into the texture of his writings. One could describe this, the ultimate Fulbright doctrine, as the view that foreign policy is a program of action intended to protect the national interest, which he defines in the first instance as the achievement and maintenance of a balance of power in world politics. All other goals of foreign policy—the promotion of economic and social well-being, for example; the encouragement of trade, cultural exchanges, and high levels of employment; and support for the realization and protection of human rights—are secondary to this first concern for the primitive security of the nation.

For a considerable group of writers, analysis proceeds explicitly from one or another version of this theory. The present chapter will concentrate on the work of three members of the group, Hans J. Morgenthau,[1] and the team of Edmund Stillman and William Pfaff.[2] Like their fellow members of the sixth school

[1] Especially in *A New Foreign Policy for the United States* (1969).
[2] *The New Politics* (1961), *The Politics of Hysteria* (1964), and *Power and Impotence* (1966).

identified in Chapter 3, they accept the general conception of foreign policy that has dominated the behavior of the American government since 1947. But they feel strongly that the basically good ideas of the Truman years—containment and reconstruction in Europe, and for some, in Korea as well—became a cancerous growth under Eisenhower, involving the United States in a hopeless, worldwide effort to stem the tide of revolution, ideology, and violence, especially in Asia and other parts of the Third World, but for some in Europe as well. When large and small nations ignored Eisenhower's treaties, doctrines, and other efforts in deterrent diplomacy, his successors had to make good on his commitments, with nightmare as a consequence. Therefore, these men argue, the United States is "overcommitted," and must reduce the reach of its foreign policy.

II

Professor Morgenthau is of course one of the best-known academic writers on international relations in the United States today. In earlier years he was a pioneer in urging American students not to mix considerations of ideology with those of power. With an emphasis and impatience that radiate his consciousness of authority, Morgenthau never tires of telling his readers that serious decisions of national policy should not be made on grounds of sentiment, but only on grounds of interest. In Morgenthau's guide for perplexed decision makers, sympathy for (or against) any people or culture is the worst of sins. He makes only one exception to his icy rule—the case of the American link to Europe, concerning which he would say that America's "vital" interest in the European balance of power is reinforced by another interest, "no less important," namely, its interest in Europe as "the fountainhead of Western civilization." [3]

[3] Morgenthau, op. cit., p. 175. He does not indicate how, in his view, feelings of this order should affect American foreign policy toward Australia, New Zealand, Israel, or a number of other countries whose peoples or cultures are linked to our own.

For reasons that are unexplained, Morgenthau's writing has acquired a new tone in recent years, that of the established American intellectual orthodoxy. Most of *A New Foreign Policy for the United States* consists of careful academic prose, but at intervals Morgenthau falls back on the vocabulary of those he used to scorn. The result is startling—a text with alternate passages in the mood of Clausewitz and of *The New York Review of Books*. Like Fulbright, Morgenthau denounces the government for the sins of "globalism," "anti-Communism," and indeed the conduct of an "anti-communist crusade"; for not noticing that communism is no longer a "monolith"; and for opposing "revolution," which he now seems to believe is the only course capable of bringing progress to the nonindustrialized countries. Perhaps this change in language explains the improbable fact that Morgenthau was recently the New Left candidate for the presidency of the American Political Science Association, where he has long been an uncompromising symbol of the Hard Line and the coldest kind of Cold Warrior.

The two layers in Morgenthau sometimes produce paradox.

In two somber chapters he stresses the dangers of Soviet and Chinese policy and contends that the "folly" of a "liberal" Western policy toward trade with China and the Soviet Union could well fulfill Marx's prophecy that the capitalists would turn out to be their own "gravediggers." [4]

> There is no reason to object to trading with Communist countries like Yugoslavia, if such trade promises economic gains and political results favorable to our interests. But it is a folly, comparable to the sale of scrap iron to Japan in the 1930s, to equip the Soviet Union and China with industrial plants and transportation systems which will then be used as weapons in the political, military, and economic offensives of Communism against the West.[5]

But elsewhere there are comments in another vein. Morgenthau cannot yet bring himself to say that the Cold War is over, or never existed, but he does sometimes indicate that the danger of

[4] Op. cit., pp. 176, 198, 196–199.
[5] Op. cit., p. 197.

Soviet expansion has diminished and that the outward thrust of Soviet power that dominated the early postwar years is nearly a spent force. In his view the "legitimacy" of the Soviet government is destroyed;[6] its power is "precarious";[7] and its "prestige" suffered "an apparently irreparable blow" as a result of the invasion of Czechoslovakia in 1968.[8] In the same spirit, he claims that the Soviet government has tried to persuade Castro to give up his support for violent revolution in Latin America, and pressed the North Vietnamese government to negotiate a political settlement in Vietnam.[9] There is no evidence to support these assertions and much against them.

There are other contradictions in his text. In one chapter he argues powerfully that the United States should pursue a policy of "masterly inactivity" toward the developing countries of the Third World or identify itself with their revolutionary movements. Morgenthau believes that genuine economic, political, and social progress is impossible in many nonindustrialized countries, because the necessary conditions for progress are incompatible with their cultures and because some are no more than "bums or beggars" and beyond redemption.[10] But elsewhere he urges that the government should engage in aid programs in order to counter the dangerous spread of Soviet political and military influence in the Eastern Mediterranean, the Middle East, South Asia, and the Indian Ocean,[11] and the spread of Chinese influence in the countries around China and in other countries where China is active.[12]

If we can put aside anomalies of this order in Morgenthau's exposition we find that his argument follows a reasonably direct line.

Morgenthau's thesis is a call to arms. Its coda, invoking "the

---

[6] Pp. 68–73.
[7] P. 76.
[8] P. 124.
[9] Id., pp. 71–72, and pp. 67–68.
[10] Ibid., p. 96.
[11] Id., pp. 67–68, 104–106, 128–129.
[12] P. 206.

first Philippic," is that the United States faces disaster unless it engages in a radical rethinking of its foreign policy and then acts on it. The creative spark of 1947, which produced the Truman Doctrine and the Marshall Plan, has lost its capacity to give life. The intellectual capital of that heroic moment is exhausted, because the issues have been transformed. The policies of 1947 are obsolete. Indeed, grown into a universal doctrine, they have become a curse.

> What is needed in 1969 is therefore a task of renovation similar to that of 1947. We must free ourselves from the burden of obsolescent policies which have become mechanical routines and embark upon a radical rethinking of the issues and of the policies adequate to them.[13]

For Morgenthau the national security of the United States—the security of its territory and its institutions—requires it now, as in the past, to support the idea of a balance of power, and to oppose hegemonial ambitions in Europe, in Asia,[14] and in another, less tangible realm as well, a realm he calls that of "the world," or of a "world-wide balance of power." [15] The problem of national safety for the United States, Morgenthau would be the first to stress, is different from what it was in Napoleon's time, or Kaiser Wilhelm's, or Hitler's, or even Stalin's. Then the United States was concerned, and in Morgenthau's opinion, rightly concerned, mainly about the possibility of hegemony in Europe or Asia that could be extended by naval power to a beachhead in the New World. That interest was a primordial interest in independence and survival—a "vital" interest, in Morgenthau's opinion, which the United States had no rational alternative but to defend. In the classical view that runs through the history of American diplomacy, a dominant power in Europe was a threat to the United States, because such a power, unrestrained by fear of its European rivals, would have the capacity to project its influence into the Western hemisphere. This is the reason why the United States

---

[13] P. 3.
[14] Id., pp. 129–130, 132, 157, 173, 193–195.
[15] Id., pp. 174–175, 193.

has hitherto remained uncommitted in the politics of Europe, and has tended to favor the weaker side during crises that might result in European hegemony. The same reasoning and the same nearly instinctive responses, he believes, have rightly governed American policy in Asia.

But political and technological change has transformed the setting in which the challenge of the balance of power now arises. The nuclear weapon on the one hand, and improved modern means of making and delivering conventional weapons on the other, have revolutionized the nature of military threats to the United States. For the first time in its history military force can be brought to bear within the United States without an invasion or a naval bombardment from coastal waters. And a rapid succession of political changes has transformed the magnetic field of world politics quite as fundamentally. As a result, Morgenthau says, the primordial vital interest of the United States can no longer be defined as immunity from invasion, or the maintenance of unchallenged American hegemony in the Western hemisphere, which was long thought to be the basic protection of the United States against invasion.

> The American interest in the European balance of power transcends today the traditional concern with the preservation of the hegemony and security of the United States in the Western Hemisphere. The United States has become a superpower whose success or failure anywhere in the world impinges to a greater or lesser degree upon its position throughout the world. This is especially so when we deal with a commitment that is so deeply rooted in tradition and vital interest as is the commitment to the European balance of power. Even if a drastic change in the distribution of power in Europe in favor of the Soviet Union did not decisively affect the U.S. position in the Western Hemisphere, it could not help but drastically affect the position of the United States in the world.
>
> In so far as the contest between the United States, on the one hand, and the Soviet Union and China, on the other, is carried on in terms of the attractiveness and effectiveness of their respective governmental systems, so spectacular a defeat for the United States and so spectacular a victory for the Soviet Union would of necessity make both the committed and the uncommitted nations of the

world dubious about the ability of the United States to compete successfully with its adversaries on all levels of social and governmental endeavor. That doubt would touch the very core of American influence and power, which from the very beginning of our history has consisted in our ability to serve as a model for other nations to emulate.[16]

What Morgenthau says in this passage about the American stake in the structure and content of European politics applies equally to our relationship with Japan, a subject hardly mentioned in his book. The American security interest in Japan is parallel in every way to its interest in Europe. If "the geographic, material, and human resources" of Japan were to fall under the control either of China or of the Soviet Union, the over-all balance among the powers, both strategic and political, would be altered quite as gravely as would be the case in the event of American failure in Europe.[17]

The American interest in China is potentially quite as real as its interest in Japan or in Europe. Like those interests, it has both a negative and a positive aspect—to discourage alliances involving China that could threaten the United States from the Pacific basin and within it, and in the long run, to develop patterns of association and cooperation with China and Japan equally—patterns that could provide the basis for a stable peace in the region, a peace in which the Soviet Union would be free to participate at all times.

Morgenthau, it is true, says it is an error "to equate the American interest in Europe with that in other parts of the world. . . . The beginning of foreign policy is to establish priorities among a number of interests, all worth pursuing, but not all susceptible of being pursued with equal commitments; for the resources even of a world power fall short of its interests." [18] This is undeniably true as an abstraction. But everything Morgenthau writes about the strategic implications of the American relation to Europe, nuclear and nonnuclear, applies also to the American relation with Japan

[16] Id., pp. 174–175. See also p. 83.
[17] See id., at p. 174.
[18] Id., at pp. 175–176.

and with China, because of their actual and potential weight in world affairs.

Morgenthau points out that a rational foreign policy must distinguish between what is desirable and what is possible, and between what is desirable and what is essential.[19] The Truman Doctrine, he argues, failed to make these distinctions. In his view the Truman Doctrine has been transformed from an ideology of military containment into a general principle of "global" policy, directed against "communism" and "revolution" everywhere. As applied by Eisenhower and later Presidents, it did not confine our interventions to those situations where resistance to Communist military expansion was both "essential" and "possible," or where resistance was "desirable" but not "essential" and could be accomplished at reasonable cost.

> For while it would be desirable to contain Communism within its present limits through the efforts of the United States, it is essential that only that type of Communism hostile to the interests of the United States be so contained. Thus I have always regarded it as essential in view of the interests of the United States that the transformation of Cuba into a center of Communist subversion in the Western Hemisphere and a military and political outpost of the Soviet Union be prevented. And on the same grounds, I find the containment of Communism in Vietnam to be desirable but not essential from the point of view of the interests of the United States, especially since this Communism is likely to be an independent national Communism after the model of Yugoslavia.[20]

It is difficult to see exactly what Morgenthau can mean by his charge that the Truman Doctrine directed American foreign policy to oppose "communism" everywhere. Clearly, he criticizes Kennedy for not carrying through the Bay of Pigs invasion of Cuba[21] in defense of an "essential" American interest, and not so clearly, he criticizes Eisenhower, Kennedy, Johnson, and Nixon (1) for making the American commitment to South Vietnam; or (2) for trying to uphold it, or (3) for trying to uphold it at excessive cost.

[19] Id., at pp. 10–12, 241.
[20] Id., at p. 10.
[21] Ibid. See also pp. 64, 123–125.

But the Truman Doctrine was not invoked to stop "revolutions," or "revolutions" identified with "communism," or even revolutions identified with brands of communism "hostile to the interests of the United States"—for example, in Syria, in the Sudan, in Algeria, in Guinea, in Iraq, in Aden, and in many other places. On the contrary, in a passage noted earlier, Morgenthau castigates the American government for not having done more to prevent the expansion of Soviet power in the Mediterranean, the Middle East, the Indian Ocean, and in South Asia.[22] The application of the Truman Doctrine thus far has been narrowly confined to certain international acts of force involving the extension of Soviet military power, or of other potentially hostile power, in places deemed to be of strategic importance to the United States: Berlin, Turkey, Greece, Korea, Vietnam, Saudi Arabia, Lebanon, Formosa, Iran, Cuba, Yugoslavia, Jordan, and Israel. Save for Cuba, all these scenes of conflict or threat are on or near the boundary of China or of the Soviet Union, and all are locations of particular strategic or tactical importance. While it is of course legitimate to criticize the American reaction in one or another of these situations as inadequate or excessive, it is impossible to characterize the pattern as one of "global" opposition to all "revolutions." By doing so, Morgenthau sets up a familiar straw man, which he can easily prove is a dead horse.

III

Our primary problem here, however, is to determine the precise content of the "new" foreign policy Morgenthau proposes for the United States and what that policy implies. For that purpose Morgenthau's characterization of existing policy is not of critical importance, except as evidence of how he would define the national interest and distinguish among "essential," "desirable," and "possible" goals for a foreign policy designed to protect the national interest by military, as well as by political, economic, and ideological means.

[22] P. 200, above.

In Morgenthau's view there are now at least two kinds of threats to the security of the United States—threats of nuclear attack or of political pressure backed by the threat of nuclear attack; and threats of conventional military power, political action, and the harnessing of revolutionary energy to hostile ends. Separately or in combination, these two classes of threat could affect the possibility of equilibrium and hence the security of the United States.

Nuclear deterrence, in Morgenthau's view, is the only way in which the threat of nuclear attack or nuclear blackmail can be controlled, at least until agreements of arms limitation reduce or eliminate the nuclear element in world politics. In order to achieve nuclear deterrence the United States must maintain the capacity to inflict unacceptable damage through retaliation against the Soviet Union or any other potential nuclear adversary. Morgenthau does not agree with certain French theorists who favor the spread of nuclear weapons on the ground that such a spread would paralyze aggression. On the contrary, Morgenthau believes that nuclear proliferation would result in "political anarchy of unimaginable proportions, followed by total nuclear destruction either piecemeal or in one single catastrophe through the coincidence of a series of preventative-retaliatory blows." [23] He therefore strongly supports efforts to limit the spread of nuclear weapons, although he acknowledges the appeal of political instincts that tend to identify national autonomy with the possession of nuclear weapons. The prevalence and persistence of such impulses, Morgenthau suggests, explain the resistance of Europeans to the processes of Atlantic Union, which would adapt alliance relations to nuclear realities and to the changed significance of geography that nuclear weapons and other changes in military technology have brought about.[24]

The nuclear problem aside, Morgenthau argues, the threats of conventional military force are different in scale and in scope from those of earlier periods, both because of the power of mod-

[23] Id., at p. 237.
[24] Id., at p. 238.

ern weapons and because the structure of world politics is entirely new: the European Concert and the European empires are nearly gone, except for the Russian and the Portuguese; Russia, Japan, and China have been transformed; and large sectors of the Third World have been Balkanized, arousing the ambitions of those who would expand, and the fears of others who react to the expansion of their rivals.

When Morgenthau seeks to fit current and prospective problems into the framework of his analysis he reaches a series of surprising and not always consistent conclusions.

One of his principal themes, for example, is that nuclear weapons cannot be used rationally as instruments of national policy, because of their destructive power. Therefore, he contends, the problem of nuclear deterrence must be separated as rigorously as possible from the problems of conventional balance-of-power politics and war; when conventional force is used in a nuclear context, as was the case in Korea, great care must be taken to insulate the two aspects of military power from each other.

Morgenthau recognizes that the separation between nuclear and conventional war cannot be complete. The possibility of escalation to the nuclear threshold can never be altogether excluded if a nuclear power is involved. The boundary between conventional and nuclear weapons can be maintained "only on the condition that the stakes of a conventional conflict are small enough to make defeat or stalemate acceptable without recourse to nuclear weapons. Korea was a case in point, and so is Vietnam. Yet Berlin and Cuba are not, and it is doubtful whether Korea would be today, and Vietnam would be tomorrow." [25] The result is a paradox in that the strong—who are proportionally much stronger today than ever before, in comparison with weaker powers—are thereby rendered "impotent" in the fullness of their power.[26] They hardly dare fight with each other. No shots have been fired between Soviet and American forces, and even in conflicts like those in Korea and Vietnam the United States has been con-

[25] Id., at p. 213.
[26] Id., at p. 214.

strained in the use of conventional power by the nuclear shadow.

It follows, Morgenthau argues, that the separation of nuclear from conventional diplomacy and warfare should be made as systematic as possible, so that an effective nuclear stalemate could be matched by comparable effectiveness in achieving and maintaining a balance of power by traditional and conventional means outside the areas where nuclear threats are relevant or credible. Thus the practice of limited war has emerged, or re-emerged. As in the eighteenth and nineteenth centuries, wars are limited by the concern that going too far could well draw new forces into the fray. Only the convincing spread of such an expectation could liberate conventional power from its nuclear shackles.[27]

Thus far the thrust of Morgenthau's analysis is unexceptionable. It should be noted, however, that far from constituting the basis for a "new" foreign policy, a fresh perception of reality to replace the "obsolete" doctrines of the Truman epoch, it is the standard wisdom of received and official doctrine presented in rather standard form.

The next step in his argument, however, is both obscure, and if I understand him correctly, highly debatable.

Morgenthau contends over and over again that "by itself the policy of peripheral military containment, appropriate to a conventional setting, has really not contained the Soviet Union and China in being applied to a nuclear setting; it has only made the threat of nuclear retaliation against a conventional attack more credible." [28] By this passage Morgenthau does not intend to criticize the American stance in Europe. On the contrary, he says that the issue that led the United States to intervene in Europe in the late forties poses itself today in novel forms, but is still the same and should be met by the indispensable combination of conventional and nuclear forces that has been developed over the years.[29] The point of that combination, however, is not to use conventional means in the event of a crisis, but to make nuclear deter-

[27] Id., at pp. 176–177, 243.
[28] Id., at p. 240.
[29] Id., at pp. 176–177.

rence credible and effective. "The Soviet Union has not been contained by the armed forces this country has been able to put in the field locally in Europe so much as it has been contained by the near certainty that an attack upon them would be countered by the nuclear retaliation of the United States." [30] In Morgenthau's judgment, only the threat of *nuclear* retaliation against *conventional* attack has kept the Soviet Union from stepping past the demarcation lines of 1945, at least in Europe.

One of Morgenthau's strongest criticisms of American foreign policy since 1953 has been that it tried blindly to apply the remedies he thought were appropriate and successful during the first decade after 1947 in Europe (and perhaps in Korea)—the Truman Doctrine and the Marshall Plan—to Asia and other parts of the world, where, in his judgment, they are inappropriate and bound to be ineffective. From this proposition, however, he reaches the conclusion that we should use in Asia exactly the same combination of policies—the Truman Doctrine and the Marshall Plan; nuclear plus peripheral conventional-force containment and economic assistance—that he believes has been successful and should be continued indefinitely in Europe.

Thus at still another point Morgenthau, having proclaimed a radical new analysis and a new policy, in the end reiterates the ideas of the State Department he scorns.

The United States, he says, has a permanent and vital security interest in preventing any one power from acquiring hegemony in Asia. That issue is posed by China. It is potentially the strongest nation in the world, and has also been committed, thus far at least, to the most virulent kind of communism, instigating and supporting communist subversion throughout the world.[31] At the same time it is China, a great power, with its distinctive history and its most distinctive sense of itself and of the outside world.

China will almost surely press, Morgenthau thinks, for the restoration of the boundaries and influence the Chinese Empire possessed before its modern decline: Taiwan and the offshore islands;

[30] Id., at p. 203.
[31] Id., at p. 189.

Outer Mongolia; the Asian territories claimed by China and annexed by Russia during the nineteenth century; Tibet, Burma, Cambodia, and Korea.[32] It is "at least possible, if not likely," Morgenthau wrote in 1969, that China will adapt its world revolutionary (and national) ambitions to political and military realities.[33] At another point he remarks that the "probability is small" that China would seek seriously to push beyond the historic regional limits of Chinese concern, because of the extreme caution that, in his view, has thus far characterized Chinese foreign policy,[34] to say nothing of the possible military reaction of the Soviet Union and the United States to such a policy.[35]

For many people, apparently, the "traditional, imperial" appetite for more territory is somehow less alarming than an appetite for territory based on the crusading zeal of a creed. The first represents a "national," "traditional," "nonideological," "limited" foreign policy; the second, more universalist, calls to mind the Huns, the Arabs, the Normans, and the Turks. But it is hard to see why one label is more reassuring than the other. There have been terrible wars both of nationalism and of religion. The menu of territorial aspirations Morgenthau lists as China's minimum, which "perhaps," or perhaps "probably," she would not wish to go beyond, is anything but reassuring. It is the kind of territorial ambition that has always led to war. And, ideological or not, is there any doubt that such an extension of China's traditional empire would be accompanied by social and political change?

If the expansion of Chinese power and influence is pursued by political rather than military means, Morgenthau contends, we should seek to contain it by strengthening the nations of Asia that are within China's reach and the nations outside Asia in which China has attempted to gain a foothold. Although elsewhere Morgenthau urges a withdrawal from what he calls the futile policy of trying to modernize many developing nations, here he is advocat-

[32] Pp. 189–190.
[33] P. 191.
[34] P. 193.
[35] P. 190.

ing massive efforts in Asia and Africa to promote the political, social, and economic strength of many nations, new and old.[36] But, he also says, we must learn to accept the political and cultural predominance of China on the Asia mainland.

If, however, China pursued either her historic regional goals or more grandiose ambitions by military as well as by political and cultural means—a possibility Morgenthau regards as unlikely, but hardly impossible[37]—it should be United States policy to counter such moves, Morgenthau contends, not by conventional means, as in Korea and Vietnam, but "by the near certainty that China as an organized society will be destroyed in the process of nuclear retaliation." [38] "It must be brought home to China, as it was brought home to the Soviet Union, that in the unlikely event it should embark on a policy of Asian or world conquest, it is bound to be at war with the United States." [39] Only such a policy, in Morgenthau's view, could be effective as deterrence.

Our interest in containing Chinese expansion, in Morgenthau's eyes, is an entirely legitimate national interest in the balance of power in Asia—a concern to which we have been sensitive at least since the time of Commodore Perry. He believes the United States should pursue that interest first through political and economic means—that is, through attempts to persuade China that her national interests would be served and her welfare advanced by policies of peaceful and cooperative coexistence with us. This, of course, has been an active goal of American policy for at least five years, and probably longer. But Morgenthau is not alone among learned writers in admonishing the government to do what it has been trying to do in any event. This is a feature of the debate about foreign policy which readers "inside" soon learn to ignore.

But the efforts to persuade the Chinese may fail, despite the wonderfully concentrating influence of the huge and growing So-

[36] At p. 206. Compare Chap. 4, especially p. 96—"As there are bums and beggars, so are there bum and beggar nations."
[37] Pp. 189–193.
[38] P. 203.
[39] P. 206.

viet armies in Siberia. Why should we use nuclear weapons if the Chinese Communist leaders continue to reject peaceful existence as "revisionism," refuse any plan for Vietnam or for Formosa short of Communist control, and continue to support guerrillas in Burma, India, Southeast Asia, and less effectively perhaps, in Africa and the Middle East?

Here, I believe, Morgenthau escapes from the discipline of his analysis.

The policy of containment we have pursued since the war—through buffer states, alliances, and limited resistance based on the use or the show of conventional force—he seems to approve at some points of his argument as rational in every sense and consistent with his basic policy of separating the nuclear from the conventional dimensions of power and policies. At other points, however, he rejects it in favor of a much greater and more direct reliance on nuclear threat.

I have the greatest difficulty with Morgenthau's return to Dulles' policy of "massive retaliation." In the revulsion against the Korean war during the early Eisenhower years the idea of the New Look policy—nuclear response to peripheral attack—was articulated. But it was never applied. And it soon became obvious, from Indo-China and Quemoy and Matsu to the prolonged agony of the Middle East, that it would not and could not work.

The New Look policy is no more convincing in Morgenthau's formulation than in Dulles'. I cannot see what interest of the United States would be served in Asia, in Europe, or in the Middle East by making every conflict a test of the credibility of nuclear weapons and by leaving the President no alternative between retreat and using nuclear force. The nuclear threat has a certain plausibility only where manifest and high priority state interests are concerned, such as in Berlin; in moments of extreme tension, such as the Cuban missile crisis; or in situations of prolonged stress and exasperation such as those in Korea and Vietnam. Between two comparable nuclear powers the nuclear threat is almost entirely incredible, as De Gaulle pointed out some years ago, and likely to become less credible with repetition—a point that Morgenthau makes effectively elsewhere in his book.

This being the case, why nuclearize every situation of conflict where serious but not necessarily vital interests of the great powers are at issue? How could it be credible under such circumstances that attacks on conventional forces or on allies would be met by a nuclear response?

Confrontation between the Soviet Union and the United States is a complex and subtle affair. It is commonplace to suppose that because the Soviet Union backed down before the Berlin airlift and certain similar tests she would always retreat when we suggested or hinted that her policies might have "grave or unpredictable consequences." The negotiations about Korea were initiated in this way.[40] But the rule of nuclear stalemate between the Soviet Union and the United States is that while the Soviets do not challenge us, we don't challenge them either. They have not yet fired at our troops in Berlin or in Germany; and they did not interfere with our supply lines or operations in Korea or Vietnam. But we did nothing to interfere with their operations in East Germany, Czechoslovakia, Hungary, or Poland, in 1948, 1953, 1956, 1968, and 1970. And we were careful to avoid shooting at Soviet forces in Cuba or in North Vietnam.

The heart of the problem is the first shot. A powerful inhibition has thus far been at work preventing each from firing the first shot at the other or from using nuclear weapons, even when, as in Korea and Vietnam, the going was rough. That rule makes modern diplomacy, not a quadrille, but a game of three-dimensional chess. There is a premium on "getting thar fustest with the mostest." The Soviet Union became exercised during the Six Day War in 1967 when the war approached Syria, where the Soviets are established in considerable force. In 1972 it is even more deeply established in Egypt.

These are the operative forces that have so far governed the behavior of both the Soviet Union and the United States in rela-

[40] Dean Acheson, *Present at the Creation* (1969), pp. 532–533.

tion to each other, since they cannot rationally fight either a nuclear or a conventional war. In this context Morgenthau's proposal is radical indeed. Where Country A, a Soviet or a Chinese proxy, attacks Country B, a country in which the United States has announced a security interest and which it has promised to defend, Morgenthau would go to the nuclear level at once with the Soviet Union or China rather than face more situations like Korea and Vietnam by helping Country B to defend itself.

I should argue, on the contrary, that bad as the disease is, Morgenthau's remedy is worse. In my view it is preferable to preserve the widest possible range of nonnuclear options in such situations, so as to give diplomacy as much time as possible and minimize the risk of miscalculation, accident, or escalation that could lead to a nuclear confrontation. This is the basic reason why we keep large conventional forces in Europe, in Japan, and elsewhere. I find the argument for continuing to do so altogether convincing. The risks of a less cautious course strike me as imprudent.

Morgenthau's answer to this contention I find mysterious, and if I understand it, horrifying.

What has actually contained the Soviet Union and China has been the threat of all-out nuclear war. Thus the military policies we have been pursuing vis-à-vis the Soviet Union and China have confused the issues of conventional and nuclear containment. Instead of using conventional force as means to the end of nuclear containment, we have tried to use them as ends in themselves. As such, the policy of peripheral military containment has performed a useful function only insofar as it has sought to discourage or counteract local expansionist policies, independent of those of the Soviet Union and China and hostile to the interests of the United States.

The paradox of the nuclear alliance reveals perhaps more clearly than the other paradoxes of nuclear strategy the nature of the dilemma and the fatal flaw in our modes of thought and action. Any attempt, however ingenious and forward-looking, at assimilating nuclear power to the purposes and instrumentalities of the nation-state is negated by the enormity of nuclear destructiveness. We have been trying to normalize, conventionalize, and "nationalize" nuclear power. By doing so, we have tackled the wrong horn of the nuclear dilemma. Instead of trying in vain to assimilate nuclear power to the purposes and the instrumentalities of the nation-state, we ought to have tried to adapt these purposes and instrumentalities to the potentialities of nuclear power. We have refrained from doing so in earnest because to do so successfully requires a radical transformation—psychologically painful and politically risky—of traditional moral values, modes of thought, and habits of action. But short of such a transformation, there will be no escape from the paradoxes of nuclear strategy and the dangers attending them.[41]

What is the "radical transformation" Morgenthau advocates in our "traditional moral values, modes of thought, and habits of action"—a transformation he characterizes as "psychologically painful and politically risky"? As I understand him, unless he has suddenly become an advocate of world government or preventive war, his sentence means that in cases of peripheral expansion such as those of Korea and Vietnam we should be willing to use the nuclear weapon against the major powers involved. Only the near certainty of such a response, he argues, could deter and contain programs of expansion like those we have experienced.

Professor Morgenthau puts the case against his own argument in another chapter. One of the main lessons he draws from his analysis is that

nuclear weapons in the hands of both superpowers are not instruments of national policy; they only provide assurance that national interests can be supported with the conventional diplomatic and military methods. In the measure that the United States is unable to utilize these methods, it will be tempted to resort to nuclear weapons. Hence, effective diplomacy and strong conventional forces are an insurance against the suicidal absurdity of nuclear war.[42]

Yet large parts of his book are given over to the puzzling themes I have quoted at length. I can attribute these inconsistencies only to the atmosphere of hysteria that has recently surrounded the issue of Vietnam.

In several passages Morgenthau's discussion of specific problems may throw light on what he really means by his stress on

41 P. 240. See also preceding discussion, pp. 237–240.
42 P. 242.

nuclear threats. Thus he frequently remarks on the legitimacy and importance of the American interest in eliminating the use of Cuba as a base threatening its security. That stress would seem to indicate that he favors a straightforward invasion of Cuba with conventional forces.

> Yet both the United States in its policy of containment and the Soviet Union in its attempt at installing offensive missiles in Cuba have dealt with territory in a nuclear setting, but in pre-nuclear terms. In a conventional military setting, control over territory has retained its offensive and defensive functions; this has become obvious, for instance, in the relations between Israel and the Arab states. But a military conflict between the United States and the Soviet Union is bound to be, and one between the United States and China is likely to be, in the nature of an all-out nuclear con-flagration. It is indeed the near-certainty of such a conflagration, if they should step beyond the lines of military demarcation of 1945 and 1949, respectively, which has contained the Soviet Union and China as well as the United States. The alliances we have con-cluded with nations at the periphery of the Soviet and Chinese empires, the military installations we have established in these countries, and the military operations we have performed there have fulfilled a political function by reassuring these nations of American protection, and they have performed a military func-tion by presenting the Soviet Union and China with tokens of our military resolution. But they have no direct military relevance in a nuclear setting, save as additional targets for nuclear attack.[43]

The campaign in Vietnam, he argues, does not serve the legiti-mate American interest of preserving a balance of power in Asia, because a victory by Hanoi would not "necessarily" expand Chi-nese or Soviet influence in the region, in view of the tensions tra-ditional to the relationship of Vietnam and China and the forces that have weakened or destroyed the centralized direction of the world Communist movement. It was plausible in 1950, Morgen-thau contends, to believe that North Korea was a tool of the So-viet Union and later of China. But he believes that no such as-sumption is possible about the present or future relationships of Hanoi to Peking or to Moscow. This is the key to the distinction

[43] Pp. 239–240.

he would make between our policy in Korea and Vietnam. "It was at this point," he says, "that our policy went astray." [44]

The sequence of this argument is decidedly mysterious. A great power need not control all aspects of the policy of another state in order to operate an effective military base from its territory. The Soviet Union is not loved in Poland or Czechoslovakia today, and it does not have monolithic control in either of those countries or in Egypt. Yet it has effective military use of their territories. And, indeed, the United States is still functioning from its base at Guantánamo Bay. The security problem in Vietnam cannot be evaded so simply. It has many facets beyond the famous question whether Ho Chi Minh was like Tito, and if so, how much, and for how long. Even if one assumes that the regime in North Vietnam would like to maintain its independence both from China and from the Soviet Union, its wars in Indochina could not continue without Chinese and Soviet assistance in supply. That dependence carries with it consequences that cannot be dismissed by the facile reiteration of the theory that the North Vietnamese are "Titoists" at heart. So are the Poles, Czechs, Roumanians, and Hungarians—and for that matter, so are the Russians. The Yugoslavs have a frontier with the West, and unlike the Czechs, have so far been able to avoid complete Soviet domination by threatening to fight when the pressure reached a point of crisis. That option is unavailable to the North Vietnamese so long as they depend on China and the Soviet Union for supplies. And it would vanish altogether if they succeed in taking over all of Indochina, thus becoming even more dependent on Chinese or Soviet backing than they are now, before the pressures of sustained irredentism and intensified anxiety.

Further, Morgenthau contends, even if the conquest of Saigon by Hanoi would alter the balance of power against us in Southeast Asia significantly, it is impossible to win a guerrilla war with some popular support save at costs we find unacceptable at the present level of hostilities or by an escalation that might draw China or the Soviet Union directly into the battle.

[44] P. 131.

But he concludes that where important interests are threatened by wars of national liberation fueled from abroad, they can be protected effectively only by a nuclear threat, ultimately "against the source and not only at one of its manifestations." [45]

Despite Morgenthau's eloquence I find myself unpersuaded.

However logical his recommendation, I cannot imagine the United States threatening such Soviet proxies as Syria, Egypt, or even North Korea with nuclear annihilation if they refuse to abandon policies of guerrilla aggression or, after the event, to disgorge their conquests. Nuclear threats are difficult enough to take seriously if issued against nuclear powers in the midst of a high-temperature crisis affecting important interests and inextricably involving national prestige. As a cold-blooded tool of diplomacy, to prevent one more slice from being taken off the salami, they seem both incredible in themselves and inadmissibly risky and destructive.

If nuclear deterrence is not a practical tool of everyday diplomacy, especially in Asia, Africa, and the Middle East, is there any hope for an equilibrium that would assure the independence of the nations of these regions? Is Morgenthau's real argument that we should wash our hands of the area roughly defined as the Third World and concentrate only on protecting the great centers of industry, and critical resources? Is this what he means by his bitter and reiterated attacks on "globalism" as an element of American foreign policy?

At first I thought this theme in his book was simply polemic sport. He has some entirely legitimate fun with the absurd vocabulary used by Wilson, Franklin Roosevelt, Senator Beveridge, and others, explaining American foreign policy in language that would make a missionary blush. I have no quarrel with Morgenthau's major premise—that a balance of power always has been and always should be the primary goal of our foreign policy, and I agree with him also that in our discussions and debates about foreign policy we should adopt a vocabulary consistent with reality, and do so as soon as possible.

[45] P. 149. See generally, pp. 131–150.

I have reached the conclusion, however, that Professor Morgenthau means something more than this in his attacks on "globalism" and "ideology" in American foreign policy.

Behind the anger and bitterness of these passages in his book is his effort to define a manageable sphere for American foreign policy and to allow the nation to disengage itself from most of the turbulence and disorder of the world.

This emphasis in the book expresses, I believe, Morgenthau's yearning for a policy that could permit the United States to escape somehow from involvement in the intractable and probably insoluble problems of an undefined area often called the Third World. By an extension and adaptation of existing policies—a better-organized Atlantic community—he thinks that Europe and the United States should somehow be able to consolidate their security as a safe, prosperous bourgeois enclave in a turbulent, revolutionary, violent, and increasingly chaotic and antibourgeois world. Presumably Morgenthau would accept the same kind of reasoning to justify a comparable policy for Japan, comparably credible because the Russians and the Chinese would understand the magnitude of the American interests at stake. Isn't this enough, he seems to be saying—a policy that is both "essential" to the safety of the nation and its institutions and within the range of feasibility? Many other goals for policy are desirable, he would say, but excessively costly in terms of effort or risk in the nightmare world that has emerged in the aftermath of empire and revolution.

Morgenthau knows too much about international politics fully to accept such a formula as a sufficient definition of the balance of power, on which he thinks it is the bedrock national interest of the United States to insist. Although he says almost nothing about Japan, he devotes a long, troubled chapter to China as a factor in American foreign policy. Similarly, the Middle East is almost completely ignored in his book, but several passing comments indicate that Morgenthau is aware of its importance to his theme.

The tension between Morgenthau's wishes and his knowledge of the world reduces him in the end to incoherence. His compass simply oscillates under the pressure of competing forces and never comes to rest. On almost every problem he supports incompatible theses with equally dogmatic conviction.

The best vantage point from which to review his argument as a whole is his summary conclusion, in which he recapitulates the results of his exercise in "radical rethinking." The conclusion consists of a list of seven principles which together define the "new" foreign policy he would have the United States adopt.

A. The first and fourth of Morgenthau's seven principles are the same. Foreign policy, he says, should be made with an eye single to national-security interests, without ideological or sentimental overtones. In the summary he doesn't mention his earlier qualification of this austere principle in behalf of nations inhabited by people of European culture.

While sound enough, if incomplete, these two principles hardly constitute a new major premise for our foreign policy. On the contrary, the United States has always in fact "talked prose" in this sense.

B. Morgenthau's second and third principles are also linked. They note that there are now three separate but interconnected kinds of threat to the security of the United States: (a) the traditional threat of hegemonial power in Europe and Asia, to be countered by the traditional methods of the balance of power; (b) the novel threat of nuclear destruction, to be countered by the novel methods of nuclear deterrence and arms control; and (c) attacks on American institutions by ideological competition and subversion from abroad, to be met by assuring the health and attractiveness of American society, and supposedly, in the case of subversion, by new police methods adapted to the new procedures of disruption. It is to be presumed that Morgenthau would have the United States counter the second and third kinds of threats not only when applied to the United States but when addressed to any country whose transfer to effective Soviet or Chinese control would significantly alter the balance of power.

These three levels of policy should be kept distinct, although they are connected. Nuclear weapons are not instruments of national policy, Morgenthau thinks, because of their destructiveness (I am sure he would add, "so long as effective nuclear deterrence is maintained"). The principles of conventional balance-of-power diplomacy and war should not therefore be transferred to the nuclear level. The nuclear weapons only provide assurance that national interests can be supported with conventional diplomatic and military methods. Since the United States will be tempted to use nuclear weapons if it cannot use conventional diplomacy and force effectively, strong conventional forces are an insurance against "the suicidal absurdity of nuclear war."

This is not a new principle, of course, but routine formulation of the official wisdom, setting out the doctrine that has been the basis for American action through thick and thin since 1947. Throughout that period—during the time of American nuclear monopoly and since—the United States government has tried to use conventional diplomacy and conventional forces, from the Berlin Airlift to Korea, Vietnam, and the successive crises of the Middle East, in ways that would protect national interests without risking the use of nuclear weapons. And from the time of the offer of the Baruch Plan to the negotiations about nonproliferation, seabeds, and space, it has sought to reduce the danger of nuclear war and to bring nuclear weapons under international control.

The difficulty with Morgenthau's second and third principles, taken together, is that they bear little or no relation to the dominant theme in the counterpoint of his book. The bulk of the book contends that the separation of nuclear from conventional force does not and cannot work in world politics today. In political or military conflicts involving the Soviet Union, Morgenthau argues, the nuclear stalemate inhibits the use of *both conventional and nuclear power* by the United States, even in those areas where interests Morgenthau would classify as "essential" are involved. At the same time, he contends that the only effective policy that has developed in the last twenty years, that of credible nuclear deterrence, *combines* nuclear and conventional force, as in NATO, on the principle that a *conventional* attack on American or Allied force would be met by a *nuclear* response. In Morgenthau's view the conventional forces in such a combination are not useful as such, but only as guarantors of nuclear retaliation. Morgenthau urges that this model, developed for Europe, should be used to prevent the military expansion of China if China should embark on such a course, through proxies or otherwise. It is his answer to the tragedy of Korea and Vietnam, which reveals the crippling limitations for the United States of limited conventional war in a nuclear setting. Thus Morgenthau contends that peripheral wars, such as those in Korea and Vietnam, could threaten American interests if they should involve Soviet or Chinese military expansion. If this should prove to be the case, the peripheral expansion of hostile power should be countered not by conventional containment, in the model of Korea or Vietnam, which he regards as unbearable, but by nuclear threat against the country sponsoring the peripheral expansion by conventional means.

He evidently assumes that a nuclear threat to prevent the take-over of Libya or Iran would be quite as effective as one to prevent the take-over of Berlin, although he also argues the inherent implausibility of the notion that we would accept bombs in New York in order to prevent an extension of Soviet power even into Berlin.

The trouble, of course, is that the restraints of the limited-war idea have not yet proved to be reciprocal. The Soviet Union is now rapidly extending its military power far beyond the demarcation lines of 1945, which Morgenthau regards as the proper boundaries of the Cold War. Employing proxies and covert methods, and taking skillful advantage of every opportunity, they have established new military positions threatening the security of the United States. In the Middle East and elsewhere, Morgenthau argues, the United States is doing little or nothing to counter these trends, being unable to use comparable methods. And where, as in Korea or Vietnam, the United States relies on the prescription Morgenthau supports in his conclusion—conventional diplomacy and conventional military power—it arouses a political storm, in which he participates.

In the text of his book Morgenthau's recommendations for the disintegration he sees coming are ambiguous and ambivalent and quite different from those in his concluding chapter: more, not less, reliance on nuclear threats; and less, not more, reliance on conventional military forces.

C. Morgenthau's fifth principle is astonishing to meet in a book by the great modern exponent of power politics. It asserts that the ideological contest among hostile philosophies and social and political systems will in the end be settled, not by military or non-military "interventions" by other nations, but by the visible virtues and vices of the rival philosophies and social systems themselves. This is certainly a pious thought, more in the spirit of Norman Thomas than of Hans Morgenthau. It hardly corresponds to man's historical experience with religion. And I wonder how Morgenthau would apply it to the careers of Lenin, Hitler, Mao, and Mussolini. Did communism come to Russia and China, to say nothing of the smaller states ruled by Communist parties, from the barrel of a gun or because the people freely chose one or the other of the competing philosophies on the basis of their preferences, after examining their visible virtues and vices? Was the experience of Germany and Italy different, in substance? And would the philosophy and social system of fascism still be in control in Germany and Italy, as they are in Spain, had there been no war, no "intervention," and no victory in 1945?

Be that as it may, Morgenthau proceeds from his axiom to the rule that "instead of embarking upon costly and futile interventions for the purpose of building nations and viable economies abroad, the United States ought to concentrate its efforts upon creating a society at home which can again serve as a model for other nations to emulate." [46] By this statement, presumably, Morgenthau is not referring to "interventions" and assistance in build-

[46] P. 243.

ing viable nations and economies, like those of the Marshall Plan, in areas he would regard as of concern to the security of the United States.

Here, once more, the thrust of Morgenthau's book bears only a tenuous relation to the principle stated in the summary. And neither the book nor the summary constitutes an adequate treatment of the looming tragedy of the development process in many, perhaps most, of the nonindustrialized nations of the Third World.

In his book Morgenthau attacks development-aid programs viciously as a waste of time and energy, since most of the countries involved are culturally incapable of economic progress, and some are "bums and beggars" to boot. Almost all, he claims, are culturally incapable of stability, probity, or democracy, and prone to revolutionary fevers which Communist nations are in a much better position than we are to exploit. On the other hand, Morgenthau also urges more ambitious, if more selective, programs of aid in "nation building" as part of the effort to contain China and the Soviet Union by nonmilitary means.

But save for a few parenthetical remarks, he nowhere indicates how he would decide in which areas of the world the United States should "intervene" to protect its national security, and those it can safely ignore as without significance to security. Is concern for the possibility of Soviet predominance in the Middle East required by our "vital" and "essential" security interest in Europe, and if so, in how much of the Middle East? Is concern for Korea, the Western Pacific, and Southeast Asia required by our "vital" and "essential" security interest in Japan, Australia, and New Zealand, and indeed in China itself? In Morgenthau's lexicon, does the United States have a security interest, "essential," "desirable," or "possible," in the Indian subcontinent, the Persian Gulf, or the troubled areas of Africa, the Caribbean, or South America, either in absolute geopolitical terms or in the context of particular trends and movements? How do we protect what Morgenthau calls our "essential" interest in making sure that Cuba is not used as a base for subversion and other activities hostile to our interests in the Caribbean? How much involvement in various parts of the Third World is required to maintain nuclear deterrence through surveillance and second-strike capacity in view of the changing technology of nuclear weapons, and of other weapons and weapon systems as well?

His book nowhere clearly answers any of these questions.

D. Principles 6 and 7 of Morgenthau's "new" foreign policy proceed from the fact that the United States and its rivals have common interests as well as rivalries, the avoidance of nuclear war being thus far the most fundamental. Steps to reduce the risk of nuclear war are preconditions to the possibility of world-politics-as-usual at the conventional level, and must never be affected by the normal vicissitudes of the political weather at lower political altitudes.

Here again Morgenthau's point is unexceptionable, but hardly new. He goes on, however, to urge that "a new American foreign policy, intent upon broadening and strengthening the area of common interests and aware of the threat to world peace and order emanating from the balkanization of large sectors of the political world, must pay special attention to the unused potential of the United Nations." [47] Mentioning the possibility of reforming United Nations voting and other features of its constitution, Morgenthau urges the United States to make "judicious use" of the organization to broaden and strengthen the area of "common interests."

The statement is interesting, for I believe it to be nearly the only place in the book where Morgenthau refers to the Balkanization and weakness of large parts of the Third World as a "threat to world peace," and therefore of security concern to the United States. Having formulated a real and intensely difficult problem, he then offers an answer that is patently no answer at all, but an evasion into a formula that has long since lost even the threadbare appearance of vitality or meaning.

The "new" foreign policy outlined in Morgenthau's seven concluding principles hardly matches the brave call of his opening pages. There he urged an act of intellectual renovation compar-

[47] P. 244.

able to the announcement of the Truman Doctrine and the Marshall Plan in 1947, which could give us new policies capable of achieving national security in a universe quite different from the world of the forties.

IV

The impassioned and sophisticated tracts of Stillman and Pfaff have the same generic background as Morgenthau's. But their intellectual scope is wider. *The Politics of Hysteria* is a thoughtful essay on the course of modern history, sensitive to its psychosocial dimensions as well as to its impact on the problem of power and peace. It is a work of quality in every sense, although it is not so original as the books of Christopher Dawson or Robert Waelder.

For Stillman and Pfaff there are two keys to modern history: (1) the many-sided reaction of non-European cultures to the experience of European civilization; and (2) the revolt against the Enlightenment, with its faith in reason and in the perfectibility of man. The revolt against reason is conducted in the name of dark gods whom Nietzsche is generally thought to have evoked. They were indeed worshiped by the growing band of his successors, Bakunin, Hitler, and the rest.

Stillman and Pfaff are aware of the mysteries of human behavior. They know that there is much more in heaven and earth than can be explained by Marxian methods. Why did Europe move out so confidently for three centuries to embrace the world and bring it within the orbit of European influence? How have the non-European cultures responded to the shock of their deep and irreversible contacts with European civilization—with its technologies, its brutalities, its ideas and modes of life, its spiritualism and idealism as well? Why has Europe now withdrawn from the adventure of the imperial mission? The tragic element looms large in their consciousness. They fear the power of evil in life, the strain of mysticism, of demonic violence, and of ideological fervor that has aroused tribes so often during this century to

226

slaughter men of alien race, or creed, or class in the name of truth.

Stillman and Pfaff sense, too, the power of deeper and more terrible urges—instincts of aggression that demand outlet without even the excuse of ideology. "What was in the air by 1914," they write, "was a spirit of violent repudiation" directed against the mild rationalism of the Enlightenment. This appetite for destruction, they say, cannot be accounted for "in any objective historical or political terms, but only by a judgment on human character. The nineteenth century had abolished war; but the peace and stability of that world perished because men could not really bear to live for a century with the kind of world they had made" [48]—a world of social progress and of unequaled cultural splendor made possible by prolonged peace. Spirits were repelled by the values of liberal civilization itself and turned in revolt to violence, brutality, and dissonance.

Like Morgenthau, Stillman and Pfaff approve the American policy of containment in Europe, launched in the late forties, and the American policy of that period in the Far East as well. Ideological war between the United States and the Soviet Union, they say, was inevitable after 1945. The nation of eighteenth-century rational optimism confronted the nation of twentieth-century messianic despair.[49] But the Truman phase of American foreign policy, in their view, was nonideological. Russia pressed outward into the chaos of the postwar world to gain control in areas of Europe from which it had been invaded seven times in three hundred years, and in Iran, in China, and Korea, and other places as well. And it threatened to sweep over, or at least to dominate, the rest.

The American response was brilliant, decisive, and entirely rational, in their judgment. The United States had to bind its fate to that of Western Europe in the interests of sheer political and military survival. A Soviet take-over in Europe would have tipped "an altered balance of forces irrevocably against the United States." Comparable trends led to comparable American commit-

---

[48] *The Politics of Hysteria* (1964), pp. 111 ff.
[49] Ibid., p. 171.

ments in Asia and the Near East—correctly, in the opinion of Stillman and Pfaff.[50]

> By 1950 Western Europe and its appendage, the Aegean Zone, was secure. In Asia (though China itself was lost and given over to a hostile dynasty) the war in Korea was fought out to a stalemate and settled; a line of demarcation was firmly drawn between two worlds. The United States, as the paramount power in the world, and as a kind of residuary legatee of the West, was materially committed to the defense of the boundaries—again, against a real enemy.[51]

Like Morgenthau, Stillman and Pfaff contend that the sensible policies of the Truman-Acheson era dissolved into the illusion of myth under Eisenhower and Dulles. The pragmatic and wholly reasonable policy of containing hostile power somehow became an irrational and universal ideological crusade against the sin and heresy of communism.

Stillman and Pfaff start their argument in the classical tradition of American puritanism. They flagellate the nation for naïveté; for sentimental and vulgar optimism; for innocence of the experience of tragedy, and for a kind of puerile anger at the ingratitude and corruption of the world.[52] These constitute an extraordinary barrage of accusations against a nation that has lived always with the moral burden of the Negro problem, and with the shadow, the reality, and now the memory of its Civil War. One would suppose that these twin forces of themselves were a sufficient experience of tragedy to mature the American people.

Ignoring Stillman and Pfaff's private vocabulary of abuse, how in fact do they define the error that converted the brilliant success of Truman in Europe, the Middle East, and Asia into what they regard as the disastrous policies brought on his successors by the Eisenhower-Dulles commitments?

For Stillman and Pfaff the focal point of the error is the belt of poor and backward states of the Southern hemisphere that have sought since 1945 to validate a renewal of power and energy.

[50] Ibid., pp. 176–177.
[51] Ibid., p. 179.
[52] Ibid., pp. 185–186, p. 222.

Most of these nations, and especially the non-European nations, are living through a period of cultural and psychological shock that has brought them close to despair and made them vulnerable to hallucination, hysteria, and disorientation. Few are succeeding in their efforts at modernization. Many succumb to policies of delusion. In Asia, in Africa, and in Latin America indigenous cultures are being buffeted and weakened by their efforts to digest the culture of the West. For one, such as Japan, that achieves an authentic synthesis, there are fifty caught up in turbulent and unstable processes of conflict, which lead them into "compensatory fantasy, [and] searches in political mythology and emotion for relief from an unmanageable and unbearable reality." [53] The links of such nations to communism are superficial and transitory. "What we see is rather the working out in public, in the affairs of civic life and the relations between nations, of the old crisis of culture and identity in twentieth century terms," often bizarre and pathological, nearly always evocative of tragedy, personal as well as public.[54]

Confronting these phenomena, American policy came "to conceive its foreign responsibilities as global and total—a near universal war, no longer against Communism, but against political and social disorder, the very bloody-mindedness of the world." [55] This effort was bound to fail, in the nature of things. It is the essence of the failure of American foreign policy that Stillman and Pfaff urge us to acknowledge and correct.

It is difficult to understand the denotation of these words, and, to discover how Stillman and Pfaff would distinguish what they regard as the sensible from the absurd applications of the Truman Doctrine, unless success alone is their touchstone. Like Korea, Vietnam is on the "line of demarcation between two worlds" which Stillman and Pfaff regard as critical—a "boundary" to defend. But what of instances where Soviet military power leapfrogs the boundary and establishes itself beyond the line of demarcation, as

[53] Ibid., p. 191.
[54] Ibid., p. 193.
[55] Ibid., p. 204.

it has done in Cuba and Egypt? Why do Stillman and Pfaff become so angry, as Morgenthau does half the time, about programs of economic assistance in nonindustrialized countries whose troubles we can never "cure"?

The Soviet Union, in their view, is a powerful and dangerous state, but in the nonmilitary sphere a less dangerous opponent than the Soviets wish us to believe. Like Morgenthau, Stillman and Pfaff claim that the Soviet Union has ceased to be an expanding or an ideological state, because of the fatal weakness in its own ideology and the deepening conflict between the Russian intelligentsia and the official dogmas of the Soviet state. This is a struggle, they conclude, the Communist party of the Soviet Union cannot hope to win. Even in the military sphere and even in Eastern Europe the risk of Soviet intervention is waning, they wrote in 1964, four years before the invasion of Czechoslovakia, and five or six before the massive intervention of Soviet arms in the Middle East and the rising tide of Soviet intervention in the Persian Gulf, the Indian Ocean, and Southeast Asia.[56]

Most of the rest of the Stillman and Pfaff analysis, like that of Morgenthau, is made obsolete by this fundamental error of judgment. It is an error characteristic of their intellectual outlook. They cannot really believe that grown men can take ideology seriously. Stillman and Pfaff conclude that the ideology of Soviet Communism is barren and irrelevant to the Russian people. Therefore, they believe, the Soviet Union has become weak and cannot sustain its pretensions to empire. It follows, they argue, that the importance of the new states in world politics has declined with what they call the relaxation of Cold War tensions.[57] They conclude that American concern with the problems of the Third World is unnecessary and that American foreign policy is overextended, both in Europe and in Asia. If the Soviet Union had given up its expansionist ambitions in order to lick its ideological wounds, they would be right. On such an assumption, the United States would not have to concern itself with the course of

56 Ibid., pp. 211–215.
57 P. 215.

events in the Third World—or indeed in Europe or the northern Pacific either. Unfortunately, their assumption has no foundation in fact.

What would they substitute for the foreign policy they condemn?

While their main prescriptive ideas are outlined in *The Politics of Hysteria*, they are more fully developed in *Power and Impotence*.

Foreign policy should start and end with the national interest, they say. It is "primarily a *defense*, a means by which the social organism defends itself against encroachments, and seeks to achieve the international environment within which it can prosper." [58]

What are the principal tenets of what they call a new foreign policy which could "ensure the external peace within which the conditions of a private national excellence may be achieved," and achieved, moreover, by an American society that remains a democracy? [59] "It may be," they write, "that the best foreign policy for America is to attend sensibly to itself." [60] Though they are powerfully attracted by this formula, they cannot bring themselves to embrace it directly.

The primary reason for their hesitation is their evaluation of Soviet (and Chinese) policy and their awareness that the risks that precipitated the American reaction after 1947 are by no means dead.

Although Stillman and Pfaff sometimes talk as if the Cold War is over and the Soviet Union in retreat, they would base American policy toward Russia on the premise that it is a hostile state, to be treated with the greatest caution and prudence for many years to come. We should guardedly cooperate with the Soviet Union to moderate tensions and the burden of arms where possible, and persuade the Soviet Union to withdraw from Eastern Europe on terms that would protect their security interests in the land ap-

[58] *Power and Impotence* (1966), p. 185.
[59] Id., and at p. 187.
[60] Id., p. 189.

proaches to Russia. We should encourage and support the autonomy of the East European states and "resist coldly, with diplomatic and military measures if necessary, extensions of Russia's
physical power . . . into new regions—for instance, any Russian
attempt to establish military bases in Latin America, or to obtain
military, territorial, or significant political concessions from
neighboring states." [61] And above all we should do nothing to
abate the consequences of hostility between Communist Russia
and Communist China.[62] They would condemn policies like those
of President Nixon toward China. In the Stillman and Pfaff lexicon, Nixon should have rebuffed Chinese overtures for American
support against the Soviet threat to China and encouraged a war in
which the Communist great powers weakened each other.

Alas for prophecies. The main issues between the United States
and the Soviet Union today are hardly the time and manner of
Soviet withdrawal from Eastern Europe. And the use of force to
prevent (or undo) the establishment of Soviet bases on the shores
of the Mediterranean, or in the Red Sea and the Indian Ocean, is
not nearly so simple nor so "cold" a proposition as Messrs. Stillman and Pfaff seem to assume. The Cuban missile crisis was far
from "cold" in any sense. Yet the outcome was a strategic victory
for the Soviet Union. No shots have been fired between Soviet
and American forces throughout the Cold War. Do Stillman and
Pfaff urge that we break this rule, with all its implications, by
driving the Soviets out of Egypt, Syria, and Algeria? If that is
how they wish us to read their sentence, they are indeed proposing a new policy.

The first principle of Stillman and Pfaff's new foreign policy is
to prevent a major nuclear war, or any nuclear war, or any large
war, and to be sure that if the first objective fails, the war will be
so limited and so controlled as to assure national survival. Here
Stillman and Pfaff differ sharply from Morgenthau. They would
eliminate all American nuclear guarantees. It is folly, they say, for
the United States to maintain nuclear guarantees for anybody,

[61] Id., p. 199.
[62] Id., p. 201.

since Soviet nuclear weapons can now reach the United States. On the other hand, the United States has a clear national interest, they believe, in defending Western Europe from Soviet control or the control of any other single hostile power. There are comparable American interests, they say, in Japan and "only a few other geographical areas where hostile control would, in material terms, jeopardize our security." [63] They carefully avoid specifying those "few other places" of primary concern to our security.

Stillman and Pfaff would also list as security interests, although less important strategically than our interest in Europe and Japan, our concern for "the security and well-being of others who are either our friends, or, even if they are not, are serious and creative societies." [64] In this class Stillman and Pfaff consider our commitment to India "unilateral but necessary," although they hasten to add that "we need to understand what we can and cannot do." It is quite clear that Stillman and Pfaff believe we cannot do much in these cases. "America should do less, not more," they say.[65] They do not name other nations that merit American protection because they are "friends" or "creative societies" or both. Should we regard Australia and New Zealand as falling into that category, or Israel, or Jordan, or Saudi Arabia, or Lebanon, or Tunisia, or South Korea, or Iran (which Stillman and Pfaff may regard as protected by the Truman Doctrine in its pure form in any event, because it is on the boundary of the Soviet realm)? They do not say.

A fundamental defect of Stillman and Pfaff's prescription is that it ignores the implacable character of the nuclear problem. How could America defend what Stillman and Pfaff call our vital security interest in Western Europe and Japan, or our less important but still important interest in India and other "friendly" or "creative" societies, without a nuclear guarantee? Could they imagine a conventional war fought in Europe by Soviet and Allied forces without escalation to the nuclear level? The possibility

[63] Ibid., pp. 186–188.
[64] Ibid., p. 188.
[65] Ibid., p. 190.

of such a war would move Europe automatically to neutrality, if not to a closer association with the Soviet Union.

Their answer would be to scrap the nonproliferation treaty and have Germany and Japan become nuclear powers. In *The Politics of Hysteria* they favor the nonproliferation treaty.[66] In *Power and Impotence* they reverse their position, deeming the risk of revived militarism in Germany and Japan to be "slight." [67] But would the Soviet Union allow Germany or Japan to become nuclear powers if the United States withdrew? Is such a development conceivable or desirable from the American point of view? Should the allies of the United States have the capacity to start a nuclear war we should have to finish? Is it plausible to argue that if the United States withdrew from Asia, Japan could "no longer expect the clear field of action in East Asia that [it] enjoyed in the first half of this century"? [68] The relative strength of Japan for such enterprises is now greater than it was early in this century, with Britain and France entirely out of Asia, and China and the Soviet Union divided, to say the least.

The Stillman and Pfaff argument ignores the most fundamental political and technological realities.

Because of the Soviet and American lead in nuclear science, Europe and Japan are now more dependent on American nuclear protection than they were twenty-five years ago, despite their economic and social recoveries. If we take Stillman and Pfaff's first principle seriously—that the primary American national interest is to prevent "a major nuclear war, any nuclear war, or any large war"—then in all prudence our course should not be to disengage from Europe and Japan, but to deepen and intensify the political integration of these three great centers of power, through methods that correspond to their deepening military, economic, and social interdependence.

Stillman and Pfaff contend that the true independence of Europe and Japan, based on nuclear weapons and large-scale conventional

[66] P. 232.
[67] P. 193.
[68] Id.

forces, has been frustrated by an American policy of keeping these nations in leading strings. No one could make this statement who has participated in American efforts to persuade the European nations and Japan to take more responsibility for their own security in recent years, or confronted their panic at the prospect that even five American air squadrons might be withdrawn. The United States has encouraged European political and economic integration since 1947 precisely in order to make a secure and independent Europe possible. In such a Europe, Germany could play a creative and constructive role. And, with British membership, the new Europe could never become a hostile force. But because of the disparity between Soviet and European nuclear strength—and, indeed, conventional strength as well—the American nuclear guarantee to Europe is precarious and incredible without the support of an American conventional presence. And from both the European and the American point of view that presence is necessary to assure diplomacy the possibility of nonnuclear options in the event of a crisis. Stillman and Pfaff's policy would leave an American President no choice except inaction or the nuclear button in the case, say, of a Bulgarian attack on Greece or a Hungarian attack on Yugoslavia.

In *The Politics of Hysteria* Stillman and Pfaff also stress the desirability of close political and military collaboration among Britain, the United States, Canada, Australia, and New Zealand—a natural collaboration, they believe, and one with great potentialities for leadership, and even regeneration.[69]

So far as the containment of China is concerned, Stillman and Pfaff would rely primarily on Japan, and they dismiss without discussion the possibility that Japan might well have other ideas on the subject. And they nowhere consider the potentiality of the tension involving China, the Soviet Union, and the United States and its allies as a force for equilibrium and therefore for peace. They do not mention the attraction to the United States of rapprochement with China, of which Dean Acheson spoke as early as 1949, in inducing all the great centers of power to accept recipro-

[69] Pp. 232–237.

cal rules of restraint in the use of force, and indeed in the pursuit of rivalry. On this fundamental issue all they say is that we should do nothing to prevent a Soviet-Chinese war—a policy at odds with the first principle of their foreign policy.

Beyond these fundamentals, Stillman and Pfaff argue, we should cancel many of the commitments that were recklessly proliferated, in their view, during the Eisenhower years. This process must be gradual and carefully done. "It is one thing to say that America is over-extended; but such allied states cannot simply be cut adrift as Americans reassess their past errors. America has its obligations, in international law and in simply humanity. We cannot abandon those who have taken our protection, or who have acted in our behalf at some cost." [70]

Stillman and Pfaff do not explain, however, how these readjustments could be carried out without inviting Soviet or Chinese expansion, such as took place in South Korea in 1950 when our forces were withdrawn.

Commitments should be kept to a minimum. Their goal should be "to restore, insofar as possible, a primary balance of power in the world, *encouraging* rather than *fighting* the growth of local strengths which might function in counterpoise to that of present or potential enemies; and, finally, to see the United States itself chiefly as a *strategic reserve*." [71]

By "strategic reserve" Stillman and Pfaff mean that the United States should rely in the first instance on local forces to resist aggression. We should use our own forces only to assist nations resisting aggression, and then only "when actual and legitimate American interest is jeopardized. . . . It will always be an open question, to be determined in the specific context, whether any local aggression justifies the American involvement." [72]

What do these words mean to Stillman and Pfaff? They indicate that "Soviet or Chinese opportunities for mischief-making" [73]

[70] *Power and Impotence*, p. 191.
[71] Id.
[72] Ibid., p. 194.
[73] Ibid., p. 195.

would be an important factor in making the decision. Should we infer from these words that Stillman and Pfaff agree with Morgenthau that the United States should have eliminated Castro? Apparently not, for Stillman and Pfaff do not regard Castro and Castroism as serious in any way. The Cuban revolution, they believe, is a diffuse and rather primitive affair, similar to Peron's a generation earlier.[74] What about Korea, or Vietnam, or Jordan, Tunisia, Saudi Arabia, or Israel, or Iran, or Burma? Scattered passages in the books give no clear sense of a consistent line.[75] We should avoid ideological interventions, not worry too much about the risks, realize that Algeria, Guinea, Iraq, Egypt, and Burma, although they have made critical statements about the United States, have not "joined the enemy camp," and in any event cannot do more than inconvenience us. Our model should be that of French policy in Algeria, which Stillman and Pfaff regard as successful, and in the event of danger, supplement our restraint with a territorial guarantee against invasion, at least for states in which they regard our security interests as high—states such as Turkey, Iran, Iraq, and Pakistan.[76]

Stillman and Pfaff attack the common view that the United States and Latin America in fact occupy the same hemisphere. Their cultures are different. There are great gulfs between them. Their economic connections do not compare in importance with those between Europe and the United States. Therefore Stillman and Pfaff urge that American policy toward Latin America be limited to the Monroe Doctrine and the enforcement of a unilateral American guarantee against external aggression. This brief and almost casual statement begs the difficult modern question—that of processes of revolution supported from abroad, or even imported. However desirable such a course might be, to revive the Monroe Doctrine today would be a major undertaking. It would produce earthquakes of excitement in Latin America. Stillman and Pfaff write as if it could be done by waving a wand.

[74] Ibid., pp. 118–119.
[75] Pp. 148–176.
[76] P. 155.

In broad outline, then, Stillman and Pfaff believe that a foreign policy strictly addressed to the protection of American interests would have us:

(1) Withdraw from Europe and Japan and encourage the development of independent European and Japanese defense policies, including nuclear weapons.

(2) Remain allied—and, indeed, become more closely allied with Great Britain, Canada, Australia, and New Zealand.

(3) Resign ourselves to a breakdown and a return to futility in the Third World as the United States and the Soviet Union, each spiritually bruised by a quarter century of Cold War, retreat to their proper realms.

(4) Remain, however, a "strategic reserve," ready to act against some but not all acts of aggression committed with conventional weapons (but not nuclear weapons)—that is, acts of aggression against countries that at the time of the event, and in its context, we decide it is in our national interest to help, but not help much.

The Stillman and Pfaff formula faithfully represents the mood of many who believe that the sound doctrine of the Truman era became folly thereafter by being generalized into a universal and ideological rule against aggression, revolution, social change, and communism. The explosion of feeling over Vietnam leads them to grope for an alternative and more restricted policy that would protect our true security interests and keep us out of unnecessary trouble.

Unfortunately, their prescriptions, like those of Morgenthau, suffer from vagueness, inconsistency, simple error, and poor forecasting. When Stillman and Pfaff published *Power and Impotence* in 1966 they thought the Soviet Union was an empire in retreat. And they fail to give sufficient weight, I believe, to the bitter reality of the nuclear problem, which makes their major proposals —the end of guarantees and the spread of nuclear weapons—prescriptions for disaster. Like Morgenthau, they finish in banality, confusion, and anticlimax.

# 8

## Does the Third World Matter?
## The Middle East: A Case Study

THE INCONSISTENCIES and contradictions of the arguments examined in the last four chapters are not their most important characteristics. They express a passionate conviction whose influence is not diminished by the incoherence with which it is explained. In a non-Cartesian world imponderables also have rights.

The conviction that runs through this branch of the literature is simple and imperative: The troubles of the Third World do not concern the security of the United States.

Many put the thesis in terms of power politics. These men say that the safety of the United States requires only that we keep Western Europe and Japan out of hostile hands. Some go further. They believe that considerations of security require us to prevent the hostile control only of the Ruhr Valley and a few like regions. Hostile control of the rest of the world's geography could not harm us, they think. The Cold War between the United States and the Soviet Union is over, or nearly over, these men say hopefully. Alternatively, they comfort themselves with the thought that the world Communist movement is no longer a "monolith" directed from Moscow. From this they infer that the emplacement in developing countries of regimes calling themselves Communist does not raise the specter of a great octopus enveloping the West in its coils, even when those regimes allow Soviet military bases to be established. Besides, they claim, the Third World is and will remain too weak to constitute a threat to the security of the United States and should not be a matter of concern even if the Communist movement regained its unity and discipline. Anyway, the world is so full of turbulence that no one hostile power, or combination of hostile powers, would in fact be able to dominate the Third World, or at least dominate it for long.

These variations on a theme are, I believe, the heart of the charge of "globalism" and "ideology" addressed to the foreign policy of the United States by many critics who should be grouped in the sixth school with Morgenthau, Fulbright, Kennan, and others of their intellectual and moral persuasion.

Some members of the fifth school reach the same conclusion by a different route. The Third World is floundering, they say, and cannot achieve progress without a "revolution." From the point of view of suffering humanity the United States should stop supporting reactionary or inadequate regimes in countries of the Third World and embrace the revolution. Oglesby and Chomsky support this view because they identify themselves with the idea of revolution and with the ideology of socialism. Fulbright and Morgenthau do not regard themselves as socialists or revolutionaries, but they are inclined to think that the nonindustrialized countries need a socialist revolution. In any event, they believe that the future of those countries is irrelevant or largely irrelevant to the national security interests of the United States.

For another group of writers the angry conviction of Third World "irrelevance" expresses racial and ethnic antipathy or disillusion with the spotty record of development-aid programs in many parts of Asia, Africa, and Latin America. And for still others it represents the view that however desirable it might be to hold back the tide of Communist advance in the Third World, it cannot be done, and we had therefore better give up wasting our substance in the effort.

Whatever its source, the opinion is widespread: The United States should get out of the Third World and stay out. No more Koreas and no more Vietnams. Repeal, revoke, and denounce the commitments to the Third World made during Eisenhower's administration. And then let nature take its course. We should resolve to stand aloof, and like a reformed alcoholic, resist every temptation to intervene.

Men of this persuasion often start their books by pointing out that there are some reasonably stable factors in world politics today: (1) the nuclear standoff between the United States and the Soviet Union makes nuclear warfare between them unthinkable; and the shadow of nuclear escalation makes it unlikely (or most unlikely, or nearly impossible) for them to engage in conventional warfare with each other; (2) nonetheless, nuclear guarantees by the superpowers retain a certain credibility, at least when backed by the presence of conventional forces and underlined at intervals by demonstrations of will. As a result, zones or spheres of influence genuinely exist—areas and countries where one of the superpowers has indicated a strong state interest which the other is willing to recognize or has been forced to recognize. Thus most people assume that neither the Soviet Union nor China would use force or the threat of force to attack Western Europe, Korea, or Japan. And it is obvious that the corresponding assumption is safe with regard to Western intentions in Eastern Europe, and *a fortiori*, in China, Cuba, and the Soviet Union themselves.

In this perspective, these American and European critics say, why should our countries concern themselves with the Third World? We are safe. No one will invade or bomb us or send us to Siberia or to concentration camps. The fate of the Third World is not a matter of importance to us.

Even if one accepts for the moment the hypothesis of indefinite standoff in the relationship between the great powers, at least so far as the use of nuclear weapons and conventional military force is concerned, what role does the Third World play in the ambitions of the Soviet Union, of China, and of other Communist states dreaming about expansion?

Khrushchev once answered the question in a famous interview with James Reston. Nuclear wars are impossible, he said: the nuclear weapon doesn't respect class differences. After Korea, conventional warfare is too dangerous. Therefore, he concluded, Communist states must rely on wars of national liberation to carry the revolution forward, especially in the Third World.[1]

The difficulty is that many parts of the Third World are protected by public declarations and demonstrations of Western interest quite as formal as the North Atlantic Treaty or the corresponding American commitments to Korea and Japan. The need for military and communications facilities, the necessity for access to raw materials, long-standing historical ties, and powerful links of nationhood, religion, and tribe connect America and Europe to many nations in Asia and Africa and of course in Central and South America as well. These connections are often suffused with the kind of emotional intensity that could detonate war—for example, the feeling in Britain, Canada, and the United States about Australia and New Zealand. And, as Professor Albert Wohlstetter has shown, technology is reducing the significance of distance as rapidly for security calculations as for economic affairs. No program of security, either by way of nuclear or nonnuclear deterrence, can today be autarkic or regional.[2]

Thus far, however, the Soviet Union, China, and Cuba, separately or in various combinations, do not respect these commitments as they are supposed to respect the American commitments to Western Europe, Japan, or South Korea. They continue to sponsor or to threaten international attacks on many of the nations of the Third World to whom the West has pledged its full support. Indeed, the pace of such campaigns has increased in recent years. They draw on the full armory of modern guerrilla warfare, using both violence and political and psychological weapons in various combinations. They sponsor proxy wars and

[1] *New York Times*, October 10, 1957, p. 11, col. 2. See also his interview with C. L. Sulzberger, *New York Times*, September 8, 1961, p. 11, cols. 4–5.
[2] "Illusions of Distance," 46 *Foreign Affairs* (1968), 242.

guerrilla wars, kidnappings, assassinations, bombings, and bank robberies. Organized demonstrators are thrown into the streets on any plausible excuse in order to demoralize and weaken government and to precipitate police violence that could rally support.

At the same time, the intellectual and moral premises of Western civilization are assaulted and eroded in journals and books of great prestige. Revolutions are incited, and every other method of political, psychological, and physical subversion and violence is employed. This is the case in Vietnam and the Middle East and in many other countries of Asia, Africa, and South and Central America today. In 1971 Mexico demanded the recall of a considerable part of the Soviet Embassy staff in Mexico City. A group of young people had been arrested in the course of robbing a bank. They talked, indeed they proclaimed their faith. They said their work was directed by the Soviet officials as part of a deliberate campaign of revolutionary violence. As students, the men arrested had gone to the Soviet Union, ostensibly to study, but in fact to be trained in the strategy and tactics of revolution. The uprising in Ceylon during the same period was organized and led by alumni of the same Soviet university. Later in the same year, informed by a Soviet defector, Great Britain ordered more than a hundred Soviet diplomats to leave the country because of their involvement in espionage and sabotage.

Is this process of national concern to the United States, Europe, and Japan? Is peace indivisible, as Litvinov used to say? Is the Charter of the United Nations a scrap of paper to be forgotten as quickly as possible? In the name of power politics, or of a broader basis for a foreign policy, should the United States and its allies respond, and if so, how?

The Middle East offers a good opportunity to test the implications of the argument for an American withdrawal from the Third World and for a policy of confining our overseas security commitments, at a maximum, to Europe and Japan.

Every region of the Third World does not, of course, have exactly the same bearing as the Middle East on the security problems of the United States. But they all have features in common, in different configurations. And they all raise common questions, although with differing degrees of urgency.

II

The Middle East is an anthology of the security problems that arise in the Third World. It is still what John Morley called it two generations ago: "that shifting, intractable and interwoven tangle of conflicting interests, rival peoples and antagonistic faiths that is veiled under the easy name of the Eastern Question." There is competition among historical claims as well as religions, secular and divine. There have been conventional wars, guerrilla wars, and coups d'état galore in recent years. The area is a Mecca for the intelligence services of the world and a theater for Soviet, Chinese, and Western rivalries, as well as the rivalries of the nations of the region. And it lives in the shadow of nuclear weapons.

"The Eastern Question" has always been part of what Duncan Hall calls the International Frontier between rival great powers. It has been a major problem of European diplomacy at least since the times of Cyrus the Great and Alexander. The Romans endured endless trouble in the East, including a bitter guerrilla war with the Jews which required a quarter of their legions before it could be won, even on the most Draconian terms. The Crusades represent one aspect of the Eastern Question for European security, the Battle of Lepanto another. The Arab invasion was as important to European history as the invasions of the Normans and of the Mongols. Turkey was a problem while the Ottoman Empire was strong, and a worse problem when it began to disintegrate. Fighting and showing the flag in North Africa and the Middle East were among the earliest duties of the American Navy. The competitive jostling for position of the European rivals in the Balkans led to a succession of small wars in the late nineteenth and early twentieth centuries, and then, of course, to the First World War itself. After that war Turkey lost more of its European territories, and its non-Turkish possessions in the

244

Near East were divided between France and Britain. As a result, French and British military forces were installed along the Mediterranean from Syria to Morocco, except for the Italian colony of Cirenaica, and in considerable depth beyond, especially in Jordan, Iraq, the Persian Gulf, southern Arabia, and the Sudan.

During the thirteen years after World War II, however, France and Britain withdrew from every one of their Mediterranean positions. Inevitably, new constellations of force emerged to fill the vacuums.

The competition of rival national claims to territory formerly within the Ottoman Empire has dominated the recent history of the region. Indeed, that story is more than a hundred years old. And now, as in earlier times, local rivalries, conflicts, and enmities, bitter in themselves, become irreconcilable when linked to the conflicting aspirations and fears of world powers.

The Algerian revolt against France in the 1950s and the effort of Egypt to eliminate the British presence in that country led to long and dangerous conflicts in which Soviet, American, French, and British policy played varying roles. The relative harmony of British, French, and American policy in the Middle East was shattered by the disaster of Suez, which left the Soviet Union and the United States virtually alone, for practical purposes, as great power arbiters and interveners in the conflicts of the region. Since the end of the Algerian affair the Soviet Union has held the center of the stage in the Middle East, playing a melodrama that could easily become a tragedy—the fate of Israel. There are other currents of rivalry in the Middle East that the Soviet Union has sought to exploit—Nasser's dream of Arab unity, for example, which frightened many who preferred their own nationhood. But all these themes of the story are influenced in turn by the explosive forces that radiate from the conflict over Israel.

The history of Israel and the history of Arab nationalism—involving the nominal protagonists of the drama—have been decisively influenced at every stage by the conjunctures of world politics. The Balfour Declaration was, among other things, an episode of the First World War. During the same period Arab nationalism was stirred to life by the British campaign against Turkey and by the Arab response to the implications of Balfour's famous statement. Both movements made their political debuts in the Middle East after the First World War—Zionism in the development of the Jewish community within the British mandated territory of Palestine; Arab nationalism in the politics of Transjordan, Saudi Arabia, and Palestine itself. As Arab anxiety about the size and energy of the Jewish community in Palestine became more acute, representatives of nearby states became involved in behalf of the Arab Palestinians and in their own behalf. These political moves, which helped to deepen the consciousness of Arab nationalism, were addressed both to the authorities within Palestine and to the League of Nations and the committees and commissions it established to grapple with the thorny conflict.

After a period of relatively slow growth during the twenties, Jewish immigration to Palestine increased rapidly after Hitler came to power. By the end of the thirties the Jewish population of Palestine had reached 30 percent. The anxiety and hostility of many Arabs became more intense. With the end of the Second World War most of the Jews who had survived the massacre wished to leave the charnel house of Central Europe. The larger part headed for Palestine, only to confront the desperate rigidity of British immigration policy, paralyzed by the competing pressures of compassion and fear. The yearning of the displaced Jews of Central Europe for Palestine was an irresistible force. So was the resistance of the Arabs to their coming. Attacks began on Jewish populations that had lived for many centuries in North Africa and the Near East. They, too, began the trek to Palestine.

Violence and counterviolence made Palestine nearly ungovernable. And these developments occurred at a time when Britain was liquidating its empire and the security positions it had established to protect its imperial communications. In 1947 Britain passed the Greek baton to the United States. At the same time, it gave up the mandate it had received from the League twenty-five years earlier and remitted Palestine to the United Nations.

Anglo-American and United Nations committees studied the

problem. Their deliberations were overwhelmed by passionate emotions—a sense of what had occurred in the German concentration camps, just beginning to sear the consciousness of the world, and a sense of fear that too large a flow of displaced persons into their own countries could produce socially dangerous counterreactions. The war had been won at immense cost. The Western nations were not yet confident that their societies were immune to the diseases that had raged so virulently in Germany, Italy, France, and Eastern Europe.

The result, combined with the enthusiasm that the Zionist ideal has always aroused in many Christian spirits, especially in Protestant communities, was the United Nations Partition Resolution of 1947. The Zionists supported that Resolution, which, despite its many inadequacies from their point of view, held out the vision of a Jewish state. For the Arabs the Resolution was a high-handed attempt by the United Nations to give away territory that did not belong to them but to the people who lived there. By the laws of natural justice, the Covenant, and the Charter, the Arabs argued, the people of Palestine, and they alone, had rights of self-determination that the General Assembly could not abrogate or ignore. With the end of the Mandate an inchoate Palestinian nation came into being. The fighting was internal to that "nation," and the United Nations should not, and legally could not, interfere.

But the world community, convened in the General Assembly, reached another conclusion. History had thrust jurisdiction upon the United Nations. There was the reality of the Mandate and of the Jewish community that had formed in Palestine under the protection of the League. And there was another reality as well—the prospect of war, if nothing was done, a prospect that affected the most important function and responsibility of the organization. It chose, therefore, to ordain a partition of the territory of the Mandate, and called for the establishment of separate Arab and Jewish states, joined in economic union, and of a separate regime for Jerusalem.

By another coincidence of world politics the Soviet Union was willing to join the United States in supporting the Resolution, which the Arabs had plainly said they would resist with force. The Soviet vote in the General Assembly and Soviet arms shipments to Israel reflected their policies of postwar expansion and their correlative interest in pushing Britain and France out of their strong points along the shores of the Mediterranean.

Thus Israel emerged into the society of nations—an active community that had become a state. Nominally, it was established by a decision of the United Nations, acting with regard to trust territories administered under its authority. In fact, like so many other nations, it was born in the travail of war—a war that those who voted for the Partition Resolution should have known was inevitable unless they acted, yet with shocking irresponsibility did nothing to prevent.

The war of 1948–49 resulted in armistice agreements between Israel and Egypt, Jordan, Syria, and Lebanon—the only political documents thus far negotiated and signed by those states. The armistice agreements were the product of conferences under United Nations auspices held at Rhodes in 1949. Those conferences, in turn, met because the Israelis made it clear that hostilities would be resumed unless the Arab nations, and above all Egypt, obeyed the Security Council's call that the parties agree on an armistice.

The war of 1948–49 had many other results, both in the Middle East and in world politics. The Arab refugee problem emerged—a burden, a curse, and a weapon of politics and of war. After Lausanne the Arab policy of not making peace with Israel crystallized and became a dogma, keeping alive the dream and hope of revenge. In turn, Israel became convinced that it was surrounded by neighbors committed to its destruction, and developed its defense capacities accordingly. With the defeat of British policy the United States became more involved, both out of sympathy for Israel and as part of the process of assuming Western leadership in the Cold War, which had already required it to act in Iran, Turkey, and Greece.

In 1956, once again, the processes of macropolitics dominated events in the Middle East. The Soviet Union had changed sides since 1947. And Nasser had come to power and started on an ambitious course of nationalist expansion incompatible with British or American policy. Understanding this fact, Nasser approached the Soviet Union well before the celebrated episodes of 1955—the Aswan Dam affair, the Israeli raid in the Gaza Strip, and the American refusal of arms to Egypt—which are popularly supposed to have led Nasser to seek Soviet support. In short, Nasser and the Soviet Union were indispensable to each other's plans of expansion, and their alliance was a matter of deliberate choice. With Soviet support, Nasser could resist Western advice or pressure. He nationalized the Suez Canal and closed the Strait of Tiran, thus blockading Israel from the south and outraging both France and Britain. France had another grievance against Egypt— Egyptian support for the rebels in Algeria in the tragic war that was straining the fabric of French life. After Nasser refused a French request to desist from his course, France resolved to act and turned to Israel as well as Britain. Thus the three states with acute grievances against Egypt came together in the ill-fated Suez campaign.

That event caused many changes in the politics of the Middle East and of the world. Britain and France fell back; the United States and the Soviet Union moved forward. Israel was perceived to be more formidable than many had realized before. With increasing emphasis, Nasser claimed the mantle of leadership in the cause of Pan-Arab unity, asserting his influence in many areas, and arousing fear and resentment as well as exaltation in the Arab world. Thus the divisions sharpened between the radical and the traditional Arab states, with momentous change ahead in Syria and Iraq, and later in other countries as well.

This quick sketch, intended only to evoke the past, recalls the main events and trends that frame the modern Middle Eastern crisis. That crisis is now the key factor in a much larger process of political struggle.

What is the crisis about? Is it a local or a regional quarrel that the United States, Europe, and Japan can safely ignore, or is it a matter of vital concern to their security?

III

The protracted conflict between Israel and some of her Arab neighbors is not the cause of the Middle Eastern crisis but its symptom and its consequence. The heart of the crisis is the process of Soviet penetration in North Africa and the Near East. Without Soviet influence, Soviet support, and Soviet arms, there would have been peace long ago between Israel and her neighbors. The Arab states would have had no alternative but to accept Israel's right to exist.

The first goal of the Soviet campaign is to achieve strategic and tactical control of the Mediterranean, the Middle East, and the Persian Gulf area. On that footing, the next step would be to drive the United States out of Europe and the Mediterranean, and to have NATO dismantled. The Middle Eastern crisis is a NATO crisis, not an Arab-Israeli quarrel. It is a fissure in the foundation of world politics—a Soviet challenge to the relationship of Western Europe and the United States, and therefore to the balance of power on which the possibility of general peace throughout the world depends.

The phrase "Middle East" is an anomaly. The Middle Eastern problem extends from Morocco to Iran and Pakistan; from Malta, Yugoslavia, Greece, and Turkey in the north, to Aden, Sudan, and beyond in the south. It is an area of major strategic importance—for its oil, its space, and its utility in transportation and communications among Europe, Asia, and Africa. Rome did not feel safe until Carthage was destroyed and Egypt conquered. Modern weapons and systems of communications, and the problem of nuclear surveillance, underline the strategic pertinence of those ancient events. Those concerned with the security of Europe have always been sensitive to the dangers of hostility from Middle Eastern positions. Even Japan is still dependent on Middle

250

Eastern oil, and therefore politically vulnerable to threats that its oil supply may be interrupted. All studies agree that Middle Eastern oil will be a factor of increasing importance to the economies of Europe, Japan and the United States for the indefinite future.

In the Middle East, as in other parts of the Third World, the dissolution of empire gave rise to a large number of weak and vulnerable states, struggling to master the techniques of modern wealth and social organization. The nations of the area vary widely in wealth, political outlook, and capacity for effective self-government. They are united by ties of culture and religion, by historic memories, and above all by pride in their Arab heritage and hostility to the colonial idea. They are divided by jealousies, and their rivalries are often tinged by violence. Some are monarchies, or traditional societies of an older kind; some, such as Iran, Turkey, Lebanon, and Tunisia, are progressive Western societies based on capitalism; others—Syria, Algeria, and perhaps Egypt and Libya as well—are radical communities governed by one or another sect of the cult of revolution, and controlled by a state apparatus that has driven older elites into exile. Almost all have military forces of increasing strength and influence, whose officers are trained either in Europe or America, or in the Soviet Union.

The most popular and inflammatory political conviction throughout the region is that the creation of Israel was an injustice to the Arabs; that Israel is the spearhead and agent of Western imperialism; and that sooner or later Israel will have to be destroyed. All must give lip service to this thesis; many believe it. In conversations with Middle Easterners one is often reminded that it took a hundred years or more to drive the Crusaders away. No Arab leader, however moderate, dares advise his people publicly that the creation of Israel has been ratified by history and that its existence is a fact of life Arabs ought to acknowledge.

As a result the Arab states have simply refused for more than twenty years any and all initiatives that might lead them to make peace with Israel. The closest they came to it was in the armistice agreements of 1949. Since 1950 or 1951, Arab policy—and especially Egyptian policy—has been, and remains, simply to refuse to make peace with Israel, relying—thus far successfully—on the political weight of their numbers and strategic position to induce the Western governments, in the end, to turn against Israel and force it to yield.

Hostility to Israel is the only political idea that can bring about Arab unity even for a short time. Even more important, it is a political force within every Arab community that can be used to arouse the masses, and weaken or destroy moderate regimes suspected of cooperating with the West—the defenders of Israel— and of being willing to make peace with Israel. Often the show of unity, even on this issue, is superficial. Many Arab leaders would gladly make peace with Israel. They realize that the idea of revenge against Israel is sterile and self-destructive, and that its true purpose is not the destruction of Israel, but the radicalization of Arab politics in Jordan, Lebanon, Tunisia, Saudi Arabia, and the Persian Gulf. But few can publicly oppose the dream of a Holy War when opinion is inflamed by the call to battle.

In its modern form the Russian interest in the Middle East was evident during the Second World War and has been an active and growing theme of Soviet policy since the war. In the Ribbentrop-Molotov meeting of 1940 Ribbentrop offered the Soviets the Persian Gulf area. Molotov put his finger in the middle of the map, on Egypt. "We want this too," he is reported to have said. The first postwar crises—the public warning bells of the Cold War— concerned Iran, and then Turkey and Greece. But Soviet policy reached far beyond the border states, even in the period of its exhaustion at the end of the war. The Soviet Union sought the mandate for what is now Libya in 1945. Then it cooperated with the United States in authorizing the establishment of the state of Israel and was an important arms supplier to Israel during the first war between Israel and Arabs in 1948–49. Starting in 1955, Soviet policy acquired new dimensions. The Soviet Union supplied arms, and, later, economic aid to Egypt on a large scale. In time this policy was extended to Syria, Iraq, the Sudan, Algeria, and the Yemen. And it led to the massive intrusion of Soviet experts—

both military and nonmilitary—into most of these countries and, at a later stage, to a direct Soviet naval and air presence at what are in effect permanent bases in the region.

One of the Soviet Union's chief weapons in this process has been the exploitation of Arab hostility to the existence of Israel as a catalyst of turbulence and of revolutionary feeling in Arab politics. There is no magic that could persuade the Arabs to give up their sense of grievance about the existence of Israel. At best, that bitter feeling will take many years to fade. It will not fade, but will become worse, if it continues to be used as an engine of radical take-over throughout the region, both by the Soviets and by their Chinese rivals.

Initially Soviet policy was simply to push at open doors in the Middle East, as in other parts of the world. In recent years, however, it has become a much more sustained and massive affair—a genuine campaign rather than a policy of taking advantage of opportunities at minimal cost. It is no longer a shadowy feint that could be reversed without embarrassment, but a major investment of resources and prestige involving the deliberate assumption of major risks.

The Soviet arms supply and other support to Egypt were the proximate cause of the 1956 war in the area; false Soviet intelligence, coupled with massive supplies of Soviet arms, played the same role in the tragedy of 1967.

Since 1955 the Soviets have skillfully used every occasion to create Arab dependency and to fortify Arab radicalism—through arms and aid; through technical assistance, especially in the military field; and through moral and political support in asserting the "injustice" of the creation of Israel and the "reactionary" and "Quisling" character of traditional or Western-oriented Arab regimes. The development of a pro-Soviet orientation in Arab opinion, despite Muslim religious antipathy to communism, was a great psychological achievement. It managed to encapsulate and indeed to bury the inconvenient facts that the Soviet Union had joined the United States in the fateful votes that launched the state of Israel, and that without Czech arms for Israel the war of

1948–49 might well have taken another course. George Kennan and other writers had assured Western opinion that there need be no Western concern about the possibility of Soviet expansion in the Middle East, because an Arab association with the Soviet Union was impossible for religious reasons.[3]

American policy in 1967 had the advantage of a comprehensive study of Western interests in the entire area against the background of Arab politics and Soviet activity. Ambassador Julius Holmes was recalled from retirement to direct the work. On the basis of that study, and the policy review it precipitated, Johnson concluded that the rising tide of Soviet penetration, and the trends in Arab politics that such penetration encouraged and fortified, threatened major American and Allied interests in the region; that the Soviet presence in Syria, Egypt, Algeria, Iraq, the Yemen, and the Sudan already constituted a substantial cloud on Allied interests; and that a continuation of the process, which could involve the Nasserization of Jordan, Lebanon, Libya, Tunisia, Malta, Morocco, Saudi Arabia, and the Persian Gulf, would present the United States and NATO with a security crisis of major and potentially catastrophic proportions. NATO military positions were being outflanked. Communications between Europe, Africa, and Asia were threatened. A disturbing Soviet fleet roamed the Mediterranean. Oil essential to the European (and Japanese) economies could be used as a lever of political coercion. And the specter of an all-out attack on Israel, with its implicit risk of general war, was becoming more and more possible, even likely. The process of Soviet penetration, and the phenomenon which the Soviets call "ultra-extremism" in Arab politics, were difficult to control or reverse, since penetration had rested thus far, save in the Yemen, not on international aggression, but seemingly on internal coups d'état and then on political steps taken by the Arab governments themselves.

In the light of that analysis, an Arab-Israeli war was perceived not as a local conflict, but as a stage in a process that threatened the security of Europe and the United States in fundamental

[3] *Memoirs, 1925–1950* (1967), pp. 317–318. See also, however, pp. 379–381.

ways. The policy conclusion that emerged was that the United States, in association with Great Britain and as many other nations as we could persuade to cooperate, should undertake a major effort to prevent the war, and after twenty years of waiting, to fulfill the urgings of the Security Council, and the promises of the armistice agreements of 1949, that the parties make peace. The protection of American and Allied interests—to say nothing of decency and the moral obligations that inhere in promises on which others have relied to their hazard—demanded nothing less. Only on that footing could one hope to contain or reverse other aspects of the process of Soviet expansion.

In the spring of 1967 the United States government began to treat the Middle East as a crisis situation. I was made chairman of an interdepartmental Control Group directed to propose policy on an urgent basis and to supervise its execution. The group met for many months in my office at all hours of the day and night. Cyrus Vance, the Deputy Secretary of Defense, and senior intelligence officers were key members, with Averell Harriman, Foy Kohler, Lucius Battle, and Joseph Sisco, my colleagues in the State Department. My executive assistant, Robert T. Grey, Jr., served as secretary for the Control Group. Walter Levy advised us on oil problems. We brought in others as we needed them, experts from the Treasury, AID, USIA, or the Department of Agriculture, depending on the agenda of the particular meeting.

On the basis of Control Group papers, reviewed in turn and approved by Rusk, McNamara, and Helms, the President met frequently with those men, Cyrus Vance, and myself, along with his own staff assistants—my brother Walt Rostow, and, while he functioned, his predecessor, McGeorge Bundy, who had been recalled to the White House secretariat for a few months during the height of the crisis in order to help cope with the burden of work. Sometimes others were asked to these meetings—the Vice-President, Henry Fowler, the Secretary of the Treasury, Katzenbach as Undersecretary of State, Battle or Sisco as the Assistant Secretaries most deeply involved.

As the crisis deepened, choices narrowed.

The atmosphere was envenomed by strange events. In May, Soviet representatives in the Middle East, including some of their senior diplomats, began to circulate rumors that Israel was mobilizing to invade Syria, by way of reprisal for acts of terrorism committed in Israel by men who had come from Syria, and indeed in many cases were members of the Syrian armed forces or were trained by them. There was no factual basis for these rumors. United Nations officials twice denied publicly that Israel was mobilizing against Syria, or indeed mobilizing at all. The United States government was convinced that no such mobilization was taking place. But the rumors spread like wildfire. Pointedly, we called these reports to the attention of the Soviet government. But they continued to circulate. The Jordanian radio and other Arab voices began to taunt Nasser for his failure to protect Syria. "You claim to be the Arabs' Big Brother," they shrilled, "but what are you doing to protect Syria from invasion?"

At this season the Soviet Foreign Minister, Gromyko, visited Cairo. Suddenly Nasser moved. An officer in the Sinai asked local United Nations officials to remove United Nations forces from the border between Israel and Egypt.

In responding, U Thant did not follow the scenario of Dag Hammarskjöld's memorandum, which everyone understood to be part of the understanding that settled the Suez crisis in 1957. Instead of consultations with the interested powers, and delay, as prescribed in the Hammarskjöld memorandum, Thant moved precipitately—and disastrously. He took the view that the United Nations forces could be removed only as a whole, and that they had to be removed at once if the nation on whose territory they were emplaced requested it. If Nasser wanted to clear the border between Sinai and Israel, he would have to ask for the removal of the troops himself, and at the governmental level, and to request the removal of the United Nations forces at Sharm-al-Sheikh and in the Gaza Strip as well as from the Sinai border.

Nasser met U Thant's terms at once. The British and American governments woke up to find that large contingents of the United

Nations forces had vanished—probably by prearrangement between Nasser and the governments involved. Despite vigorous
American and other protests, there was nothing to be done.
Humpty-Dumpty had fallen. Nasser immediately sent forces to
occupy Sharm-al-Sheikh and proclaimed that force would be used
to deny the Strait of Tiran to Israeli shipping.

There are many theories about Soviet motives in precipitating
this crisis.

One is that the Soviet government intended all that happened—
the war, the Egyptian defeat, the increased dependence of the
defeated Arabs on Soviet assistance, and a Soviet presence in the
area which gradually became imperial in its scope and reach.

A variant of this theory is even more malign. During the week
of the Six Day War a high Soviet official had a conversation with
a Western diplomat in Moscow. "What a disaster," he commented. "We thought Israel would be in trouble and the United
States would be drawn into a war against the whole Muslim
world. We thought it would be worse for America than Vietnam.
But we underestimated the Israelis and overestimated the Egyptians. And the United States says it is neutral. What a disaster."

What an idea.

A second theory hypothesizes that the Soviet Union assumed
that U Thant would follow Hammarskjöld's procedure. During
the period of delay the Western powers would press frantically to
head off a war and persuade Israel to acquiesce in concessions that
would amount to a political triumph for Nasser and for the Soviet
influence behind him—submitting the international character of
the Strait of Tiran to the International Court of Justice, for example. The Soviets could then claim, as they did after Suez and on
other occasions in recent Middle Eastern politics, that a Soviet
threat had obtained satisfaction for the Arabs that could have
been obtained in no other way. And they could do so in perfect
safety, because they were confident that the Hammarskjöld procedure would be followed and that their bluff would not be
called.

A third theory rests on Mrs. Murphy's celebrated law—if anything can go wrong, it will. As usual, it seems the most convincing.

When Nasser closed the Strait of Tiran, in May, there were only two courses open to the United States and its allies—to allow the war to explode or to take responsibility for opening the Strait of Tiran by escorting merchant vessels headed for Israel through the strait, past the gun emplacements at Sharm-al-Sheikh. If nothing was done, Nasser's decision to close the strait made war inevitable, in the light of the agreements of 1957 which resolved the Suez crisis. The trial of Egyptian Field Marshal Amer, and other sources, make it clear that Nasser was aware of this fact. Indeed, he was probably counting on it as a lever to induce the great powers to squeeze a political victory out of Israel for him without a war.

The critical character of the problem reflects both the inherent importance of the area to Israel and the history of the struggle to establish Israel's right to exist.

Sharm-al-Sheikh controls access through the Strait of Tiran to the Israeli port of Eilat on the Gulf of Aqaba. The strait is narrow. It connects the Red Sea to the Gulf of Aqaba. The gulf had always been regarded as international waters—part of the high seas. But in recent years states all over the world have been claiming larger and larger areas as "territorial waters." Four states border the Gulf of Aqaba—Jordan, Israel, Egypt, and Saudi Arabia. If they were conceded the right to claim territorial jurisdiction as extensive as that claimed by a number of other states, the Gulf of Aqaba would consist only of territorial waters and cease to be international in character.

The dispute concerned international law and the maritime nations, directly and fundamentally. The Strait of Tiran is by no means the only narrow strait in the world connecting parts of the high seas. The 1958 Convention on the Law of the Sea had reiterated the classical doctrine that such a strait was an international waterway, but several nations, including Egypt, had abstained from voting or objected. And there was doubt as to the decision the Court at the Hague might reach in view of the character of the controversy and changes taking place in the pattern of international practice.

Furthermore, since Egypt had kept the Suez Canal closed to Israeli shipping despite two Security Council resolutions, the Strait of Tiran was Israel's only direct route to East Africa and Asia, and its most important source of oil. Closing the strait was in effect an act of blockade.

Egypt's announcement that it would use force to close the strait had another set of consequences. In 1957, in deference to Arab sensitivity about seeming publicly to "recognize" Israel, to "negotiate" with Israel, or to make "peace" with Israel, the United States took the lead in negotiating an understanding between Israel and Egypt, on the basis of which Israel withdrew its forces from the Sinai. The terms of the understanding were spelled out in a carefully planned series of statements made by the governments both in their capitals and before the General Assembly and in supplemental letters, aide-mémoires, silences (in the presence of statements by others), and other classical diplomatic devices.

The understanding consisted of a number of elements. Israel withdrew from the Sinai, and United Nations forces were placed along the border, in the Gaza Strip, and at Sharm-al-Sheikh. Dag Hammarskjöld wrote a famous memorandum summarizing his conversations with the chief nations involved. That memorandum laid down the procedures of consultation and delay to be followed should Egypt ever request the withdrawal of the United Nations forces. The Suez Canal and the Strait of Tiran were to be open to Israeli shipping. The United States, France, and Great Britain guaranteed the international character of the Strait of Tiran —a pledge de Gaulle repudiated in 1967. In due course, it was understood, Egypt would make peace.

In 1957 Israel made it clear that if force were used to close the strait, it would regard itself as justified in responding with force, as an act of self-defense authorized under Article 51 of the United Nations Charter. The British, French, and American guarantees all supported this position. No nation opposed it.

The United Arab Republic, it is true, never took formal public responsibility for this understanding, as it refused to recognize Israel or to deal directly with her. But in every other sense Egypt was a party to and beneficiary of this arrangement, through which Israeli withdrawals had been secured. But the Egyptian commitments of the period were broken one by one, the last being the request for the removal of the United Nations forces, and the closing of the Strait of Tiran to Israeli shipping in May 1967. That step, it was clear from the international understandings of 1957, justified Israeli military action as self-defense against an act of hostility deemed by the world community to come within the scope of Article 51.

As Johnson remarked in May 1967, "If any single act of folly was more responsible for this explosion than any other, I think it was the arbitrary and dangerous announced decision that the Strait of Tiran would be closed." While the Soviet Union coldly supported Nasser in every forum, it was reticent, as a maritime power, to defend—or even to discuss—the legality of his action in closing the Strait of Tiran.

Shortly after the Strait of Tiran was closed in May we advised the President that he had to choose between two lines of action: to allow war to break out, because war was inevitable, in the matrix of history, unless we moved effectively to prevent it; or to join with as many other nations as possible in fulfillment of Eisenhower's commitment, by deploying a naval and air force to convoy vessels through the Strait of Tiran. We had reason to suppose that such convoy operations would not be opposed. But the risk had to be faced that hostilities might develop.

Johnson chose the option of action—a decision with immense implications in view of the controversy over Vietnam then raging in the country. And his instructions set into motion a program of diplomatic action, of Congressional consultation, and of military planning and preparation, which was pursued with the utmost urgency. Johnson received assurances of Eisenhower's full support in the effort. The pledge, Eisenhower said, was a debt of honor for the United States.

The United States, Great Britain, the Netherlands, Italy, Canada, Denmark, and a number of other states sought to head off imminent war with all the speed they could muster. They pressed the Security Council for a resolution that would have called on the U.A.R. to keep the strait open. France's refusal to support this resolution—a signal of French Middle Eastern policy well before the Six Day War[4]—meant that the issue could not be forced to a vote to test the Soviet's willingness to exercise its right of veto. A statement of the maritime powers was prepared reaffirming the international character of the strait. Talks with the United Arab Republic and other Arab states were urgently pursued in quest of an understanding that would have restored the situation. And against the contingency that these political efforts might fail, the United States, Great Britain, Australia, the Netherlands, and some other countries began to prepare an Allied naval operation to keep the strait open and thus defuse the crisis.

The idea of an Allied naval escort plan to carry out the guarantees of 1957 was first broached by George Brown, the British Foreign Minister at the time, a man of vision whose foibles and eccentricities, extraordinary as they are, are more than outweighed by his good sense and courage. Brown's idea received strong support in many parts of the American government. Both Johnson and Rusk were convinced and vigorous advocates. Abba Eban came to Washington at the end of May to discuss the proposal, and the Israeli Cabinet accepted his recommendation that Johnson have a little more time to complete his political and military preparations for putting the plan into effect.

At the same time, the United States was engaged in active discussions with the United Arab Republic, including direct exchanges between Johnson and Nasser. The Six Day War broke

[4] It is frequently asserted that France turned against Israel because in President De Gaulle's view that country did not follow his advice "not to fire the first shot."

out on Monday morning. On the preceding Saturday Egypt announced publicly that it had accepted an American suggestion and that on the following Wednesday the Vice-President of the Republic, Zechariah Moheiddin, would go to Washington for talks about the crisis.

While these approaches and others were being urgently pursued, events took over. Mobilization and countermobilization pushed the closing of the Strait to the periphery of things. Algerian and Iraqi troops moved into the menacing circle around Israel. Jordan's armed forces were placed under Egyptian command. The cry of Holy War was sounded. Meanwhile the planning and political preparations for the Allied naval action proceeded. But the risks of further delay grew more and more ominous. The explosion occurred before the naval escort plan could be put into operation.

The three weeks before June 5, 1967, is a perfect theme for the study of war as a psychosocial phenomenon. Step by step, and with increasing menace, Nasser acted and spoke like a man intending and preparing to make war. His words and conduct aroused primal fear, in Israel and elsewhere. He said he was about to launch the final battle and destroy Israel. And his actions were consistent with his public words, although Egyptian offensive dispositions in the desert were not quite complete when the Six Day War began. Diplomatically, Nasser said that while he was willing to listen to proposals for peace, fate was in the hands of Allah.

The air was full of emissaries and reports. The atmosphere became highly charged. Misunderstandings and misperceptions—normal to crises, and hideously dangerous—occurred, and some were not discovered until much later.

As intelligence alarms about imminent hostilities became more frequent, there were exchanges with the Soviets, the Israelis, and the Egyptians on the subject, heavy and foreboding on the Soviet side, feverish and immensely tense with Israel and Egypt. Johnson and Rusk pressed like demons to keep Egypt and Israel from firing the first shot, and to put the naval escort plan into operation. We recalled Guy Mollet's grim joke about Suez: "The British planned as if we were getting ready to invade Normandy. If they had only let me send in a couple of battalions of the Foreign Legion on tramp steamers, we could have finished the job in a few days." But we were talking about a naval demonstration in support of our diplomacy—an escort operation that might have involved American vessels and aircraft in hostilities in an area where a Soviet presence and a Soviet commitment were realities. We had reason to believe that Egypt would not have fired on the American flag, and that large parts of the Egyptian government would have been immensely relieved by such action as a face-saving excuse not to go to war. But what if our information proved to be wrong?

The President's inherent authority to take such steps as necessary to the conduct of foreign relations was confirmed in this case by Congress' Middle Eastern Resolution of 1957, which had been reaffirmed in 1961. And the leadership of both houses of the Congress, and of both parties, was briefed and consulted. Because of the intensity of the debate in Congress and the country over the constitutional foundation for the war in Vietnam, however, the President preferred to reinforce the policy of Eisenhower's Middle Eastern Resolution with a new resolution, specifically authorizing the use of force if the President found it necessary to protect the national interest and carry out the commitments of past Presidents in the situation that had emerged.

It may well be that the United States was prevented from acting in time to head off the Six Day War by the hesitations and delays implicit in this consequence of the Vietnam debate in the Senate and in the country. The decision to obtain a new Congressional resolution despite the clarity of the old one required time, and prevented immediate action in a situation that would not wait on the tensions of our politics; perhaps, of course, the crisis was addressed to those tensions, so far as the Soviets and the Egyptians were concerned. Never was the wisdom of the founding fathers more evident to me in their policy of giving the President wide latitude in the conduct of foreign affairs. I believe that my worst mistake at the time, for which I have the deepest regret, was in not fighting this decision even harder than I did.

It is often said that the Six Day War was an accident. That is not true. It resulted from Soviet and Egyptian miscalculation, which is quite a different matter. Those nations sought certain goals, possibly—probably—without war, but most definitely through the threat of war. Their goals were incompatible with peace, to say nothing of their obligations under the Charter.

Unfortunately, both the intelligence and the politics of the situation made Nasser's threats credible. To Nasser, and to the Soviets, the existence and independence of Israel had become more than an ideological offense, and the embodiment of what Arabs regarded as a historic injustice. Geographically and politically Israel blocked Nasser's ambition to consolidate the Arab states into a Pan-Arab union—a political entity that would be far more than a league or a consultative body. With Israel in his path he could not effectively coerce Syria, Jordan, Iraq, and Saudi Arabia, and seize the fabulous wealth of the Persian Gulf. His Yemen adventure had failed. He had to weaken or destroy Israel, or give up the Pan-Arab dreams which had become his central passion.

As the trial of Field Marshal Amer made clear, Nasser had carefully prepared his move in 1967. Politically and legally Egypt was ready to challenge the international character of the Strait of Tiran and to use that issue as a first step in forcing an Israeli retreat—a retreat that would have the effect, inevitably, of weakening the link between Israel and Iran. Militarily Egypt's effectives and their equipment were far more numerous than those of Israel.

On the first day of the fighting in 1967 President Johnson announced that American policy was to move not only for an end of hostilities but for a beginning to peace. The Arab-Israeli conflict, he said two weeks later, had become a burden and a threat to world peace. The time had come to bring it to a definitive end.

This position, different from the American posture in 1956–57, has been decisive to the diplomacy of the subsequent period. In the Middle East the word "peace" is not a cliché, but the essence of a far-reaching policy—that of requiring Israel's neighbors to give up all claim of a right to make war against her, and finally to accept Israel's right to exist.

When hostilities erupted on June 5, 1967, the Soviet Union blocked American cease-fire proposals for several days until it realized what was happening in the field. Then, when the cease-fire resolutions were finally in place, a major diplomatic campaign, extending around the world, was brought into focus, first in the Security Council, then in the General Assembly, then at Glassboro, and finally back in the Security Council.

Johnson's style in diplomacy is illustrated by many facets of the handling of this tense and explosive situation. In conciliatory talks with Arab, Israeli, European, and Soviet representatives, he stressed, over and over again, that the position at Sharm-el-Sheikh had to be "what it was"; that the United States was unalterably opposed to the use of force; and that it would be "true to its word"—that our commitments stood. With all the formidable force of his personality, he pressed for peace.

His decision not to attend the special meeting of the General Assembly during June, 1967, was characteristic of his method. Over our opposition, the Soviets had suddenly shifted the Middle East debate from the Security Council to the General Assembly, and let it be known that Kosygin was coming. Johnson was urged by all hands to go as well, "to demonstrate our respect for the United Nations."

After thinking it over, he decided not to go. We had opposed the General Assembly debate as premature, to say the least, since the Security Council had not exhausted its capacity for action. If he did go, the President remarked, Wilson and de Gaulle would surely come also, and there would be no way to avoid a Four Power meeting, at which de Gaulle would support the Russians, Wilson would be of divided mind, and he would be alone. "I'll stay here," he said, "and make a speech on Monday, before the Assembly opens. And see to it," he added, "that only Eban answers Kosygin in the General Assembly. He can take care of himself. It will be David against Goliath."

And so it was arranged. On June 19, 1967, an astonished convention of school teachers heard the President make a major speech, in which American policy toward the Middle East was decisively outlined. And Eban, one of the great orators of the time, responded to Kosygin in New York.

On November 22, 1967, the Security Council passed a unanimous resolution calling on the parties to reach an agreement that would definitely settle the Arab-Israeli controversy and establish conditions of just and lasting peace in the area. That resolution was achieved after more than five months of intensive diplomatic effort on the part of the United States, Great Britain, Denmark, Canada, Italy, and a number of other countries. The history of that effort gives the text an extremely "plain meaning."

A number of positions emerged. Their interplay, and the resolution of that interplay, are reflected in the document.

The Soviet Union and its chief Arab associates wished to have Israel declared the aggressor and required under Chapter VII of the Charter—that is, under threat of sanctions—to withdraw to the armistice demarcation lines as they stood on June 5, in exchange for the fewest possible assurances: that after withdrawal, Israeli maritime rights in the Strait of Tiran would be "no problem" (sometimes the same thought was expressed about the Suez Canal as well); and that after Israeli withdrawal, the possibility could be discussed of a document that might be filed with the Secretary General, or a Security Council resolution, that would finally end any possibility of claiming that a "state of belligerency" existed between Israel and her neighbors. This position was asserted without regard to the fact that the Security Council had twice explicitly denied that any state could claim "belligerent" status or "belligerent" rights in the Middle Eastern conflict.

The Israeli position had four major elements. In the Israeli view the Arab governments had repudiated the armistice agreements of 1949 by going to war. They believed that the parties should meet alone and draw up a treaty of peace. So far as territorial problems were concerned, they contended that negotiations should begin, not with the armistice demarcation lines, but with the 1967 cease-fire lines. Until negotiations actually began, Israel should not weaken its bargaining position by publicly revealing its peace aims, although the Prime Minister and the Foreign Minister did state publicly and officially that Israel had no territorial claims as such, but was interested in the territorial problem only insofar as issues of security and maritime rights, and, of course, the problem of Jerusalem were concerned. Meanwhile Israel began its administration of Jerusalem, the West Bank, the Golan Heights, the Gaza Strip, and Sinai as the occupying power under the cease-fire resolutions, justifying its policies "at the municipal level," and without annexations, in the perspective of that branch of international law.

The United States, Canada, most of the Western European and Latin American nations, and a large number of nations from other parts of the world supported a different approach, which ultimately prevailed.

In view of the taut circumstances of May and June 1967, no majority could be obtained, either in the Security Council or the General Assembly, to declare Israel the aggressor. The question of who fired the first shot, difficult enough to resolve in itself, had to be examined as part of a sequence of Byzantine complexity: the false reports of Israeli mobilization against Syria; the removal of U.N.E.F. forces from the Sinai and the Gaza Strip; the closing of the Strait of Tiran; the mobilization of Arab forces around Israel, and the establishment of a unified command; and the cycle of statements, propaganda, speeches, and diplomatic efforts that marked the final weeks before June 5. Before that mystery, sober opinion refused to reach the conclusion that Israel was the aggressor. In view of the political orientation of the United Nations, no serious attempt was made to obtain a resolution declaring the United Arab Republic to be the aggressor.

Second, the majority opinion both in the General Assembly and in the Security Council supported the American view, first announced on June 5, 1967, and stated more fully on June 19, 1967, that after twenty bitter and tragic years of "war," "belligerency," and guerrilla activity in the Middle East, the quarrel had become a burden to world peace, and that the world community should finally insist on the establishment of a condition of peace, flowing from the agreement of the parties.

Third, the experience of the international community with the understandings that ended the Suez crisis of 1956–57 led to the conclusion that Israel should not be required to withdraw from the cease-fire lines, except as part of a firm prior agreement dealing with all the major issues in the controversy: justice for the refugees; guarantees of security for Israel's border and for her maritime rights in the Gulf of Aqaba and the Suez Canal; a solution for Jerusalem that met the legitimate interests of Jordan and of Israel and of the three world religions that regard Jerusalem as a Holy City; and the establishment of a condition of peace.

Fourth, while the majority approach always linked Israeli withdrawal to the establishment of a condition of peace through an agreement among the parties, the question remained, "To what boundaries should Israel withdraw?" On this issue the American position was sharply drawn, and rested on a critical provision of the armistice agreements of 1949 with Egypt, Syria, and Jordan. Those agreements provided that the demarcation line "is not to be construed in any sense as a political or territorial boundary, and is delineated without prejudice to rights, claims or positions of either Party to the Armistice as regards ultimate settlement of the Palestine question." The wording of the armistice agreement with Lebanon is slightly different, although its tenor is the same. Many other provisions of each agreement make it clear that the purpose of the armistice was "to facilitate the transition from the present truce to permanent peace in Palestine," and that all nonmilitary "rights, claims, or interests" were subject to later settlement as part of the transition from armistice to peace. These paragraphs, which were put into the agreements at Arab insistence, were the legal foundation for the controversies over the wording of paragraphs 1 and 3 of Security Council Resolution 242 of November 22, 1967.

That resolution, promulgated under Chapter VI of the Charter —that is to say, as a call for an agreement of peace—finally received the unanimous support of the Council. It was backed in advance by the assurance of the key countries that they would accept the resolution and work with Ambassador Gunnar Jarring to implement it.

It is important to recall what the resolution requires. It calls upon the parties to reach "a peaceful and accepted" agreement that would definitively settle the Arab-Israeli controversy and establish conditions of "just and lasting peace" in the area, in accordance with the "provisions and principles" stated in the resolution. The agreement required by paragraph 3 of the resolution, the Security Council said, should establish "secure and recognized boundaries" between Israel and its neighbors, "free from threats or acts of force," to replace the armistice demarcation lines established in 1949 and the cease-fire lines of June 1967. The Israeli armed forces should withdraw to such lines as part of a comprehensive agreement settling all the issues mentioned in the resolution, and in a condition of peace.

On this point the American position has been the same under both the Johnson and the Nixon administrations. The new and definitive political boundaries should not represent "the weight of conquest," both administrations have said; on the other hand, under the policy and language of the armistice agreements of 1949 and of the Security Council Resolution of November 22, 1967, they need not be the same as the armistice demarcation lines. The walls and machine guns that divided Jerusalem need not be restored. And adjustments can be made by agreement, under paragraph 2 of the Security Council Resolution, to guarantee maritime rights "through international waterways in the area," and equally, to guarantee "the territorial inviolability and political independence of every State in the area, through measures including the establishment of demilitarized zones."

This is the legal significance of the omission of the word "the" from paragraph 1 of the resolution, which calls for the withdrawal of Israeli armed forces "from territories occupied in the recent conflict," and not "from *the* territories occupied in the recent conflict." Repeated attempts to amend this sentence by inserting the word "the," or equivalent language, failed in the Security Council. It is not legally possible, therefore, to assert that the provision requires Israeli withdrawal from *all* the territories occupied under the cease-fire resolutions to the armistice demarcation lines. In the fall of 1968, Soviet ambassadors both in Washington and at the United Nations indicated that this view of the resolution was acceptable, and that they could agree to "insubstantial" modifications of the Armistice Lines of 1949 as part of a "package deal" leading to peace. The next day, their commitment was withdrawn.

This aspect of the relationship between the Security Council Resolution of November 22, 1967, and the armistice agreements of 1949 likewise explains the reference in the resolution to the rather murky principle of "the inadmissibility of the acquisition of territory by war." The murkiness of the idea, stated abstractly —as was the case in the resolution—arises from its failure to distinguish between territorial changes brought about by hostilities that violate Section 2(4) of the Charter and those that are justified under Article 51. Moreover, the principle is difficult to reconcile with the practice, which has almost become a rule, of basing cease-fire and armistice lines on the actual position of troops after hostilities, and then having these lines become actual political boundaries, occasionally with small modifications. This was the case in the Middle East, in Indochina, in Korea, and in Central Europe. Whatever the full implications of the idea might be as applied to the Middle Eastern situation in 1967, it would necessarily permit the territorial adjustments and special security provisions expressly called for by the Security Council Resolution of 1967 and the armistice agreements of 1949.

The resolution provided that the Secretary General should appoint a representative to consult with the parties and assist them in reaching the agreement required by paragraph 3 of the resolution.

The prolonged controversy about who has "accepted" the resolution is worth noting, for it sheds light on the intentions of the parties. It was never a real issue, since the key parties to the hostilities had given advance assurance that they would cooperate with the Secretary General's representative to promote the agreement called for by the resolution. Shortly after Ambassador Jarring had begun his consultations in the area, however, the question emerged in the form of Arab insistence that Israel indicate its "acceptance" or its "implementation" of the resolution before discussions could proceed. One version of these proposals would be that Israel withdraw to the armistice demarcation lines as they stood on June 4, 1967, in advance of negotiations on any other problem of the resolution. This position violates the text of the resolution and recalls the experience of broken promises the text reflects. It is, however, the interpretation of the resolution from which Egypt has not yet publicly budged.

Throughout 1967 and 1968 Ambassador Jarring and the representatives of many governments sought to persuade Nasser to enter into negotiations or discussions that might result in progress toward agreement under the resolution. Given the theory of the resolution, it is impossible for the parties to take serious negotiating positions on "secure and recognized boundaries" before they grapple with security arrangements and guarantees of maritime rights. The problem of borders would look altogether different to Israel, manifestly, if it was clear that the Sinai and the West Bank were to be completely demilitarized. And other problems under the resolution—that of refugees, for example, and the consequences of a state of peace—require negotiation and agreement, not simply formal compliance with the resolution.

But thus far each initiative has had the same outcome: in the end the United Arab Republic has simply balked, in the pattern of Egyptian policy since Lausanne, on the problems of making a definitive peace with Israel.

A good deal of the early diplomatic history of the problem is reported in Foreign Minister Eban's comprehensive speech to the General Assembly on October 8, 1968. The Israeli position is summarized in the statement of May 1, 1968, made to the Security Council by the Israeli Permanent Representative to the United Nations.

In declarations and statements made publicly and to Mr. Jarring, my Government has indicated its acceptance of the Security Council resolution for the promotion of agreement on the establishment of a just and lasting peace. I am also authorized to reaffirm that we are willing to seek agreement with each Arab State on all matters included in that resolution.

On May 31, 1968, Foreign Minister Eban reiterated this statement in the Israeli Parliament.

Corresponding statements have been made publicly and privately by other parties to the conflict, but without specific reference to the requirement of "agreement" in paragraph 3 of the resolution.

There is great skepticism among the parties, a skepticism altogether natural against the background of more than twenty years of history. The Arabs fear that Israel has no intention of withdrawing, even to secure and recognized boundaries; Israel fears that the Arabs have no intention of making peace. Many Israelis perceive the Arabs, and especially Egypt, as determined to destroy them, with Soviet help. Many Arabs perceive the Israelis as committed to a policy of indefinite expansion.

But Israel has said repeatedly and officially that it has no territorial claims as such; that its sole interest in the territorial problem is to assure its security and to obtain viable guarantees of its maritime rights; and that even on the difficult issue of Jerusalem it is willing "to stretch its imagination" in the interest of accommodating Jordanian and international interests in the Holy City.

These assurances by Israel have been the foundation and the predicate of the American position in the long months since June 1967. If the Arabs are skeptical of Israeli professions, their remedy is obvious; put them to the test of negotiation. They could be sure, as Prime Minister Golda Meir remarked in 1970, that the position of the United States in the negotiating process would come more than halfway to meet their claims.

To this point, however, it has proved impossible to initiate the final stages of the processes of consultation and negotiation that are necessary to the fulfillment of the resolution. The reasons for the stalemate are obvious, but rarely stated in public. The basic obstacle to peace has been the continuation and intensification of terrorist activities, supported or condoned by Arab governments, and the policy embodied in the Khartoum formula approved by the Arab states in 1967: "No peace, no recognition, no negotiations." The principal tactical responsibility for the absence of peace is the policy of the government of the United Arab Republic. It has said it is ready to carry out the Security Council Resolution "as a package deal" in all its parts. But until the summer of 1970, at least, it refused to say it was willing to implement the provision of the resolution requiring it to make an agreement establishing peace. President Sadat did then take the important step of stating his willingness to sign an agreement of peace with Israel. But as these lines are written, in the spring of 1972, Egypt still rejects procedures of consultation and negotiation accepted by other parties to the dispute, as a way of achieving the agreement required by the resolution. And in words and in military actions it still proclaims the view that the Security Council Resolution requires Israel to withdraw to the lines of June 4, 1967, before it undertakes even the vaguest and most impalpable of countersteps.

In short, the government of the Arab Republic of Egypt has simply refused to implement the resolution. It is backed in that posture by the Soviet Union, prodigious supplies of arms, and some 20,000 Soviet military "advisers." Egypt could not have persisted in this stand for long against the will of the Soviet Union. Under these circumstances, given the nature of Arab opinion, no other party to the conflict could move toward peace.

In this connection, Secretary of State William P. Rogers' comment in January 1970 is illuminating. He stated:

> We have never suggested any withdrawal until there was a final, binding, written agreement that satisfied all aspects of the Security Council resolution.
>
> In other words, we have never suggested that a withdrawal occur before there was a contractual agreement entered into by the parties, signed by the parties in each other's presence, an agreement that would provide full assurances to Israel that the Arabs would admit that Israel had a right to exist in peace.

Now that is what has been lacking in the past. The Arabs have never been willing to do that; and if that could be done, we think it would be a tremendous boon to the world.

Now, we have also provided that the security arrangements would be left to the parties to negotiate, such as Sharm-el-Shaykh, and the Gaza Strip, the demilitarized zone, and so forth.[5]

It is easy to understand the Soviet position, and that of Egypt, in terms of a policy of political and military expansion that threatens not only Israel but Syria, Jordan, Lebanon, Iraq, Saudi Arabia, and the states of the Persian Gulf. They have gained positions and aroused forces that seem for the moment to enhance their influence and diminish that of their rivals. Arab raids and Israeli reprisals have generated an atmosphere of turbulence and of violence that is dissolving many sectors of Arab society and bringing more and more extremists to power.

It is not, however, a posture easy to reconcile with the terms and purposes of the Security Council Resolution of November 22, 1967, or with their professed willingness to see peace come to the area.

The absence of peace strengthened Egypt's position and that of the Soviet Union. New and more radical regimes have taken over in Libya and the Sudan. The government and society of Lebanon and of Jordan are weakened by the pressures of anti-Israeli feeling and the guerrilla movements that have flourished as a result.

In April 1969 the Egyptian position moved far beyond a passive refusal to implement the Security Council Resolution of November 22, 1967. At that time President Nasser denounced the cease-fire proclaimed by the Security Council in June 1967—a cease-fire that Nasser had of course accepted at the time and agreed to respect until peace was made. It was that cease-fire that stopped the remorseless surge of the Israeli armed forces in June 1967. But in 1969 Nasser proclaimed a "war of attrition" against Israel and tried to carry it out.

Inexplicably, the United States and its allies did nothing. They did not even summon the Security Council into emergency ses-

[5] 62 State Department Bulletin, 1970, pp. 218–219.

sion to call on the parties to respect the cease-fire and meet in a conference to carry out the peacemaking resolution of November 22, 1967. Nor did they concentrate their fleets in the Eastern Mediterranean and put mobile reserves on the alert in Germany, in Malta, and in Libya, where the United States and Great Britain still had bases.

The paralysis of American and Allied policy at this point strengthened the impression that the American government was controlled by a small group of isolationist senators, and that the United States would do nothing to resist the destruction of Israel and Soviet domination of the entire Middle East. From such impressions fatal miscalculations grow.

Israel, of course, reacted to Egypt's renewal of open warfare in 1969. In a devastating series of raids she asserted supremacy in the Egyptian air space and inflicted heavy casualties on the Egyptian armed forces. The Soviet Union had already arranged to assign Soviet pilots to combat roles in Egypt and to supply Egypt with more and more sophisticated antiaircraft missiles, while rejecting all efforts to restore the cease-fire of 1967. Meanwhile the Arab guerrillas, especially those influenced by China, sought to prevent peace, to destroy the regimes in Jordan and in Lebanon, and indeed to precipitate general war.

Nonetheless, in the summer of 1970 Secretary of State Rogers obtained Soviet and Egyptian assent to the renewal of Ambassador Jarring's mission, in the setting of a cease-fire and stand-still agreement for at least ninety days. The formula for a negotiating procedure accepted by Nasser in 1970 was considerably stiffer, in terms of the vocabulary of Arab politics, than one he had refused in the spring of 1968. According to Jarring's report to U Thant of August 7, 1970, that formula pledged the parties to join in "discussions to be held under my auspices, according to such procedure and at such places and times as I may recommend, taking into account as appropriate each side's preference as to methods of procedure and previous experience between the parties." [6] The formula that Egypt rejected in 1968 contemplated only a "confer-

[6] *New York Times*, August 8, 1970, p. 2, col. 8.

ence," without specifying its modalities or giving Jarring the last word on its format. Nonetheless, for reasons that have not been revealed, Jarring has not yet used his apparent power under this formula to convene a conference of the parties.

Why did the Soviet Union and Egypt decide to accept the American proposals, even nominally, in 1970? Military events, Chinese pressures, and Egyptian second thoughts about the risks of complete Soviet control in their country all must have played a part in the decision. The war of attrition had been a disaster for Egypt. But concern about American intervention must have been decisive. While the introduction of Soviet pilots and missiles improved the Egyptian military position somewhat, the event had aroused President Nixon, Congress, and American public opinion. Senators who opposed the President on Vietnam publicly urged him to take a strong stand in the Middle East and pledged their support for such a policy. And President Nixon issued warnings whose credibility was enhanced by his successful actions in Cambodia.

At a minimum, Soviet uncertainty about the future course of American policy indicated a cooling-off period.

But should one assume that there is no more to Soviet policy than a cynical zig or zag? Objectively, one should judge the conjuncture of events in the summer and late fall of 1970 and the winter of 1970–71 to be more favorable to the possibility of peace than has been the case for a long time.

The death of President Nasser, and the outcome of the explosion in Jordan in the fall of 1970, strengthened the chance for peace. President Sadat cannot hope to claim President Nasser's Pan-Arab prestige for a long time, and he should be more cautious and more concerned with internal problems than his predecessor. The king's position in Jordan is stronger than it has ever been. He has demonstrated that both the military and the political strength of the guerrillas was exaggerated. As for Syria and Iraq, both countries were suddenly required to confront military realities. There has been a noticeable shift in the temper of Arab politics since the fall of 1970, despite the steady military buildups along the Canal. The withdrawal of Iraqi troops from Jordan is perhaps the most significant and most hopeful straw in the wind since 1967.

Soviet policy, of course, remains the key to peace in the Middle East as it is in so many other areas. In many ways, it is still an enigma—threatening, but not foolhardy; ominous, but shot through with hints of promise as well. In both my tours of duty in the State Department, and in my United Nations experience, I was a conspicuous and even notorious practitioner of the doctrine that we must at all costs maintain continuous contact with the Soviet Union and pursue every opportunity to reach fair agreements with her. During my service in the Johnson Administration, I was an energetic exponent of this diplomacy for European questions, for Vietnam, and for the Middle East.

The United States has no alternative but to follow this course. The greatest danger in such diplomatic approaches, however, is self-deception. Many Americans, carried away by optimism, are prone to assume that the Soviets really seek the same goals we want to achieve. Hundreds of hours of amiable conversation with Soviet diplomats during all three of my adventures in the bureaucracy convincingly demonstrate the contrary. The worst errors of our policy, in my experience, stem from the exuberance of wishful thinking. The American mind longs to see the Soviet Union as a friend, and resists the conclusion that Soviet policy is what it is —a strong and ambitious force for expansion, but also a cautious one, which can be deterred only by the calm (and preferably secret) confrontation of unacceptable risks, always accompanied by the offer of fair and moderate alternatives, sensitive to the Soviet Union's legitimate preoccupations.

In the Middle East, unfortunately, the Soviet Union has thus far rejected every offer for a peaceful settlement of the Arab-Israeli dispute, although, after Glassboro, it did join in the vote for the Security Council Resolution of November 22, 1967, and it has thus far held back from the course of unlimited proxy war. The goals it is pursuing in the area profoundly threaten basic— indeed vital—American and NATO interests. It is illusion to suppose that they will be modified or abandoned without the deployment of credible military deterrence, or basic changes in other aspects of the situation.

IV

The details of a peaceful settlement between Israel and her neighbors have been exhaustively canvassed. There is no mystery about them. With a will for peace, they should be easy to resolve.

So far as Egypt is concerned, the problem of peace is simplicity itself. Egypt has no claim to the Gaza Strip, which it occupied as a result of the fighting twenty years ago. Israel has no substantial historic claim to the Sinai peninsula, although Egyptian title has some historic ambiguities. Israel does have a claim, under the Security Council Resolution of November 22, 1967, to arrangements that would "guarantee" Israel's right of passage through the Suez Canal and the Strait of Tiran. And it has a claim, under the same resolution, to security arrangements, including demilitarized zones, which would assure the safety of the "secure and recognized" boundaries to which its forces would eventually withdraw.

There are many ways in which these ends could be assured. The complete demilitarization of the Sinai, patrolled by the United Nations forces, or conceivably, by joint Israeli-Egyptian patrols, would perhaps be the simplest and most effective. Short of such a solution, the leasing of security positions by Egypt to Israel at Sharm-al-Sheikh, and elsewhere, is another possibility.

Perhaps the most practicable procedure would be to combine these ideas. The parties could agree to a timetable extending over a considerable period of time. Its goal would be Israeli withdrawal by stages, pursuant to the agreed timetable, during which conditions of true international peace would be established. Throughout the transition period and after the ultimate Israeli withdrawal, either to the armistice demarcation lines or to new borders that did not deviate substantially from them, the Sinai would be per-

278

manently demilitarized. Such a plan would most fairly balance the dilemmas and anxieties posed by the tragic history of the last twenty-four years.

It is probably impossible to make progress on the terms of a peace between Israel and Jordan in the absence of a movement toward peace with Egypt. The dynamics of Arab politics and rivalry are generally thought to be too volatile to permit such a development. But in the Jordanian case again, the elements of peace are obvious: some agreed adjustments in the armistice demarcation lines, as part of the movement from armistice to peace; demilitarization of the West Bank; an open economy and free movements of peoples between the two countries; access to the Mediterranean for Jordan; and a special regime in Jerusalem that would give suitable recognition to its relationship to both countries and to the international religious character of the Holy Places. Ambassador Lewis Jones has suggested that an international private foundation be established to take administrative charge of the Holy Places and to preserve and restore them as monuments available to all the world. It is a promising idea, perhaps too sensible for the irrational politics of the Middle East.

So far as Gaza is concerned, it could well become part of Jordan, in a context of peace.

Viewed objectively, the nominal issues that block peace between Israel and Egypt are pitifully trivial: a military presence in a desert area nearly devoid of population. In their setting of history they are issues of pride and dignity for Egypt, and of life and death for Israel, which once before evacuated the Sinai in reliance on international promises, only to find herself threatened from the area, and alone.

In the perspective of the campaign of Soviet expansion in the Middle East, however, these problems take on another cast. The nominal issues are not the real issues. The process of Soviet expansion has passed beyond Israel's reach. Israel cannot contain the Arab masses if the Soviet Union arouses them to fury and provides their air cover and their cutting edge. That force can be contained only by the credible assertion by the United States, hopefully backed by some or all of its NATO allies, that it cannot and will not accept Soviet predominance in the Middle East.

v

The moral of this drama, I suggest, is that there is no way to isolate the quarrels of the Third World from the security concerns of Europe, the United States, and Japan, unless the Soviet Union, China, and Cuba should abjure policies of imperial expansion and undertake to live according to the spirit and the letter of the United Nations Charter. From the point of view of American, European, and Japanese security, every part of the Third World is not exactly comparable to the vast arc between Morocco and Iran. But most such regions have comparable potentialities, many more ominous than those of the Middle East.

Some geographical positions in the Third World have inherently important strategic implications, from the points of view of land, naval or air warfare, space communication, and nuclear deterrence. Others have inescapable links to the nations and peoples of the West, historical ties and economic importance of special weight and sensitivity. The Western security interest in most areas of the Third World, however, is contextual. Such countries become important to the security of other states, not in themselves, but in relation to trends and to the policy of their neighbors. It would be absurd to say that a Communist regime in Syria would in itself threaten the security of Europe or the United States. The security problem for the West begins to emerge if Syria becomes a base from which guerrillas attack neighboring states and seek to provoke war among them. It becomes radically more acute if Syria acts as a proxy for the Soviet Union in providing a staging area in a process of indefinite subversion, attack, and expansion. Yugoslavia presented one set of problems to the West when it was an enthusiastic member of Stalin's team, quite another when it established its independence of Soviet rule and then received Western support. In both roles it was a Communist state.

The historic shift of Chinese policy in 1971, from complete independence toward rapprochement with the United States, is perhaps the most dramatic as it is potentially the most important of all such changes in the map of world politics.

Above all, when viewing war as a psychological phenomenon—that is, as a violent response to fear and rage—episodes of this kind have to be considered in relation to each other. The German attack on Poland in 1939 was not in itself more serious as a blow to British and French security than the occupation of the Rhineland, of Austria, and of Czechoslovakia. But it provoked the war precisely because the sequence was finally perceived as part of a process that could only end, unless it were stopped by force, in the accumulation of overwhelming power in German hands, and hence in the domination of Britain and France by Germany.

In the Middle East all three aspects of the security problem are important. Middle Eastern oil is vital to the economies of Europe and Japan and of marginal use to the economy of the United States. The strategic space of the Middle East is of critical importance to the security of NATO. Soviet hegemony or near hegemony in the area would make the position of NATO vulnerable, and render communication with the Near East and the Far East expensive, slow, and chancy. As President Pompidou has said, the Soviet presence in the Mediterranean threatens "the underbelly of Europe," and constitutes a situation like that of the Cuban missile crisis. These are words of tremendous resonance. But they are not exaggerated. The cumulative spread of Soviet influence, country by country, over a period of more than twenty years, has created a sense of unease in Europe and America that could easily become panic.

Western ties with many states of the region are old and deep. And its relationship to Israel is complex and explosive. That relationship has powerful psychosocial dimensions on both sides. Some derive from the history of Christianity and the role of anti-Semitism in Western culture; others from the experience of genocide, so vivid in the nightmares of Western man. Ambiguities characterize Western attitudes toward Israel and Israel's attitudes toward the West—feelings of identity, attraction, resentment, admiration, fear, and guilt. They would make a dangerous mixture if Israel were being beaten to her knees by Arab states, with Soviet pilots and officers in the battle. Whatever men may imagine in advance, I believe Europe and America, and many other countries, would not stand by were another chapter of massacre to be written in the strange history of the Jews.

The apparently endless troubles of the Third World are the heart of the anguish over foreign policy in the West today. This is the case, not because the United States wrongly applied to Asian problems the ideas of the Truman Doctrine and the Marshall Plan developed for Europe, but simply because the pressures for the West implicit in Soviet, Chinese, and Cuban programs of expansion are intense, and are becoming more intense.

The Middle East is a case in point. Whether the Arab-Israeli conflict erupts in another outburst of open warfare, or, as is more likely, is resolved by a political settlement generally consistent with the Security Council Resolution of November 22, 1967, the Soviet campaign of expansion in the Middle East, and Chinese rivalry with the Soviets for control of revolutionary movements in the area, will be a major problem of American and NATO policy for years to come. The pressure will end only if the Soviet Union and China finally accept—or are forced by events to accept—the logic of peaceful coexistence and of détente. In the absence of concerted and determined Western counterpressures to achieve that end, the region will face a condition of spreading anarchy, which, on past form, would almost surely erupt in war.

# 9

## Peace as a Problem of Law

THE TASK OF PEACE among the nations is like that of peace within a free society.

By definition, the idea of peace is linked to the idea of law. Arbitrary power may maintain order in society for a time without the regularities of law, but peace is beyond its reach. While the concept of law pervades the social process too completely to be held for long by a single definition, in its simplest sense law *is* a system of peace. Perhaps we should say that law is *the* system of peace—a peaceful way to resolve social conflicts and make social policy through known procedures and in accordance with known and accepted principles—an alternative both to tyranny and to anarchy. Thus every system of law is a reticulated body of custom and of ideas—a pattern of social behavior on the one hand, and of rules to guide and direct behavior on the other.

It follows that each society has its own legal system, for in each society the configuration of custom, history, values, and ideas is necessarily unique. This is true even for societies closely linked in background and experience, such as Denmark and Sweden, for example, or Scotland and England, or Louisiana and Minnesota. Each legal system has certain common features and all share several common norms. But in each the shadings, the tone, and the emphasis are different.

A human society is a living organism animated by ideas—by beliefs, habits, customs, values, and perceptions of the external world. Perhaps "beliefs" is the most comprehensive word to describe ideas of this order, which run along the nerves of society like signals. In the end, the beliefs that a culture shares as a collectivity determine its response to events, pressures, and threats, and govern its choices among possible policies. For each culture, as for each individual, the past is inescapable. Its response to each new stress is influenced in considerable part by favorable and unfavorable elements in its collective memory of earlier behavior. Thus each community follows its own particular path. That path is not a rigid linear projection of the past. Each culture is capable of change, at its own pace. But the path defining the range and purpose of possible change is greatly affected by the past.

For example, several recent presidential elections represent deviations from the pattern of the past. Franklin Roosevelt was elected four times, breaking a tradition that went back to Washington. And in 1960 the American people chose a Catholic as President for the first time. In the first case the deviation was repudiated and the tradition reaffirmed. An amendment to the Constitution now forbids a President to be elected more than twice. It embodies the strongest principle of the American polity—the distrust of power. But Kennedy's election vindicated principles of equality and religious tolerance which are among the animating notions of the Constitution. After his election there was no impulse in the society to return to the earlier practice, always understood to be a shameful breach of the principle of equality. On the contrary, there was nearly universal relief in the triumph of an ideal that nearly everyone accepts as right.

It is common to suppose that a society in this sense cannot be deemed to exist without a center of sovereign authority. The view of law as sovereign command leads to the conclusion that international law is not really "law," and that international politics are not governed by its rules, because the society of nations has no sovereign. This familiar opinion reflects the power in our minds of ancient symbols of royal, and indeed of divine, authority. International law is enforced about as effectively as national law, both as the embodiment of mores—that is, of customs deemed right—and as an influence upon them. Effective law-making occurs in many societies, such as that of the United States, where the wafer of sovereignty is broken into hundreds, if not thousands, of pieces. In such societies, societies of pluralism, the authority to declare and to interpret laws is dispersed among a multitude of institutions, public and private. In the United States, for example, the sovereign prerogative is shared by the President, Congress, and the Supreme Court on the one hand, and by officials of states, counties, cities, universities, churches, corporations, trade unions, and dozens of other private and semiprivate groups on the other. Similarly, the evolving rules of most branches of international law are declared and applied with a good deal of consistency by national and international courts and tribunals, by governments, by organs of the United Nations, and by learned writers of books and articles, who are treated with somewhat more deference in international than in domestic law.

The respective role of habit and command in the effectiveness of law can be seen in another perspective. The most sovereign of sovereigns cannot promulgate any laws that happen to catch his fancy. No matter how completely a ruler's power is concentrated and respected, he cannot obtain obedience to rules that depart too far from the pattern of custom, or require people to behave in ways they consider wrong, save at the cost of totalitarian coercion. He could hardly legitimize polygamy in a religious society of monogamy, for example, or stamp out polygamy if his people were attached to the custom as a matter of faith. No society can function without at least a marginal invocation of the police. But in a free society, obedience to law, like the law itself, springs in the main from custom. In a pluralist society, laws that correspond to its mores, or represent aspirations for the law that society is willing to see translated into patterns of actual behavior, can become effective without much use of police power. But this result can be attained only if its diffuse law-making and law-enforcing institutions accept their responsibility and assert their will.

In this perspective, the peace of law implies a certain quality of relationships within society, an atmosphere of confidence and tranquillity, such that no citizen within the domestic order, and no state within the international order, need seriously fear violence from his fellows. Peace, that is, is a condition of society characterized by the expectation of general obedience to law. Without that expectation men and nations live in a state of unease. They are preoccupied by the thought that they may be exposed to unpredictable hostility from one source or another, and must devote more and more of their substance and attention to minimizing that danger.

But a pattern of general and spontaneous conformity to law posits the general acceptance of a vital and unified system of common belief, shared by all except a few malcontents on the fringe of society, and perpetuated by strong institutions, directed by a confident and faithful elite. When a society loses faith in its system of values, and the capacity to generate a sagacious leadership, it loses what the Chinese call the mandate of heaven. At that point aggressive impulses slip their shackles, and peace becomes impossible.

Peace is a matter of degree. We consider a domestic society to be at peace even though it contains a number of practicing burglars or pickpockets and there are a few brawls on Saturday nights, and occasional assaults or even murders. The most peaceful of free societies sometimes endure periods of social turbulence —strikes or other demonstrations that become riots, or outbursts of protest that involve disorder. Phenomena of this kind are not necessarily evidence of disintegration in the underlying harmony of custom and values that constitute the society and define the state of peace within it. More often they are signals warning authority that the law-in-fact has fallen behind the pace of change in men's minds and spirits—that its ideas no longer correspond to the prevailing code of social justice, and that change in the law is needed to restore a climate of general acceptance of law.

The pattern of conformity to the law becomes frayed when the law-in-fact—the law at the end of a policeman's nightstick—departs too much from the grooves of custom and of ideals customarily regarded as right. But the process of reorienting and restoring law after a transforming social experience—a war, a plague, a moment deemed glorious—or after a change in prevailing concepts of justice, is not a departure from the peace of law, but its vindication, even though the process involves turbulence approaching the edge of violence. Similarly, when the peace of law is breached, one should distinguish violence that is contrary to law from that which enforces it and restores the tranquillity of peace.

Many situations illustrate these distinctions. The two or three decades before 1914 offer as vivid an example as any.

It has been the fashion, looking backward, to think of the period immediately before 1914 as a golden age of peace and progress in Europe and in the United States and in the world at large. So it was. But it was also a period of intense social conflict, and of considerable violence as well, within Britain and the United States and on the continent of Europe. In world politics, of course, it was the moment before the political system of the nineteenth century collapsed irretrievably.

The prevailing recollection of La Belle Époque is drawn in glowing colors and suffused with nostalgia. In the vision of memory the progressive spirit reigned, and Western culture flourished in every realm. Asquith, Lloyd George, Theodore Roosevelt, and Woodrow Wilson were its political symbols. There were strong progressive or social-democratic parties in Western Europe, and for a moment, even a Duma in Russia. In the Far East, Japan was brilliantly adapting Western technology to its ancient civilization, through a process that seemed to offer only hope, as universities and parliamentary government flourished and the Anglo-Japanese alliance held Japan firmly in the orbit of peace. In China the promising revolution of Sun Yat-sen seemed to put that great country on a comparable path.

A few gloomy and detached observers—Nietzsche and Brooks

Adams, for example—perceived the rebirth of tragedy. But the dominant mood was quite different. There was a nearly universal confidence in the capacity of the liberal spirit, and of democratic institutions, to achieve economic and social progress under conditions that respected and protected human liberty. Social legislation was the order of the day. Trade unionism helped to promote equality among the classes within each Western society. Education was the magic key. It would enable parliaments to fulfill a law of social evolution that science itself guaranteed would always be governed by liberal and humanitarian principles of progress.

For all its optimism, however, and all that genuinely was accomplished, the atmosphere of the period was also one of turbulence, causing great anxiety. In Britain there were painful battles with the suffragettes. The Irish question poisoned politics and led to a mutiny in the Army. A wave of strikes convulsed the nation, and in 1910 there was a constitutional crisis over the House of Lords. The experience of the United States was scarcely less disturbed. Anarchists and Wobblies frightened respectable citizens. Bombs were thrown and Presidents assassinated. There were prolonged depressions, bitter strikes, lynchings, and other forms of social violence.

Yet in both Britain and the United States, when war came, society demonstrated exceptional solidarity at the level of national feeling. Some wonder whether the First World War itself resulted from the same processes that caused so much turbulence in the domestic social life of the prewar period. Writers of this cast of mind would characterize these processes as a degeneration of faith that weakened the restraints of civilization against violence. Others ask whether the sense of national solidarity achieved by the war could have been restored without it.

I am skeptical about such theories. Social violence was a familiar phenomenon throughout the nineteenth century; indeed, it was even more familiar in earlier centuries. In the European revolutions of 1830 and 1848, and in the American Civil War, it reached peaks that seemed to menace the continuity of cultures.

But cultures are robust, with an extraordinary capacity for emerging from the ruins and rebuilding their hives even after hideous catastrophes. After each shock of the nineteenth century the societies of the world returned to familiar patterns. And both in the nineteenth and in the twentieth centuries democratic politics proved capable of adapting society to new claims generally accepted as fair.

There is obviously a limit to the amount of crime, disaffection, and disorder that can be considered compatible with a condition of social peace. If phenomena of this order achieve a certain frequency—that is, if disobedience of law becomes common, notorious, and of continuous importance both to public and to private life—if the atmosphere of society, once disturbed, does not tend to return to its own norm of peace, then we say that society is disintegrating into a state of anarchy or civil war, as the case may be. If prolonged, the experience of anarchy or civil war can destroy the ideological basis of a society, the loyalty of its citizens to their common code of shared habits and values.

Manifestly, periods of violence may also be the consequence, rather than the cause, of erosion in the ideological basis of a culture. Deeper currents may be at work, moral and intellectual attitudes sapping the faith of men in ideas, in models, and in institutions previously accepted as authoritative. There is much to consider in the thesis that democracy itself, by transferring power to the masses, may be the instrument of its own destruction, by making possible what Ortega called a revolt of the masses against rule according to civilized norms.

Cultures have vanished under the impact of such changes in consciousness, as Philip Rieff points out. In circumstances of this kind, he says, the superego of the culture disintegrates, and society loses its capacity

> to organize the moral demands men make upon themselves into a system of symbols that make men intelligible and trustworthy to each other, thus rendering also the world intelligible and trustworthy; [and] to organize the expressive remissions by which men release themselves, in some degree, from the strain of con-

forming to the controlling symbolic, internalized variant readings of culture that constitute individual character.[1]

A degree of tension between these forces of moral control and of release-from-control is inevitable in all cultures, Rieff argues. Cultural revolutions occur when the symbols of release become more compelling than those of control. Then culture may reach a genuine breaking point. The culture ceases to

> maintain itself as an established span of moral demands. Its juris-diction. contracts; it demands less, permits more. Bread and cir-cuses become confused with right and duty. Spectacle becomes a functional substitute for sacrament. Massive regressions occur, with large segments of the population returning to levels of de-structive aggression historically accessible to it, as in the case of Germany during the Nazi period, or ancient Rome when it be-came less a city than a mob.[2]

Must we accept Rieff's vision of the older Western culture, rooted in the value system of religion, now dissolving into anarchy under the hammer blows of rationalism and the new reli-gion of science? I think not, although all must agree that the doom he perceives is a possibility.

I suspect that Rieff overestimates the importance of religion among the sinews of the superego of Western cultures. The uni-fying power of the national idea, and of the value system it prescribes, retains its power, despite changes in the style and vocabulary of patriotism. And so do men's ties to the more diffuse societies, and societies-within-societies, to which they belong. The secular religion of human compassion and social cooperation, rooted in the ethical tradition of the Western cultures, has, if any-thing, increased in influence during the last few generations. This is true as well, in my opinion, for the creed of liberty. It is a severe and lonely creed. And it has always had enemies—those who yearn for the fellowship of communes and the thrill of participating in Nuremberg party rallies. In the cultures that have lived by liberty, however, it remains a fighting faith.

[1] *The Triumph of the Therapeutic* (1966), pp. 232–233.
[2] Id., p. 234.

To be sure, balance between moral demands and personal freedom has shifted. But neither the necessity for social cooperation nor the ethic of social cooperation has been destroyed. In some ways the most astonishing and dramatic aspect of social experience during the last fifty years is the capacity of societies to recuperate after catastrophes. The restoration of Western Europe as a moral entity after the agonies and degradations of the period that ended in 1945 is in itself evidence that the Decline of the West, if it finally occurs, would be an act of suicide, not of fate. The probabilities are just as great, I should suppose, that the transformations Rieff perceives and describes are not mutations but weak and strong branches on a living tree, which still has the capacity to impose its own shape on the new growth.

In any event, men must plan, and governments must act, on the assumption of social continuity, which implies the possibility that peace can be restored. In the United States, at least, I am persuaded that prodigious energies are available to assert the vitality of an abiding faith in the social order that has evolved from the Grand Design of those who wrote its covenants and established its habits. I should venture the same judgment for most of the other cultures of the world—the Russian, the Chinese, and the Japanese, surely, and those of Western Europe as well.

Peace, obviously, is never the only goal of social organization. Defense, justice, wealth, personal liberty, creativity, glory—all these are goals that each society also seeks to satisfy in accordance with its own scheme for ordering values. Cultures that attach a high value to personal freedom necessarily develop complex patterns of social organization. They must arrange to establish and preserve a dispersal of power among the institutions of society in order to minimize the risk that the state, or any other center of authority, be tempted to dictatorship.

The American people are particularly expert in this art. All the constitutional and quasi-constitutional arrangements of American society reveal the same overriding concern with the problem of power. Pluralism is the dominant rule for the organization of government, business, labor, education, and religion. Political power is divided among the states, the local authorities, and the nation, and divided again, within each governmental unit, among legislative, executive, administrative, and judicial organs. Capitalism is justified not only on economic but on social and political grounds —not only because of its supposed efficiency, that is, but as a device for dividing power and encouraging equality. The antitrust laws and those governing banking and many other sectors of the economy seek to prevent an undue concentration of economic power and to keep economic opportunity open to all who want it. No one group has ever controlled the labor movement or either political party for long. And education is directed with extraordinary autonomy by thousands of school boards, church bodies, departments of education, and boards of trustees.

Thus for the United States, or for any other society whose goal is not only popular sovereignty but the enforcement of protections for personal liberty, peace is not a simple matter of command. To fulfill such goals requires a complex and sometimes turbulent process of making decisions, without which the autonomy of the individual would always be under threat. In societies of this kind, peace can prevail only when policy comes close to reflecting the relative strength of contending and independent social claims. Men are free, that is, because authority expresses not the arbitrary will of a sovereign but the consensus of a balance of power.

The balance of power within democratic societies is never static. It responds to changing technology, to changing ideas of social justice, and to changes in the condition of the external world. The appetite for power leads each contending set of institutions toward self-aggrandizement. But in the United States the social system contains counterweights, which, thus far at least, have functioned effectively to prevent any class, region, or set of institutions from becoming a Minotaur.

Each culture differs in the way it ranks peace among the values it seeks to secure through its system of law. Some tolerate a greater degree of disorder than others, and correspondingly insist on a wider area of liberty for the individual. Many prefer a more rigid structure of hierarchy, and insist that the individual be closely and continuously identified with community purposes through collective institutions that dominate both his working and his private life. Others prefer the looser but more lonesome patterns of individualism. Each culture, however, must seek to achieve what it regards as a state of peace, for no society can expect to fulfill its ideas of social justice under conditions of chaos, or indeed to survive, save as a prison.

The state of peace need not be somnolent. A society can be flexible and imaginative in adapting itself to changing ideas of social justice without losing the discipline of peace. Peace is not the enemy of social change, nor yet of personal freedom. On the contrary, neither personal liberty nor social progress based on personal liberty can be imagined without social peace. The societies that have been most successful during this century in protecting a generous field for personal freedom and in fulfilling vigorous programs of social justice—Britain, the Netherlands, and the Scandinavian countries—have also been successful in achieving and maintaining social peace. They have done so, however, by insisting on the restrained methods of law and democratic politics, achieved over centuries of experience, which embody and express an overriding will to live in common. Methods of direct action, and above all recourse to violence, are enemies of what Ortega called the basis for civilization—"the radical progressive desire on the part of each individual to take others into consideration." [2a]

II

Is it permissible to view the problem of peace within free societies as comparable in any way to the problem of peace among autonomous nation-states, each anxious to be secure and independent in its internal affairs? Can we compare the problem of protecting smaller nations against interference in their internal affairs with that of protecting the liberties of an individual in the domestic order of a free society? Is it rational to talk about international

[2a] José Ortega y Gasset, *The Revolt of the Masses* (1922, 1930, 1932, anniversary edition, 1957), p. 76.

293

peace as a condition of international society characterized by the expectation of general obedience to the law of that society? Do the states that preside over the fate of man constitute a society at all, or are they snarling packs of rival wolves, each hating and fearing the others and waiting for a chance to conquer them? If they constitute a single society, even in a limited sense, do its members share a sufficient number of mores and values to generate a system of law—that is, can we discern, even as a potentiality, a pattern of practice they accept as right, one that is effective in guiding the bulk of behavior and in predicting what behavior the society will in fact permit or require in the future?

The members of international society are nation-states, fiercely committed to the tradition of national autonomy or "sovereignty," which has proved itself to be the toughest and most successful of modern creeds. Many are organized in accordance with different social philosophies whose devotees tend to regard their rivals as pagans or heretics. Under these circumstances, is there a feasible way to reconcile the tradition of national sovereignty with the requirements of international peace? Or is peace conceivable only if world society is organized under a single imperium, or under the rule of two or three imperial leagues, whose patterns of rivalry, bargaining, and cooperation would themselves constitute a kind of peace, perhaps the only kind of peace that can be imagined? In short, is peace compatible with much autonomy for the nation-state, or do the facts of life in the modern world permit peace only at the price of far-reaching limitations on what used to be regarded as the immutable privileges of sovereignty?

In earlier centuries people did not visualize the communities to which they belonged as part of a universal international society. For the Romans and the Chinese alike, barbarians began at the frontiers of the empire. The distinction has survived into modern times. It was once customary to identify the parts of the world governed from Europe, or closely linked to it, as "Christendom," leaving the rest in a shadowy limbo. In the international law of the Western nations no more than a generation ago it was commonplace to describe certain areas as "barbarous" and "anarchic," and outside the circle of membership in the "family" or "society" of "civilized nations."

Before 1815 one could describe the parts of the world oriented toward Europe as a society or community in a limited sense, but not one genuinely capable of peace, save as a persistent hope. For many centuries after the breakup of the Roman Empire international law and international politics acknowledged without serious qualification the sovereign freedom of rulers to slaughter their neighbors at will. All efforts to distinguish lawful from unlawful war had failed to gain acceptance. War was taken to be the prerogative—indeed the supreme sport—of princes and of the nation-states that succeeded them. The phenomenon of war occurred in response to the impulses, ambitions, and the fears of rulers—wars of conquest; wars to assure the legitimacy of royal succession; wars of glory; wars of religion and other ideologies; wars for national freedom; wars of boredom, of adventure, of excitement; wars of panic, to prevent changes felt to threaten the possibility of independence or to secure what were considered the necessary conditions of survival or security.

In this setting, international peace could only be described as the state of international society in the absence of open war.

The anarchy of international politics was somewhat mitigated by the influence of men's ideas about the nature of power. The theory of power has the sanction of a wisdom so ancient, and so familiar, that it is considered almost a matter of instinct. The weak huddle together for protection against those who are both predatory and strong. Rivalries are manipulated to produce stalemates, and stalemates sometimes last long enough to become habitual. Organizing new coalitions of king and people to overcome the centrifugal influence of feudalism, ambitious men combined feudal fragments into larger units, stirring new national loyalties to life in the process. The size and strength of these units, and the mysterious appeal of their nationalism, generated a pressure to form units of corresponding size and of corresponding ideological attractiveness. Thus in the new world of international politics after 1945, the European states, crowded between two vast superpowers, responded with new intensity to the appeal of the ancient idea of an integral Europe. If one state becomes strong enough to coerce others and is seized by the mania for conquest that occasionally afflicts men and nations, those who are threatened shift their alliances in order to discourage disturbances of the peace—as China did in 1971, seeking American support against the Soviet Union.

While international politics during the centuries dominated by this pattern could hardly be described as "governed" by the principles of the balance of power, there was a tendency toward equilibrium constantly at work. If the equilibrium of peace was rarely achieved, or, when achieved, did not last long, the yearning for peace was a factor of significance among the causative influences in the political universe. Commercial interests almost invariably pressed in the direction of peace; sometimes religious influence did too, as did the policies of those occasional wise rulers who for one reason or another abominated war and were immune to tunes of glory. The pressures for peace were opposed, and often overcome, by contrary impulses. Peace or war resulted from the interplay of these forces. The laws that permit us to predict economic behavior, or the weather, are hardly more exact.

During this period international law developed a considerable body of rules to prescribe how force should be used, but not when it could be used. They defined the rights and duties of states and of individuals both in peace and in war. Some of these rules were codified in treaties or conventions or in texts viewed as authoritative. All were enforced with reasonable consistency by national tribunals as part of the municipal (that is, the internal or domestic) law of each nation, which is deemed to include the law of nations. Later, international tribunals developed, which undertook to decide cases submitted to them on the basis of generally accepted rules of international law. These rules dealt with the rights, privileges, and responsibilities of states under conditions of war, peace, and neutrality, and with the capacity of citizens and aliens to live, to travel, and to trade within the society of nations, under each of these conditions. They represented the acceptance by all states of principles that qualified but did not genuinely limit their freedom to use force.

In the aftermath of the French Revolution the great men of Vienna radically transformed the system of international politics, and therefore of law. They thought they were restoring legitimacy, conservatism, and the Old Regime. But they danced to the melodies of philosophers they professed to hate. Prudently and cautiously, they sought to organize international society in ways that could prevent a repetition of Napoleon's adventure and the chronic intrigue and instability of the eighteenth century. They were concerned, too, about another danger, which has become familiar again—the threat of social revolution as a demonic international force. In those simpler days it was believed that the pestilence could originate only in France.

In order to achieve their prudent and limited goals, however, they started down the road to Utopia—hesitantly and pragmatically, but unmistakably. Their operative code was that of Castlereagh and Metternich. But their dreams were the dreams of the Czar Alexander, who foresaw a universal commonwealth of men living in peace as brothers in the spirit of Christian piety.

During the nineteenth century the creed of eighteenth-century Enlightenment gradually became the dominating influence in the social policy of Western civilization, and not only of Western civilization. With magnificent optimism, men began to storm Bastille after Bastille in the name of rationality and reform. Custom and tradition were not viewed as the binding fibers of a living social organism, but as vestiges of superstition, irrational excrescences to be swept away as rapidly and completely as possible. War itself was a favorite target for the reformers. The notion of enforcing the peace through collective security was an integral part of the generalized movement for social improvement that makes the nineteenth century in retrospect seem to have been a heroic age of moral action, as it was of cultural achievement. The peace movement was propelled by the same impulses, and fed by the same ideals, that led societies to undertake wide and cumulative changes in other social habits. In an environment of general peace the ideas of the Enlightenment altered the human condition. Slavery and serfdom were abandoned; equality for women was proclaimed; religious toleration became the general rule. The suffrage was extended and often became universal. The lot of the poor improved, and educational opportunities multiplied. The texture of human sensibility changed. New attitudes led to the disappearance of public hangings and other forms of brutality. Capital punishment was limited, and sometimes abolished, and a systematic reform of the criminal law undertaken. The treatment of prisoners, lunatics, animals, and children became less callous, and a thousand other advances in the code of social justice were recorded.

The humane ideas of the Enlightenment—and above all the idea that rational social reform was possible—came to dominate the agenda of politics in democratic societies, and dominate it still. In the name of progress, man's conception of social justice was transformed. The long, slow struggle to make custom conform to the principles of the Enlightenment altered the atmosphere and the social structure of every European society and of many Asian and African societies as well. Trade unions emerged, and political parties based on the strength and dignity of the workingman—a new estate in the constellation of political power within modern societies. The welfare state developed, providing for the poor amenities and protections which had earlier been available only to the rich. To achieve these ends—in housing, education, health, and social insurance—taxation achieved a radical redistribution of wealth and income, on a scale novel to human experience.

No wave of the wand, no sovereign command, could make the rules of modern humanism prevail instantly over customs and attitudes having the force of immemorial law. There was no magic through which the abolition of slavery could produce immediate equality for the Negro in Western societies, above all in Protestant societies, and especially in the United States. The status of women slowly improved, but has nowhere become one of genuine equality with men. Educational opportunity did not quickly alter patterns of class and of motivation. For all the earnest teaching of economists, the strength of independent trade unions has not thus far produced wage levels compatible with full employment at stable prices in any of the Western economies.

The balance between success and failure in the effort to assure international peace has been perhaps less favorable than in other phases of the nineteenth-century movement of reform. The relative success of the Concert of Europe as a principle of diplomacy between 1815 and 1914 provided the Western world with an environment of comparative stability and security, and a climate of confidence, which made all other aspects of the process of reform possible. But since 1914 the aspirations that began to influence events after the Congress of Vienna have suffered terrible defeats. As a body of ideas, however—the source of a system of law—they remain the only coherent and conceivable theory of peace for international society. They were the matrix from which the Covenant of the League and then the Charter of the United Nations emerged.

Beyond its prescriptions about the use of force by states, the United Nations Charter contains many provisions defining the rights and duties of states—their duties of cooperation and their commitment to certain broad social goals and policies. But those aspects of the Charter, benign as they are, are secondary. The fate of the United Nations, like that of the League of Nations before it, turns on the effectiveness of its influence for peace—the influence of the Charter, viewed as a code, on the behavior of nations; and the influence of the institution, when a threat to the peace develops, as a way of mobilizing and deploying the forces in world politics willing to take national responsibility for peace.

The Charter declares a universal rule against force as an instrument of national policy, save for self-defense—a rule applicable to member and nonmember states alike. But is there in fact a society of nations capable of peace, a society whose constitutional structure is outlined in the Charter? Or is the Charter no more than a statement of hope that someday a society built around the ideas of the Charter may develop?

In attempting to consider whether the world is a single social entity, even for the limited purposes of the United Nations Charter, one's first impression is of cultural diversity almost to the point of irreconcilability. Many cultures—those of China, Japan, Russia, and the United States, for example—have been absorbed for considerable periods, and to differing degrees, in trying to accommodate European technology and European civilization to their own traditions. Comparable processes of interaction can be watched in many regions of Asia and Africa, where they began under the influence of empire. Now these ancient divisions among the cultures of the world are being intensified by differences of ideology and outlook. Some governments led by revolutionary parties believe that the Charter should be interpreted to allow them to initiate what they regard as "just" wars, that is, wars to overthrow bourgeois societies or to liberate colonies. Others are still stirred by religious concepts of Holy War. And many believe that the "inherent and inalienable natural right" of peoples to form nations must be accepted as an exception to the strict rule of the Charter. At the same time, the Europe-centered world order has been dissolved, new powers are jostling for pre-eminence, and the poorer countries everywhere are seeking to use modern technology and the science and philosophy from which it is derived.

But beyond the evident fact of cultural diversity, and perhaps of growing cultural diversity, is an equally evident pressure for worldwide integration. That pressure has been at work for several centuries and has steadily increased in intensity. It includes the realms of politics and economics, but extends beyond them. Its dynamism has elements of mystery, which cannot be explained by the development of transportation and communication or by economic interests. How, for example, can one account for the actions of Europe and the United States during the last century in pressing China and Japan to join the European states system, even as partial members? Neither greed nor fear really explains these events. They represent human impulses for excitement, adventure, and curiosity, more like the motives of explorers and scientists than of stay-at-home merchants.

Whatever the causes of the movement may have been, the nineteenth century witnessed a steady and continuing increase in the size of the operative social unit as farms gave way to factories; villages to towns and cities; regions, provinces, and small states to large nations, and then to international groupings, integrated by a network of social, cultural, and economic relations, and above all by relations of security. It witnessed also the emergence of two ideas that were given increasing recognition. The first was that the universe of international law was and had to be the entire world; the second declared that some forms of war should be recognized as illegal—that is, that membership in a world political system of nominally sovereign states carried with it a restraint on sovereignty as it had been traditionally understood.

The premise of the Charter of the United Nations is that a universal world community exists—a human society like any other, animated by a core of shared customs and beliefs—and that the main lines of its public international law are drawn from that core of shared ideas and declared in the Charter. Manifestly, the concept of a "community" for the purpose of this hypothesis is a limited one. The body of ideas shared, say by North Korea and Denmark is not an extensive one; the ideas they share are not drawn from the same religious and intellectual tradition or from the experience of living together in the immemorial grooves of the same cultural pattern.

Nonetheless, there is a sense in which North Korea and Denmark can be regarded as members of the same society.

First, they participate in a world economy that is becoming more and more integrated, and is integrating at an accelerating rate. They participate in that economy differently. Denmark is the more deeply engaged. But in the long run even North Korea could be greatly affected by the existence of world markets for goods, services, and capital.

Secondly, they participate also in a worldwide network of communications whose bombardments cannot be escaped, or even seriously controlled. Despite the best efforts of censorship and propaganda, their minds are formed by exposure to a flow of reports and images more uniform than has ever been the case before. Broadcasts, travel, the movement of students, books, and tapes propagate changes of mood and style throughout the world at a pace that can hardly be credited. At almost the same moment genuine Levi's become the *dernier cri* for young people in Moscow, San Francisco, Rio, Tokyo, and Warsaw. The same phenomenon makes the same writers, actors, furniture, haircuts, and ideas fashionable simultaneously in nearly every corner of the world.

Third, both Denmark and North Korea participate in different ideologies, different systems of ideas about how to organize social life. Those ideologies have international links.

Finally, both countries share life on a planet shadowed by changes in the military art. Neither one can be assured of immunity from general war.

In the end, as Raymond Aron has said, the risk of nuclear war is the decisive fact.[3] A universal world community does exist today. The basis for its existence is necessity, not cultural history, necessity rooted in the nature of modern technology, and above all, the technology of modern war.

A community in this sense should be deemed to exist because there is no alternative. Its existence reflects and corresponds to the deepest and strongest of all social facts, "the nature of things."

What ideas and values are shared by the members of this tenuous and tumultuous community? Some live by the Charter as law; others profess to do so, although their overriding loyalty is to an ideal of revolution that requires, or at least approves, international assistance to revolution—a plain violation of the Charter, deemed to put all responsible for such policies in breach of the Nuremberg principle. Still others violate the Charter more openly, as North Korea did by invading South Korea in 1950, and as the Soviet Union did by invading Hungary in 1956 and Czechoslovakia in 1968.

Nonetheless, the system of world politics does generate and sustain a considerable degree of pressure against the use of force as

[3] *Peace and War* (1967), Part III.

an instrument of national policy—not a completely effective restraint, obviously, but not one that can be dismissed as entirely nugatory either. There is a pattern of prevailing practice with regard to the use of force by states, despite the frequency of conflicts of ideology and of interest. That pattern has varied from time to time during the last twenty-five years. The dams of restraint may break down altogether. On the other hand, the tensions of the triangle involving the Soviet Union, China, and the Western allies may inhibit the illegal use of force by China and the Soviet Union more severely than is the case today. In that pattern of usage by states one can trace the ideas about peace and war that the members of the world community in fact share. Their ideas are not accurately reflected in the language of the Charter, nor yet in their propaganda, but in the wordless diplomacy of the Cold War.

In that experience one can discern the possibility that all the nations could be brought to accept common rules of mutual restraint in the pursuit of national or ideological ambitions. This goal has not yet been reached. It cannot be reached without hard and sustained effort. But the experience of the last twenty-five years, bitter as it has been, teaches that it is not chimerical to try. Unless agreement is reached soon on minimal rules of order for the conduct of rivalry among the nations, the degree of fragile order achieved during the last generation will crumble at an accelerating rate. It follows that general war, or total war, would then be nearly inevitable, for reasons of panic or fear that have been familiar at least since Thucydides—reasons whose dominance, when anarchy threatens, has been demonstrated three times at least in this century. Such war, should it come, would surely destroy first the nations of greatest power in world politics, although it is hard to imagine exempted enclaves in such a holocaust.

For these reasons I believe it is realistic to posit the existence of a universal world society, and the necessity for national action addressed to consolidating and confirming it as a single polity, based on a limited but effective code of public law.

Manifestly, international society in this perspective is one of dispersed power, pluralist beyond even the planned pluralism of American society and government. The ultimate sovereign of that society is hardly a prince or principality, nor yet Leviathan, but the power of coalitions that form almost instinctively, but often too late, when nations are gripped by the fear of being over-whelmed. What Ortega y Gasset wrote about Europe with re-markable prescience in his essay "Unity and Diversity of Europe" applies now to world society as a whole.

Ortega's paper was published in English in 1941 from his exile in Buenos Aires. It had been written, Ortega said, "in my coun-try's difficult times," that is, during the Spanish Civil War of the thirties. The preface is dated December 1940—the most somber and difficult moment of Europe's "difficult times"—after the fall of France and before the tide of war had begun to turn against Hitler and Mussolini.

It is a striking comment on Ortega's discipline that he was able at that juncture to assert the essential homogeneity of Europe, as it had been perceived by Montesquieu and Gibbon, among others.

> [F]or a long time the peoples of Europe have actually made up a society, a collectivity, taking these words in the same sense as when applied to the nations separately. This society has all the attributes of any: there are European manners, European customs, European public opinion, European law, and European public power. But all these social phenomena appear in a form appropri-ate to the stage of evolution reached by European society as a whole, which is obviously less advanced than that of its component parts, the nations.[4]

> [T]he real government of Europe, ruling in its flight through history the swarm of peoples, industrious and belligerent as bees, that rose out of the ruins of the ancient world [is] the greatest secret of modern politics, [the European balance of power, for Europe] is not a "thing" but a balance . . .[5]

> I therefore suggest that the reader spare the malice of a smile when I predict—somewhat boldly, in view of present appearances —a possible, a probable unification of the states of Europe . . . It

[4] *History as a System, and Other Essays* (1941), Norton ed. 1962, p. 51.
[5] Id., pp. 54–55.

is historic realism that has made it clear to me that the unity of Europe as a society is not an "ideal" but a very ancient daily fact, and having seen this fact one cannot but confront the probability of a general European state. As for the occasion that will suddenly bring the process to a close, it might be almost anything: a Chinaman's pigtail appearing behind the Urals, or a shock from the great Islamic *magma*.[6]

Manifestly, the unity of world society, conceived in these terms, is different in texture from that of Europe in the thirties, even though Europe at that moment seemed divided to the point of schizophrenia, under governments directed by Hitler and Léon Blum, Mussolini and the benign socialists of Scandinavia, Stalin and Stanley Baldwin.

Can we dare to visualize the partial and unwilling unity of world society as the source of a system of law capable of achieving and maintaining peace? Can we dare not to?

### III

Our secular age has had to examine realities about the nature of man, and the nature of power, which have been resisted and pushed aside for more than a generation. Loyal to the optimism of the age of reason, we have been unwilling to acknowledge that there are some ailments that science cannot cure. But our experience of war and tyranny since 1914 has forced us to confront brutal facts about the phenomenon of war and the fragility of civilization, which we have preferred to dismiss as superstitious echoes of a less enlightened time.

In earlier centuries, men steeped in religion and in history lived with evil as a familiar. They would have found nothing strange and nothing new in Freud's observation that instincts of aggression were universal and all-pervasive, and that it must be an unending preoccupation of social policy to curb them or to direct them into socially constructive forms of expression—through competition and emulation, for example, which play positive roles in the development of societies.

[6] Id., pp. 52–53.

Men are not gentle, friendly creatures [Freud wrote] wishing for love, who simply defend themselves if they are attacked, but . . . a powerful measure of desire for aggression has to be reckoned as part of their instinctual endowment. The result is that their neighbour is to them not only a possible helper or sexual object, but also a temptation to them to gratify their aggressiveness on him, to exploit his capacity for work without recompense, to use him sexually without his consent, to seize his possessions, to humiliate him, to cause him pain, to torture and to kill him. *Homo homini lupus;* who has the courage to dispute it in the face of all the evidence in his own life and in history? This aggressive cruelty usually lies in wait for some provocation, or else it steps into the service of some other purpose, the aim of which might as well have been achieved by milder measures. In circumstances that favor it, when those forces in the mind which ordinarily inhibit it cease to operate, it also manifests itself spontaneously and reveals men as savage beasts to whom the thought of sparing their own kind is alien. Anyone who calls to mind the atrocities of the early migrations, of the invasion by the Huns or by the so-called Mongols under Jenghiz Khan and Tamurlane, of the sack of Jerusalem by the pious Crusaders, even indeed the horrors of the last world-war, will have to bow his head humbly before the truth of this view of man.

The existence of this tendency to aggression which we can detect in ourselves and rightly presume to be present in others is the factor that disturbs our relations with our neighbours and makes it necessary for culture to institute its high demands. Civilized society is perpetually menaced with disintegration through this primary hostility of men towards one another. Their interests in their common work would not hold them together; the passions of instinct are stronger than reasoned interests. Culture has to call up every possible reinforcement in order to erect barriers against the aggressive instincts of men and hold their manifestations in check by reaction-formations in men's minds. Hence its system of methods by which mankind is to be driven to identifications and aim-inhibited love-relationships; hence the restrictions on sexual life; and hence, too, its ideal command to love one's neighbour as oneself, which is really justified by the fact that nothing is so completely at variance with original human nature as this. With all its striving, this endeavour of culture's has so far not achieved very much. Civilization expects to prevent the worst atrocities of brutal violence by taking upon itself the right to employ violence against criminals, but the law is not able to lay hands on the more discreet and subtle forms in which human aggressions are expressed. The time comes when every one of us has to abandon the illusory anticipations with which in our youth we regarded our fellow-men, and when we realize how much hardship and suffering we have been caused in life through their ill-will. It would be unfair, however, to reproach culture with trying to eliminate all disputes and competition from human concerns. These things are undoubtedly indispensable; but opposition is not necessarily enmity, only it may be misused to make an opening for it.[7]

Freud contended that hatred and the impulse to destroy were not the only instinctive forces governing men's lives. Social groups are also held together, he wrote, by strong positive emotions, by the example of the heroes, prophets, and ideas they share, by a sense of communion in a common history and a common destiny. The members of a group identify themselves with these symbols of a common purpose intensely, and they commit to them their strongest energies and ambitions. Emotional ties of this order are more than the repressed and diverted instincts of aggression. There is another force at work, Freud thought, that of civilization as a "process passing over human life." [8] He called this force Eros, following Plato and St. Paul,[9] as the power in man which opposes "the energy of the death instinct." [10] Eros, the force of life, he concluded, aims at

binding together single human individuals, then families, then tribes, races, nations, into one great unity, that of humanity. Why this has to be done we do not know; it is simply the work of Eros. These masses of men must be bound to one another libidinally; necessity alone, the advantages of common work, would not hold them together. The natural instinct of aggressiveness in man, the hostility of each one against all and of all against each one, opposes this programme of civilization. This instinct of aggression is the derivative and main representative of the death instinct we have found alongside of Eros, sharing his rule over the earth. And now, it seems to me, the meaning of the evolution of culture is no longer a riddle to us. It must present to us the struggle between Eros and Death, between the instincts of life and the instincts of destruction, as it works itself out in the human species. This struggle is what all life essentially consists of and so the evolution of

[7] *Civilization and Its Discontents* (1930), pp. 85–87.
[8] Id., p. 102.
[9] *Group Psychology and the Analysis of the Ego* (1922), pp. 38–39.
[10] *Civilization and Its Discontents*, p. 101.

civilization may be simply described as the struggle of the human species for existence.[11]

In the intellectual and moral climate of this century many factors resist the acceptance of these ancient truths about the nature of war and society. Rational optimists, liberated from what they regard as the burden of religion, refuse to believe that man can be evil as well as good. For them, still, man is born virtuous and is malformed only by society. If only men could live in a state of nature, or in a cooperative society structured to eliminate greed, ambition, rivalry, and selfishness—to say nothing of the seven deadly sins—social justice would prevail, and war would vanish from the earth.

It is paradoxical, but not remarkable, that modern man has been attracted both by Marx and Freud—both intellectual prodigies, both rebels against orthodoxy, both endowed with the peculiar charisma that permits men to enlist acolytes and found schools.

The Marxist Freudians and the Freudian Marxists have developed a considerable literature that attempts to reconcile seemingly irreconcilable themes—Freud's plea for civilization, despite the discontents it must impose upon man by way of restraining or controlling his instinctual gratifications, and the Marxist argument for revolution, which would release "class hatreds" and other forms of aggression and put civilization itself at risk for the sake of goals deemed more important. Freud saw chaos and brutality as the only possible alternative to "civilization," which for him was the bourgeois culture he knew, gradually improved in ways which did not weaken the authority of its civilizing institutions. Marx and his followers proclaimed Utopia as a feasible alternative to bourgeois civilization—a Utopia that could be achieved only by destroying bourgeois society and all the institutions that give it strength. Freud thought it indispensable to curb "the rebelliousness and destructive passions" of the masses and "to promote the feelings of identification" between the masses and their rulers; Marxist strategy, of course, depends upon methods having precisely the opposite purpose and effect.

[11] Id., pp. 102–103.

It is hardly surprising that the literature seeking to synthesize Marx and Freud abounds in paradox. Some identify Freud's instinct for aggression as a disease of capitalism, not a universal trait of man. Their reasoning recalls the Polish joke about the difference between capitalism and socialism. "Capitalism," the story goes, "is a system for the exploitation of man by man. Under socialism it's just the other way around."

The same writers often contend also that the success of capitalism, having produced universal "affluence," in their view, has made it no longer necessary to support Freud's emphasis on the need for civilization "to call up every possible reinforcement in order to erect barriers against the aggressive instincts of man and hold their manifestations in check by reaction-formations in men's minds." Men no longer need to work so hard, they urge, in order to build or to preserve civilization. Therefore, they contend, Freud's arguments are obsolete and his rather severe puritanism unnecessary.

The conviction that the Western nations are not merely rich but affluent survives daily exposure to the obvious facts—the declining standards of education, health and health services, domestic order, and amenity; the probability that the standard of housing is declining; the cumulative impact of inflation. The average standard of living in the advanced nations is probably falling, by measures more sophisticated than pure counting. In the world at large the economic situation is far worse. Manifestly, the world's chief economic problem is poverty, not abundance. And its chief need is hard work, not leisure, as the Germans and the Japanese understand.

But here as elsewhere myth is more important than reality.

Even if affluence were a fact, however, its presence would not affect Freud's argument for the restraints of civilization. The increase in crime, which is degrading the quality of life everywhere without respect to "poverty" and "affluence," would alone suffice to destroy the argument of the Freudian Marxists against Freud.

As a reviewer in the (London) *Times* Literary Supplement remarks, the efforts to reconcile Freud and Marx, even at their most brilliant, constitute "a brain-splitting experience . . . one of the more stunning displays of intellectual jugglery of our day," erecting in the end an "utterly false" image of Freud's thought.[12]

Yet the effort persists, attesting men's passionate loyalty to systems of ideas which for one reason or another enlist their devotion. Both Marx and Freud are integral parts of the modern mood, and have a tenacious grip on the modern mind.

It is difficult to perceive an intellectual reason for the importance of Marxism as a doctrine. The major analytical tools of Marxism have long since vanished in economics, although occasionally an economist can be found trying to reconcile what he does with what the master said. In quality, such exercises come close to the literature that seeks to accommodate Marx and Freud. They permit the writers to say they are still "Marxists," although the theories they actually use in their professional work bear no relation to those of Marx.

Each of Marx's principal concepts has failed to gain a place in modern economic theory.

The theory of surplus value (and hence of labor exploitation) disappears in the light of contemporary macroeconomics, dealing with flows of expenditures, both in real and in monetary terms. Since the total of expenditure rises and falls through time, and the shares of different groups and classes in total output change, no one has been able to measure, or even define, surplus value as a quantity or a concept.

The principle of diminishing returns, on which Marx and Lenin rested their theories of imperialism, has been repealed over and over again by technology. Capital is not irresistibly drawn to colonies and developing nations by the prospect of returns far higher than those possible in developed nations. On the contrary, investment prospects in the advanced nations, even in their agriculture, remain consistently attractive, and it is difficult to obtain capital for the developing world, save for raw materials. There is no professionally respectable evidence for the argument that imperialism is a profitable outlet for surplus capital generated by the

[12] January 8, 1971, p. 26.

inevitable running down of the advanced economies, controlled by the iron law of diminishing returns, and tending inevitably toward monopoly.

The evolution of economics has been no kinder to Marx's trade-cycle theory. Marx based his trade-cycle theory on the concept of monopoly and on the assumption that capitalist economies would inevitably fall under the control of monopolies. Monopolies, Marx thought, would repress investment and preside over incurable situations of unemployment and crisis, which could be postponed for a time only by imperialism and war.

But the degree of monopoly in capitalist economies has almost surely declined since 1900, under the influence of cheaper transportation, the development of competing products, and the policy of the law. Interregional and international trade brings European and Japanese cars even into Detroit. Steel faces the competition of glass, aluminum, and plastics; railroads wither under the competition of the road, the river, and the air; even banks are hard pressed by insurance companies, mutual funds, and other financial institutions. Few modern companies, if any, have the degree of assured monopoly power possessed by many, both in large and in small markets, in 1900. And in any event, monopoly has proved to be no more than a secondary factor in the processes of adjustment we call the trade cycle. As J. K. Galbraith once remarked, "Were it possible to prevent depressions by compensating for the deficient purchasing power of the worker with (say) public spending, then capitalism might be workable. Instead of revolution there would be a budget deficit." [13]

The power of Marxism as a creed can be explained by man's craving for monistic explanations of the social process, and by the appeal of a theory that purports to have the authority of scientific law. It has another attraction. It is also a theory that would legitimize and even encourage the discharge of aggressive feelings in the sacred name of progress.

As an explanation for war, Marxism suffers from all its intellectual defects as a theory of economics, and some additional defects

[13] *The Affluent Society* (1958), p. 67.

as well. There surely was commercial rivalry between Britain and Germany before 1914, for example. But there was also commercial rivalry among the Allies in that war—Britain, France, Russia, and the United States. In any event, as Germany and Japan have now demonstrated again, energy and imagination devoted to economic activity is a much better way to get rich than going to war.

But the persistence of Marxism as a myth, despite its intellectual failure, is a phenomenon of importance. There can be no scholarly justification for theories of social development that claim the sanction of science in predicting the evolution of society in accordance with fixed laws determined by the relationship between one or two selected variables. In this respect the optimistic social Darwinism of Herbert Spencer and the pessimistic social Darwinism of Marx stand on the same intellectual base. They are equally inadequate as hypotheses that might explain the complex processes of social change. As models of the social process they rest on too few propositions, and on propositions, moreover, too simple, too abstract, and too remote from reality to be useful.

Against the screen of modern experience, Marx's social theory has proved to be as sterile, and as shallow, as his economics and his theory of war. States ruled by Communist parties seem to suffer more than the bourgeois states from illegal internal violence and to be at least as prone as the bourgeois states to external violence, even against other states ruled by parties that are also called Communist. In this area Freud is much closer than Marx to the heart of things.

It is one of the appalling commonplaces of human experience, as Freud pointed out, that a group of men within a society, or a whole society, can be swept by a wave of regressive feeling to abandon the restraints it has carefully built into its collective morality and embark on terrible adventures in destruction. Thus all systems of law recognize mobs as "dangerous beasts"—masses of men who can be suddenly aroused to acts of hostility no individual member of the mob would dream of committing alone. Modern history, like that of other centuries, is full of depressing instances of the phenomenon: communal massacres in India, Indonesia, and Turkey; the frenzy of Germany under Hitler, and of other nations possessed by the urge to war.

Clemenceau's eyewitness account of a day in the life of the Commune, March 18, 1871, describes phenomena that have since become commonplace.

> Suddenly a terrific noise broke out and the mob which filled the courtyard of No. 6 burst into the street in the grip of some kind of frenzy.
> Amongst them were chasseurs, soldiers of the line, National Guardsmen, women and children. All were shrieking like wild beasts without realizing what they were doing. I observed then that pathological phenomenon which might be called blood lust. A breath of madness seemed to have passed over this mob: from a wall children brandished indescribable trophies; women, disheveled and emaciated, flung their arms about while uttering raucous cries, having apparently taken leave of their senses. I saw some of them weeping while they shrieked louder than others. Men were dancing about and jostling one another in a kind of savage fury. It was one of those extraordinary nervous outbursts, so frequent in the Middle Ages, which still occur amongst masses of human beings under the stress of some primeval emotion.[14]

The eruptions of men and of nations into violence are never "caused" by the factors that historians usually list as their nominal occasions. The archduke was murdered many times before 1914 without precipitating the response of general war. Nor can the living conditions of students in American universities be seriously considered as more than a ritual excuse for the contagious waves of riot that have so gravely wounded those institutions in recent years. Writing of the Revolutions of 1848, A. J. P. Taylor said, "After forty years of peace and stability men were bored; they wished to translate into real life the poetry of Victor Hugo and the music of Berlioz."[15] Hearing a Parisian mob shout "Vive la guerre" in 1870, Clemenceau thought of geese following a cook and shouting, "Vive le pâté de foie gras."

In its search for justice through peace, civilization deploys its

---

[14] Jean Martet, *Georges Clemenceau* (1930), p. 182.
[15] *From Napoleon to Stalin* (1950), p. 34.

most powerful influences to form the consciences of men and the value systems of society. The prestige and authority of religion, law, custom, education, and the family are combined to fortify the power Freud calls Eros, and to curb that of death. But over and over again in history, and more and more frequently during the last sixty years, the seemingly eternal structures of civilization have been eroded or swept away by primitive impulses of hatred. In the name of optimism and faith in the perfectibility of man, we have seen revolutions consume their children and millions more; in the name of Utopia, the prison state; in the name of freedom, orthodoxy and censorship; in the name of progress, poverty and monotony; in the name of peace, the endless war of all against all. We have become hardened to the parade of idealists betrayed. But they still try, and try in vain, to persuade the exalted among us that the God of Utopia has failed once more.

In his important memoir Joseph Berger, former member of the Comintern and survivor of twenty-one years in Soviet prisons and camps, describes his sense of shock in discovering that

> public opinion and the workers' movement in the West have not come to the conclusions which we in the prisons and camps considered obvious and inescapable . . . [that] once the truth about conditions in the USSR became known abroad the idea of saving humanity through socialism would be discredited for ever, and the main idea of the October Revolution, which Lenin saw not only as a national revolution but as a beginning of the liberation of all humanity, would be rejected and disproved.[16]

Despite the inhumanity, hypocrisy, and cynical manipulation that seem inevitable once "revolutionary expediency" is made the ultimate test of policy, Berger found after his escape that "powerful apparatuses of deceit and obscurantism" still operate in the West, and that the bitter experience of the Soviet Union has not yet inoculated humanity against "any further bacchanalia of lies and deceptions by 'socialists.'" His study and experience of the revolutionary movement for fifty years, he says, reveal nothing to compare with the "confusion and absurdity . . . to be found in

---

[16] *Shipwreck of a Generation* (1971), p. 271.

the so-called 'New Left' movement in a variety of countries at the present time. The worst forebodings of the 'lost generation' of revolutionaries, to which I belong," he writes, "have been exceeded in some of the events of the last few years, in particular in a number of universities in the West." [17]

Of this phenomenon, Ortega once remarked:

> The people of Attica suffered from too much intelligence. Acuity of mind is a sublime restlessness, almost an exalted form of neurasthenia, which easily disintegrates an organism. Consequently, in Athens all traditions were soon done away with and the social body embarked at once upon an era of utopian reforms which eventually destroyed it. That is why Attica preserved but scanty remains of its primitive organization . . .
>
> If the state, as cannot be denied, since history proves it repeatedly, is disintegrated by an excess of intellectual acuity and restlessness, it, conversely, reaches its highest degree of stability and permanence in a moderately intelligent nation which possesses a definite talent, the strange innate talent of ruling. Such was the case of Rome, as today it is that of England. And, notable resemblance, both nations are characterized by their maniacal conservatism.[18]

Ortega's thesis is strikingly paralleled by that of Rieff in his *Triumph of the Therapeutic*, which argues that the rationalist attack on the old religious culture has weakened the attraction of its models and the discipline of its moral demands, so that the culture of the West has probably lost its capacity to survive at all. What has replaced it, Rieff says—a social faith in personal freedom as a good in itself, and in wealth—cannot generate a sense of unity, a code of morals, and a communal purpose that can attract the loyalty and enthusiasm of men. It is nothing, and it stands for nothing. It lacks confidence in itself, and is both impoverished and weak.[19]

[17] Id., p. 272.
[18] Op. cit., pp. 34–35.
[19] Chap. 2.

IV

With regard to international war as distinguished from war within society, writers who had witnessed times of trouble often wrote in tones of despair. Thucydides, whose book is as much a tract for our times as it was for his, thought it was "a general and necessary law of nature to rule wherever one can." [20] Hobbes concluded that the quest for power sometimes, or perhaps always, had a more limited cause: fear. "A general inclination of all mankind," he wrote, was "a perpetual and restless desire of Power after power, that ceaseth only in Death. And the cause of this is not always that a man hopes for a more intensive delight, than he has already attained to; or that he cannot be content with moderate power; but because he cannot assure the power and the means to live well, which he hath present, without the acquisition of more." [21] Thucydides recognized the pervasive influence of this motive in his famous analysis of the causes of the Peloponnesian War. The war was not caused, he said, by the episodes and maneuvers of conflict which preceded it. "What made war inevitable was the growth of Athenian power and the fear which this caused in Sparta." [22] At least where one is not dealing with wars of conquest, such as those of Napoleon and Hitler, launched for their own sake, the impulse to strike out has often been released from the restraints that hold it in check by feelings of suffocation and threat, by a fear that the world will slide into chaos and unknowable risks will materialize unless one fights while there is still time.

But Hobbes' quest of "Power after power" is not a universal law. Different cultures have shown different patterns of reaction, both generally and at different periods of their history. Sweden was the scourge of Europe under Charles XII, as France was

---

[20] *History of the Peloponnesian War*, Rex Warner trans. (Penguin, 1954), Book V, Ch. 7, p. 363.

[21] *Leviathan*, Book XI.

[22] *Peloponnesian War*, supra note 20, Book I, Chap. 1, p. 25.

under Napoleon. Canada and Iran perceive different risks in their proximity to a great power. Power is not good or evil in itself. It can be used for good or evil. Acton's famous aphorism—that power corrupts, and absolute power corrupts absolutely—is only half true. Each state tends to use power in accordance with the rules and norms of its own culture. But all nations, like other groups of men, are subject to intermittent fevers of aggression, during which restraints against violence are dissolved, and they can be led to act out their dreams of glory, or of death. Such fevers have been epidemic in this century. The law of nations can hardly assume that they have vanished and that the rules of the United Nations Charter will enforce themselves.

It follows that peace is a problem of politics and law, and not of economics, ideology, or social virtue. It follows also that the central problem of peace as a problem of politics and law is the control of power. If one's goal is not simply the absence of war but a condition of peace compatible with the independence of nations, then the course of prudence is that power be organized so that no state likely to succumb to hegemonial ambition be in a position to achieve hegemonial power.

Achieving and preserving a balance of power is the indispensable first step. It is not enough to guarantee either peace or freedom. Much more is required. But international society, like any other society, can only achieve peace when its structure and its mores make it possible for those who want peace to insist on respect for basic and minimal rules of public order.

# 10

# *What's to Be Done?*

It is no more than fair, after examining the theories of others, that I should try to bring together here, by way of summary, a brief statement of my own notions about American foreign policy—what I believe its major premise should be, and how that major premise should be applied to the problems of the world in which we have no choice but to live.

As any reader who has come this far will know, I consider the national interest to be the only acceptable guide for foreign policy. There can be no distinction in this regard between "conservatives" and "liberals." These are important words to which many are passionately attached. They suggest real differences of outlook and temperament about many problems—the perfectibility of man, and the proper boundaries between order and liberty, for example; and the strength of one's response to the appeal of tradition and reform. But they have no application to foreign policy. Foreign policy can be wise or foolish; realistic or quixotic; too zealous or not zealous enough; measured or intemperate; too slow or too fast. But there is no meaning in the usage that describes some foreign policies as "liberal" or "idealistic" and others as "conservative" or "cynical."

In this realm the only appropriate standard, as Justice Holmes pointed out long ago in another connection, is what makes sense. Citizens who are genuinely liberal or genuinely conservative about many issues of domestic life can come together with equal conviction behind policies intended to protect the safety, prosperity, and freedom of the nation.

Of course one should conceive the national interest in this sense broadly, in the perspective of the national character. The United States has always responded to suffering abroad and protested against outrage. Its sympathies are engaged by Don Quixotes and repelled by cold and worldly artists of power. Memories of Philadelphia and Valley Forge draw us toward all who defy kings and fight empire. But in its broad lines, foreign policy is intended to safeguard the basic interests of the nation as a nation. That is the only test, I believe, that can justify sending the armed forces into battle.

Manifestly, we have never quite swallowed this doctrine completely in handling our foreign affairs. We often say that politics should stop at the water's edge. But we have always had favorites in foreign quarrels too. The Jeffersonians were supposed to have been pro-French, and the Federalists pro-British, during the Napoleonic Wars. There were waves of national sympathy for Kossuth and Garibaldi during the nineteenth century, and a serious division of sentiment about Germany and the Allies during the First World War. Many Americans were troubled in both world wars by the necessity of alliance with the Russia of the czars and of Stalin. Nonetheless, I believe it is fair to conclude that in the main our actions in the field of international politics have been motivated finally by interests rather than by feelings alone, although we have rarely defined those interests with precision. We did not go to war in 1917 or 1941 because some of us, or many of us, had affinities of blood or spirit with the cultures of Britain, France, or Russia. After all, many of those who died had quite different attitudes.

What is the national interest of the United States in world politics today? As I have pointed out elsewhere in these pages,[1] im-

[1] See pp. 85–86, 201–205, above.

munity from invasion is no longer a sufficient measure of national safety, if it ever was.

President Washington warned the nation against foreign entanglements in his Farewell Address. But his admonition was not intended to be absolute. The United States should not commit itself, he urged, "in the ordinary vicissitudes of [world] politics, or the ordinary combinations and collisions of [its] friendships and enmities." But he and his contemporaries knew from vivid experience that the safety, and indeed the existence, of the United States necessarily depended upon the effective functioning of the balance of power, and that we had to be concerned with extraordinary events that threatened its vitality or survival. It was not by accident that these astute men sought French help in their revolution against British rule, and then turned to France's rivals when they (and the French) had won. They knew, too, that the Bourbon king of France had not supported the American revolutionaries because he was a secret republican at heart. Like Palmerston, they understood the fact that in the world as it was then, and is now, nations have interests, not friends.

Washington's precepts measure our interest in world politics today as wisely as they did in the period when potential threats were calculated in terms of the speed of sailing vessels.

The goal of American foreign policy, I should suggest, is a system of world politics assuring a state of general peace, a system within which the United States could continue to develop as a free and democratic society. American democracy can be safe at home, to recall a speech by Senator Fulbright, only in a world of wide horizons, organized under the Charter of the United Nations—a world of balanced power, tolerant of different social systems, flexible in allowing and encouraging social progress, but free of the threat of change achieved by external force. There can be no safety, no national freedom, and little chance of democracy if we are forced to live as a garrison in Fortress America, hemmed in by missiles, alone and armed to the teeth in a world of hostile or resigned states.

At a minimum, therefore, the most primitive and direct national interests of the United States require it to help restore and preserve a balance of power in the world, and a political process through which basic rules of public order would be respected and generally enforced.

No such system of law and politics now exists. And no system meeting this standard can conceivably be developed without powerful, sustained, and difficult efforts by the United States. The struggle to achieve such a system is not an act of benevolence or charity on the part of the United States but one of self-preservation in the most fundamental sense—self-preservation as a nation and as a free society.

For the present pattern of power and of ambition in the world, and the prevalence of ideas glorifying the international use of force as an instrument of national and ideological aggrandizement, make the task of peace more difficult, and more problematical, than at any time since the first decade of this century.

Why can't America be safe at home behind a shield of ICBM's and Polaris submarines? Because it is extremely doubtful whether nuclear weapons can be used. The nuclear deterrent has to be preserved, in a condition of nuclear stalemate at least, as a safeguard against nuclear blackmail. But after Hiroshima no American President could bring himself to use nuclear weapons unless hideously pressed, and even then the issue would be in doubt. Uncertainty about the use of nuclear weapons can be a deterrent in situations of ultimate tension, such as the Cuban missile crisis. But the Soviets cannot believe that the United States would risk using nuclear weapons to prevent one more slice being taken off the salami. During the years between 1945 and the middle 1950s the American nuclear monopoly did not prevent Soviet take-over in Eastern Europe or the threats to Iran, Greece, Turkey, and Korea. Nor has nuclear stalemate, more recently, prevented processes of Soviet or Chinese penetration in the Middle East, Southeast Asia, and elsewhere. And if we were to arrive in the final nuclear redoubt, surrounded by an overpowering array of passive, neutral, or hostile nations, and divided at home by plausible appeals for "cooperation" and "compromise," would we then opt for Götterdämmerung and use nuclear weapons, knowing that we should be bombed in return? Or would we bitterly accept the wave of the future?

The answer, I think, is obvious.

The vision of safety under siege in Fortress America is a terrible illusion.

Thus far the balance of nuclear forces has neutralized nuclear power as a credible diplomatic influence, save perhaps during crises in which major passions are deeply engaged. The preservation of that balance, and of the nuclear stalemate that it brings about, must remain the first task of American foreign and defense policy. It is a task of far-reaching implications, since nuclear technology never stops changing, and stalemate must be monitored from more and more distant and sometimes exotic stations. But, as Hans Speier has written, if the Soviet Union accomplishes a technological breakthrough in the military field or surpasses the United States in nuclear power,

> it might not be necessary for the Soviet Union to wage war in order to reach its political objective. It could "win" by creating and exploiting the fear of nuclear war in a far more effective manner than it has done in the past . . . Recklessness may replace prudence at any time in high places. Nor have passion and error been eliminated from human affairs merely because man can afford less than ever not to be reasonable and prudent.[2]

The nuclear weapon, then, does not radically change the problem of peace. It complicates it with a new dimension. But it remains true, now as in the past, that to minimize the possibility of general war, and to maximize the possibility of remaining a free and democratic nation at home, we have no choice but to function in world politics at two levels: one, that of conventional diplomacy and conventional weapons, seeking to gain general acceptance for a stable equilibrium, based on understood limits for international conflict; the other, which affects the first but is also distinct from it, the level of nuclear deterrence and nuclear control.

[2] *Force and Folly* (1969), p. 4.

It is often said that the concept of the balance of power is immoral and should not be the foundation for the foreign policy of an idealistic nation. If the argument of Chapter 9 is sound, however, the principle of the balance of power is the key to any system of law, domestic or international, that seeks to assure liberty in peace. For world politics it is the only alternative to international anarchy on the one hand, or to a Roman solution for the problem of international peace on the other. I cannot understand why international peace, and its correlative principle of not interfering in the internal affairs of other states—the two basic principles of the United Nations Charter—should be regarded as an unworthy or immoral goal for the foreign policy of the United States, or one lacking in "idealism."

II

What does the concept of the balance of power imply, as a principle of American foreign policy?

The magnetic field of world politics is arranged in different configurations from those of 1919, 1939, or 1947. The nature and the distribution of power and the character of international politics are changing, and changing rapidly. In the 1830s Tocqueville saw that Russia and America would become giants in world affairs, as Napoleon had a generation earlier. They did not, however, foresee the development of China and Japan, the decline of Europe, the end of empire, and the emergence of many of the newer threats to the possibility of peace.

I can detect nothing in the pattern of change that would allow the United States an easy escape from the kind of policy it has pursued since 1947. Like the pain of making a living, in Acheson's phrase, the job of safeguarding the interests of the nation in a changing world is endless. There is no simple cure for it, no aspirin that can make it go away. Congressional resolutions cannot repeal the fact that hostile and expansionist powers are pursuing programs that would radically alter the balance of power and leave the United States isolated on its own continent. Great shifts in the balance of power have always drawn the United States into war. There is no reason to doubt that Thucydides' maxim about fear as an ultimate cause of war still applies to the affairs of men.

The best, indeed the only remedy against the emergence of such fear as a fever is to prevent the convulsions that are its cause—to continue steadily to insist on the achievement of a reasonably stable system of peace in world politics, based on a dispersal of power, and the enforcement of understood rules as to the limits of rivalry.

Many who accept this premise as a valid definition of the purpose of American foreign policy often add that times have changed since the late forties, when Truman and Acheson laid down the broad lines of the foreign policy the United States has followed ever since. The Communist movements of the world are no longer so tightly controlled as was the case then, they point out—implying, at least, that they are less of a threat to the balance of power than they were in Truman's time. Of course the division among Communist parties and nations offers Western diplomacy certain opportunities. But it by no means guarantees their success. The pressure of Soviet, Chinese, or Cuban ambition is still felt in many parts of the world. That pressure, backed by arrays of conventional and nuclear force, and the full panoply of political, psychological, and guerrilla warfare, has increased in intensity since the Sino-Soviet split. It is hardly obvious why the pressures arising from the rivalry of several revolutionary parties, movements, and nations should be easier for the West to manage and contain than was the case when the world Communist movement was firmly under Soviet control. Both in economics and in labor relations, competition, even among the few, is hardly less turbulent and dynamic than monopoly or duopoly.

The interplay of these factors and rivalries has become the central theme of world politics.

The primary structure of the problem of power for the next ten years or so is what is often called the Sino-Soviet-American triangle. It would be more accurate to describe it as a pentagon, including Japan and Western Europe as well as China, the Soviet Union, and the United States as principals.

The Soviet Union is allied with the nations of Eastern Europe, and with Cuba, Syria, Egypt, and other Middle Eastern states. It will surely seek to establish at least a cooperative, and conceivably an allied, regime in China, as opportunity may occur or be created.

It is fashionable in Western Europe and the United States to believe that the Cold War is over, that détente prevails, and that the Soviet Union is pursuing a policy of collaboration with the West, both in the field of nuclear arms and on other subjects. I have been unable to find any evidence to support such a view either in my Washington experience or in the literature. True, the NATO governments no longer engage in vituperation with or about the Soviet Union. But Soviet propaganda, at home and abroad, is still written in vitriol. We have simply stopped listening.

Limited agreements with the Soviet Union, particularly in the field of nuclear weapons, have been achieved, and others may still be achieved, for it is decidedly in the Soviet interest to induce the United States to limit its military and research expenditure, to control its own armaments budget, and to prevent Europe, Japan, and some other countries from becoming nuclear powers. Michel Debré, when he was Minister of Finance, once remarked that what the world needed most was a trade union of finance ministers to suppress the scientists. Like every other country, the Russians show signs from time to time of complaining about the high and rising cost of military technology. "They weep and weep, but still they spend."

Thus the possibility of nuclear agreement is kept alive, while the Soviet Union pursues a program of imperial expansion based on ambitious programs of military expansion, particularly striking in the fields of sea power, space technology, and nuclear energy. The buildup of Soviet sea and air power, and of nuclear capability, has no parallel in world politics since the Kaiser's bid to challenge Britain on the seas during the years before World War I. Nuclear warfare has been avoided in the period since 1945 because the persistent pressure for the expansion of Soviet control has paused before an occasional American threat of reprisal with overwhelming force.

But Soviet energy presses outward, patient and ingenious, flowing around obstacles, taking advantage of every opening. It can be stopped only by the calm deployment of unacceptable risks. The underlying balance of forces is changing as the West flags. The nature of Soviet pressure is changing as well. Soviet policies of expansion are far more sophisticated and difficult to contain today than was the case in 1949, when they were no more than the glacial outward movement of a land mass—first in Iran and Turkey, then in Greece and Berlin, then in Korea. An invasion of Western Europe is not now a serious possibility, at least while there are strong NATO conventional forces in being. But Europe has been outflanked in the Mediterranean, and perhaps in the northern seas as well, by a process of penetration that poses major problems for the defense of Allied interests in the Mediterranean and the Middle East, in Iceland, in Norway, and in Europe as a whole. The true Soviet goal in Western Europe, one should suppose, is not occupation, Polish style, but West European neutrality and disarmament and American withdrawal both from the Continent and from the Mediterranean. Such a policy would reduce Western Europe to the political status of Finland, and make her resources fully available to the Soviet Union.

In the Far East, Soviet policy has been, and remains, caught up in a dilemma whose contradictions were evident in the conflicts over Korea, Indonesia, and Vietnam, and are now brought into even more vivid and portentous focus by its quarrel with China. The dilemma is implicit in the basic problem of the balance of world power. If Soviet control expands too quickly or too far, as was the case in Korea, it may stir a response from the United States, Japan, or Europe, or all three together. But if the Soviet Union moves to abate the risk, it will be charged with revisionism and collusion with the West, and may lose its leadership in the movement of worldwide revolution to China and to Communist parties oriented to China.

The United States and the Soviet Union have parallel national interests in limiting Chinese expansion. A consciousness of those interests dominated Soviet and American policy toward India after the Chinese demonstration on the Indian frontier in 1962. It remains to be seen whether the Bengali revolt of 1971 will genuinely alter that pattern. From the point of view of national interests, the Soviet Union should surely have followed the same course with regard to Indochina, insisting on the inviolability of the arrangements for French Indochina that emerged from Geneva in 1954 and were confirmed by the Soviet agreement with the United States over Laos in 1962. But the attractions of American misery in the Vietnam morass were apparently irresistible to Soviet policy-makers. They may also have been concerned that China would have moved into North Vietnam if Soviet influence were weakened or withdrawn, as had proved to be the case in North Korea fifteen years before. In fact, the Soviets supported North Vietnam's effort to change the Geneva arrangements by force, and refused to liquidate the adventure, as they did finally in Korea, when North Vietnam failed.

This Soviet policy, as the British say, has proved to be "too clever by half." Its consequences are potentially disastrous for the Soviets. Their tactical success in Vietnam has led to strategic failure in a larger theater. By building up their conventional and nuclear forces in Siberia to a level of clear threat, and their growing presence in Southeast Asia, they forced China to turn to the United States as the only power on earth that could deter a Soviet attack on China itself. For China and the United States have parallel interests in limiting Soviet expansion, exactly like the interests the United States and the Soviet Union share in limiting Chinese expansion. The heavy Soviet hand in Siberia has compelled China to change its foreign policy, for the time being at least, in order to obtain American backing, and thus persuade the Soviet Union that its nuclear and nonnuclear threats against China involve unacceptable risks.

In recent years the Soviet Union has increased both its nuclear capability and its conventional military presence on all fronts—in Siberia and Outer Mongolia, in Central Europe, in the Mediterranean, and in the Atlantic and Indian oceans. It apparently believes that it has restrained China by its nuclear threats, or at least imposed certain limits on Chinese policy for the period of the next few years, before Chinese nuclear weapons could constitute a major threat to the Soviet Union. To take advantage of this short period of time, the Soviet Union has been pressing a bold and risky strategy in the Mediterranean and in Europe, in order to achieve the disintegration of NATO and the withdrawal of United States forces from Europe and the Middle East before undertaking a showdown with China. In Europe and the Middle East, Soviet policy has recently had a new urgency, which can be explained only by its policy of pressing for the neutralization of Europe and the end of NATO while China is still relatively weak; the United States weary and uncertain, after the ordeal of Vietnam; and Europe still not genuinely united as a political and military force.

While China has no overt allies as yet, it does have important political associations both with governments seeking a Chinese counterweight to Soviet dominion, such as those of North Korea, Roumania, North Vietnam, and Albania, and with guerrilla movements and governments willing to precipitate revolutionary action against American or Soviet interests.

In 1971 China moved dramatically to obtain American support against the Soviet Union. Naturally, it will seek to pay as little as possible for American efforts to prevent Soviet aggression against China. But it is inconceivable that help so vital to Chinese security should not involve—so far as China is concerned—at least a Vietnam settlement compatible with American policy; a Formosan settlement that respects long-standing American commitments, and Japanese and American security interests; and an understanding about Korea based on the principles and interests that led the West to resist the conquest of South Korea in 1950. The Chinese government has explained its approach to the United States in terms of an article by Mao Tse-tung published in 1940. Just as it was proper then to seek American help against Japan, the article contends, so it is proper now to unite "with forces than can be united with while isolating and hitting at the most obdurate enemies." [3] Thus, the Chinese argue, it is entirely compatible with revolutionary principles to obtain help from an imperialist power not now committing aggression against China in order to confront the imperialism that presents the greatest danger to the country.

This major event illustrates the classical mechanism of the balance of power at work. The potentialities of conflict between two powers, or two power groups, must take into account the possibility of reaction by a third. The Soviet Union must be concerned about Chinese reactions if it becomes dangerously involved in Europe or the Middle East, and about American, Japanese, and NATO reactions, as well as the risk of explosions and rebellions in its Central European empire, if it should undertake to destroy the Chinese nuclear establishment or should become embroiled with China in other ways. China cannot expect to obtain American, European, and Japanese backing to head off the rising threat from the Soviet Union unless it accepts and respects the interests of those nations.

The United States has assured the Soviet Union that its rapprochement with China does not imply an alliance against the Soviet Union. No such alliance is now conceivable, or desirable. But an understanding between China and the United States to oppose any hegemony in Asia, and to deter a Soviet attack against China, is the heart of the matter. Under these circumstances, the most appropriate posture for the United States is that stated by Acheson in his famous and controversial speech after the withdrawal of American forces from Korea in 1949, in which he said that no person can guarantee areas where there is no American military presence against attack, but "should such an attack occur . . . the initial reliance must be on the people attacked to resist

[3] *New York Times*, August 22, 1971, Sect. I, p. 5, col. 1.

329

it and then upon the commitments of the entire civilized world under the Charter of the United Nations" [4]—a formula whose potential was demonstrated in Korea.

The Soviet Union must oppose these implications of the Chinese turn toward the United States. Its support for the Hanoi offensive against South Vietnam during the spring of 1972 was a preliminary answer to the United States, to China, and to other nations dependent upon American support. If that offensive should succeed, and if the United States were to withdraw from Asia, pro-Soviet forces in China would be strengthened, and the promise of China's new policy would fade.

The tensions of this triangular relation, which during the next decade should also involve Europe and Japan as effective allies of the United States, offer great hope for a degree of peace that could meet the security needs of the United States. The dynamics of response and counterresponse require both China and the Soviet Union to confront the fact that now, as always, there are limits to the possibility of imperial expansion. Under the circumstances of modern life the path of wisdom and prudence is that of stalemate, stability, détente, and peaceful coexistence under the rules of the United Nations Charter.

But Western policy cannot assume that these hopes are self-fulfilling. On the contrary, there is no chance they will be achieved unless they are pursued with energy through a diplomacy necessarily backed by force.

In many ways the situation recalls that of the late thirties, when Britain and France gingerly explored the possibilities of a relationship with the Soviet Union in order to deter Hitler. Had that approach been followed with greater conviction, could the war of 1939–1945 have been prevented?

III

However rational this bleak conclusion may be, the state of public opinion in the West after Korea and Vietnam creates a new crisis

[4] State Department Bulletin, January 23, 1950, p. 116.

in international affairs—a crisis of understanding, and of will. Many insist on believing, or at least on saying, that the "Cold War is over"—a view quite as absurd, in the light of reality, as its opposite, the thesis that there is a Communist agent of one persuasion or another under every bed and behind every protest and demonstration. And after more than twenty years of unremitting pressure, men are no longer so convinced as they were in 1945 that stopping small aggressions in distant places will in fact prevent major wars.

The crisis of opinion mainly concerns the relationship of the industrialized nations of the Pan-Atlantic community to the Third World. Many writers ask whether the rich nations have a genuine security interest in assisting the nations of the Third World to preserve their territorial integrity and political independence against take-over in any form, whether by Communist nations or by other conquerors. Our concern with the nations of the Third World, they say, is sentimentalism or worse, based on Western feelings of guilt about colonialism and slavery. We in the West should liberate ourselves from these feelings and realize that there is little or nothing we can do to influence the future of the new nations, which should be allowed to find their own way as best they can.

Many, of course, resist arguments of this kind, on grounds both of security and of humanity. They wonder at least about new countries in strategic locations, if nuclear war has not made such considerations obsolete, and about the spread of epidemics of aggression. Are the small nations of Asia and Africa successively threatened by coercive intervention—Thailand, Burma, Tunisia, Kuwait, Israel, and many others—each in the position of China in 1931 and of Ethiopia in 1935? Were the convictions of 1945 about what should have been done in the thirties to prevent World War II valid then? Are they valid now?

To put the issue in this way is not to compare the various would-be conquerors of the moment to Hitler or to the military regime of the thirties in Japan. The threat to the equilibrium of peace can come in many forms. The question, rather, is whether

331

processes of aggression are cumulative, generating fears and anxieties that in human experience have inevitably led to armed resistance and then to spreading war.

It would be foolish to conclude that the West has a vital security interest in the independence of every small nation of Asia, Africa, or South America. But it would be equally foolish to assume that there is nothing to fear in the strategy of surrounding the "cities" by occupying the "countryside"—that is, the strategy of neutralizing the great centers of industry in Europe, the United States, and Japan by occupying large parts of the Third World. President Nixon has said that Soviet "predominance" in the Middle East, for example, would be a matter of "grave concern" to the United States. He is quite right. The same reasoning would apply to such sensitive areas as the Persian Gulf and Southeast Asia, and to others as well.

The problem of policy with respect to the Third World, then, is inordinately difficult: How to define a policy, short of the complete enforcement of the Charter, that would minimize the risk of miscalculation, and therefore of war? I am not at all sure that it can be done, save on the basis of mutual restraint—the policy of agreed abstinence, which characterized both Soviet and American policy in Africa for a few years after the Congo crisis. Any alternative, as the experience both of Vietnam and of the Middle East attests, is necessarily so ambiguous, and its signals and alarm bells so liable to be misinterpreted or ignored, as to be nearly unworkable.

The risk of both regional and general war would be much less, obviously, if the United States and its allies could obtain a universal acceptance of Article 2, paragraph 4, of the Charter: that all nations "refrain in their international relations from the threat or use of force against the territorial integrity or political independence of any state, or in any other manner inconsistent with the purpose of the United Nations." In the absence of miraculous conversions, this goal could be achieved only by the deployment of credible arrays of deterrent force. Under such circumstances, those who would breach the rule would confront the certainty that the rest of the international community would contest such breaches, in the pattern of the Korean war, or go further, if the habit of breach is not broken, by reprisals against those responsible. In the end, such a course would pose the question whether the nations upholding the charter should threaten to denounce Article 2, paragraph 4, as it applies to themselves, unless it is honored reciprocally.

"Spheres of influence" is the traditional name for a second, and perhaps more practicable, policy of peace. Its shortcoming, if the reasoning of Chapter 8 is correct, is that it must be nearly universal to be effective under the circumstances of modern life. The dynamics of Balkanism, now evident throughout the Third World, would require a policy of spheres of influence to approximate that of enforcing the Charter.

The West has tried both peace through universal rules and peace through mutual respect for spheres of influence. Neither approach has worked. The rules of the Charter have been breached over and over again. And while the West refrained from interfering in the affairs of Eastern Europe, the Soviet Union has not respected the interests or the commitments of the West in Berlin, in Cuba, in Korea, in Vietnam, or in the Middle East. The troubled history of the last twenty-five years has not produced an atmosphere of peace. Understood limits for the process of rivalry have not been accepted by the Soviet Union, by China, or by Cuba. It is by no means self-evident that Soviet policy would even respect the manifest state interests of the United States in the continuity of its relationships with Western Europe and Japan.

IV

Under these circumstances what is to be done?

In 1968 I published a short book, *Law, Power, and the Pursuit of Peace*. Its theme was that we were in the midst of a major crisis in international affairs such as those of the decades before 1914 and 1939. I argued that change was urgently required in the foreign policy of the United States and of its allies "if its great aim, the achievement of peace, is to remain in our grasp." [5] In the shadow of Korea and Vietnam, American opinion was in revolt against the burdens the nation had carried since 1945. No one could tell how far that revolt would take policy. But the American deterrent, the sole force keeping the general peace since 1947, had been put in doubt, while the pattern of events was more ominous and more difficult to control than was the case in the late forties and early fifties.

The argument of *Law, Power, and the Pursuit of Peace* was that the minimal security of the United States could be protected only by establishing a new balance of power in the world, and achieving the reciprocal acceptance of rules of restraint that could limit conflict and assure the nations that the underlying equilibrium of force would be respected; that thus far neither the Soviet Union nor Communist China had accepted this prudent idea as the basis for a policy of coexistence, although neither one had declared full-throated war against it either; and that while the United States could not be expected indefinitely to respect these rules without reciprocity, the strategy of our foreign policy should continue to press both China and the Soviet Union to accept the logic of peaceful coexistence.

Under these circumstances, I contended, there was only one prudent course capable of containing the pressures of Soviet or Chinese expansion, and preserving the hope of peace. It was to achieve closer concert in our alliances, both in Europe and in Asia, and a more equal sharing of their burdens and responsibilities. For reasons that may or may not be rational, American opinion will accept collective responsibility just as strongly as it resents having to do the job alone. Therefore the remedy for the isolationist yearnings of the American soul, and, in any event, the equitable principle for dividing the costs of security over the long run, was a process of transforming our alliances. Through political understandings of this kind, I urged, the United States should "become in fact the junior partner in regional coalitions to assure

[5] P. xiii.

stability and development in areas of the Free World now threatened with conquest or chaos." [6]

Formally, the transformation of our alliances was in train in 1968. But the process moved slowly, given the continuity of social habits and the grip of old ideas on men's minds.

These perceptions were the heart of Johnson's strategy, often stressed in the official speeches of the Johnson Administration. Nixon has now made them the central feature of the Nixon doctrine.

The effort of writing this book did not lead me to a different conclusion. On the contrary, it confirmed its urgency. I should still contend that the United States and its allies have no real alternative but to renew their commitment to the line of policy they have followed since 1947. The acceptance of reciprocal rules defining the outer limits of conflict must be pursued as the explicit goal of that policy. Given the strength of national and ideological ambitions at work in world politics, such acceptance can be achieved only by the patient and restrained firmness that has characterized Western insistence on its rights in Berlin, and on the defense of Iran, Western Europe, Korea, and South Vietnam.

One can hope for better and more sophisticated handling of the political and military applications of that policy in the future. One can try to convince the Soviet Union and China that there is no workable alternative to the policy of the Charter of the United Nations, which forbids not only traditional imperial expansion but international support for revolution. One should use the major opportunity opened up by China's request for American assistance to deter an ominous Soviet threat, in 1971, as the basis for bringing this conviction home to both countries.

Another factor works in the same direction—the fear of nuclear proliferation and the implications of the Non-Proliferation Treaty. The treaty imposes an obligation on the Soviet Union, the United States, and Great Britain—an obligation to protect nonnuclear signatories against nuclear threat. The United States

[6] Id., p. 116.

would face the issue in its most acute form if the Soviet Union made an overtly nuclear threat against a nonnuclear signatory. But this dimension of the treaty emerges from the shadows whenever the Soviet Union threatens a nonnuclear power. The treaty would become a curse if it were to be used as a screen behind which nonnuclear powers are systematically invested, through "Wars of National Liberation," or otherwise. The treaty can survive only if it reinforces these pressures for accommodation and leads to a degree of political cooperation among the nuclear powers, and an end of expansionist adventures such as the Soviet program in the Middle East.

But success in these efforts is by no means assured. And at best it will be slow. What is required for success in this effort is not trivial, after all; it is nothing less than acceptance of the Charter, and therefore abandonment of the idea of international support for revolution. Without that principle, true "co-existence" is impossible.

It follows that a deepening and strengthening of the Western alliance system, and corresponding change in the structure of American relations with Japan, are essential to a strategy that would have more than a token chance of success. Rightly or wrongly, American opinion resents the fact that so large a part of the burden of defense for the last twenty-five years has been borne by the United States, while many of the beneficiaries of that effort have been able to concentrate their resources and energies exclusively or nearly exclusively on economic development and trade. The explosive character of the changes in American economic policy announced on August 15, 1971, derives from this bitter feeling. Unless basic change in the structure of our alliances is achieved soon, the risk of irrationality and of imprudence in American policy will increase.

The monetary explosion of August 15, 1971, illuminates the nature of the problem. On that occasion the United States broke a pattern of international cooperation in whose successful continuity all the nations of the world, developed and undeveloped alike, have a vital interest.

The international monetary system as it has functioned since 1945 had become obsolete.

To have built a progressive world economy out of the ruins after 1945 was a brilliant achievement, accomplished over twenty-five years by a few key officials and the responsive energy of private business. Habits of cooperation among governments and central banks crystallized around their work. So did more and more liberal policies toward trade and investment, which in turn stimulated an extraordinary expansion of international economic activity as an engine of economic development.

Of course mistakes were made. Of course the practice of international cooperation is difficult and sometimes exasperating. Of course the level of international investment is not yet high enough to achieve full employment everywhere. And of course change is needed in the arrangements that have served so well since Bretton Woods.

But the changes that are needed can be achieved only by patient cooperation, not by abrupt unilateral action that threatens a retreat to anarchy—a course of economic folly that would fray the political relationship with Europe and Japan on which the hope of peace, and of development in the Third World, ultimately depend.

The economies and societies of Western Europe, the United States, Canada, Japan, and a number of smaller countries are now more integrated than their monetary institutions. For implacable reasons, the process of their integration will accelerate. But the economy of this emerging social unit—the Pan-Atlantic Community—cannot function unless its monetary system is genuinely unified.

First, the nuclear weapon makes Europe and Japan more dependent on American protection than in 1949, despite their economic and social recovery. American troops are stationed in Europe and Japan primarily to make nuclear deterrence credible, and to minimize the risk of recourse to nuclear weapons during crises. Under present and foreseeable conditions, deterrence is impossible without such deployments. While the tensions of the

Soviet-Chinese-American triangle may produce stalemate, stability, détente, and peaceful coexistence, policy cannot assume that these goals have already been achieved.

But keeping troops abroad affects the balance of payments as well as the budget. None of the palliatives thus far used, from military purchases to offset loans, can free security planning from balance-of-payments restraint, as Lend-Lease did. After ten years of futile negotiation, nothing short of such a solution is acceptable.

Second, the scale of investment and travel within the Pan-Atlantic Community has produced a degree of business and social integration which in itself compels monetary consolidation. Normal movements of funds between the subsidiaries and home offices of international companies are sometimes large enough to offset national monetary policy. Private and public investment, and the payment of interest and dividends, are on a scale beyond anything experienced since the era of monetary integration before 1914. And the volume of private travel has become a major factor in international accounts. Like security expenditures, most transfers of this kind are independent of exchange rates.

Third, a central bank of central banks is also needed to help rationalize, harmonize, and discipline the movement of wage rates within the community. No Western society (save Japan) has thus far succeeded for long in achieving wage rates compatible with full employment at stable prices. None has been willing as yet to adopt Keynes' proposal of fixed money wages, despite the superobvious fact that rising money wages do not increase labor's share in national income, but simply require government to choose between unemployment (caused by higher wage rates) and enough monetary inflation to restore full employment at higher prices.

When wages increase at different rates in different countries, the modern system of fixed exchanges becomes unmanageable. Education in economics is the only ultimate cure for the absurdities of Western wage-making. The only feasible course meanwhile is monetary unity.

Beyond all the other objections to a system of floating exchange rates—more uncertainty and speculation, higher interest rates, less trade and investment—it cannot work save at the price of even more rapid inflation.

Removing the last international restraint on wage-making would finally transfer monetary management from the central banks to the trade unions and start a race of competitive devaluation no one could win.

A consciousness of economic interest, and the facts of economic life, are limiting the damage caused by Nixon's economic moves during the summer of 1971, and once more pressing the Pan-Atlantic nations into patterns of closer economic integration.

The same centrifugal and centripetal pressures are visible in allied diplomacy and defense policy. In 1945, anyone who predicted that sizable American forces would still be in Europe and Japan in 1972 would have been regarded as nearly committable. Roosevelt thought it would be impossible to keep American forces abroad for more than a few years. But the forces are still there, despite powerful opposition, because the problem of nuclear deterrence makes it inconceivably dangerous to remove them.

Nixon sometimes speaks as if the popular "dumbbell" theory were in fact a feasible alternative to closer unity among the Allies. That theory contends that alliance relationships should be loosened, so that Western Europe and Japan, as autonomous nuclear powers, could operate in world politics in their own orbits, allied to the United States, but independent of it too. Under those circumstances, there would be five major centers of power and influence in the world, not three—the Soviet Union, China, the United States, Western Europe and Japan. Their orbits in world politics would be harmonized, and collisions avoided, these men argue, by a Gaullist law of celestial gravitation, upon which we could safely rely to maintain equilibrium.

As a matter both of fact and of theory, this view is a fantasy. Politics are not governed by mechanical principles of gravitation, celestial or otherwise. In any event, there is no way in which Western Europe could soon become an effective political entity, or catch up with the United States or the Soviet Union as a nu-

339

clear power. The implacable consequences of the nuclear weapon, without regard to any other factors, mean that there is no real alternative to a policy of accelerating the processes of alliance integration, through institutions which do not yet exist.

v

Can men bring themselves to confront and accept such unpleasant facts in time by rational analysis alone, without the shock of disastrous alarms, like the invasion of Poland in 1939 and the attack on Pearl Harbor in 1941? The fate of those who sought to arouse the West to danger before both the First and the Second World Wars is not an encouraging recollection. In retrospect, the small band of men who were right—Eyre Crowee, Robert Vansittart, Winston Churchill, and a handful of soldiers—have earned respectful footnotes for their efforts to prevent those tragedies. But they were not heard. Is it man's destiny not to believe in his intelligence enough to live by it?

It is difficult to predict the impact on American foreign policy of the strains and frustrations associated with the anguish of Korea and Vietnam. It is hard to imagine our repeating the follies of the twenties and thirties. But we may. After all, we did so once before.

If we do try to escape down the rabbit hole into the nineteenth century, if we stand by and do nothing to prevent cumulative and threatening gains in Soviet power in the Middle East, or of Chinese power in Asia, war is almost certain to follow, for the same reasons that led to war in Europe as a result of the American withdrawal from world politics thirty years ago. Wars come, in the perspective of history, when panic touches nerves of animal passion—when men feel threatened or cornered, or fear a slide toward chaos if they fail to strike out. The Cuban missile crisis of 1962 is a good example of this psychological mechanism at work.

In *Law, Power, and the Pursuit of Peace*, I said:

> The explosions of feeling and of protest in 1968 have been remarkable events—signals of dissatisfaction at a time when West-

ern societies, at least, have never been more active in moving toward the fulfillment of their social goals. Historians may look back on 1968—as they do on 1848—as a year in which the deepest wishes of mankind were made manifest. Namier called 1848 the Revolution of the Intellectuals. It is striking that students and intellectuals have taken the lead in articulating and dramatizing the diverse dreams of mankind.

All over the world, there are visible and sometimes violent manifestations of human stress and concern over the trend of events. In most cases, these manifestations reflect the yearnings of generous and idealistic spirits. In some, they betray feelings of hostility, bitterness, frustration, and the desire for revenge. In many countries, the demonstrators seek liberty and social advance. Occasionally, they manifest man's universal taste for violence, and his instinct of destruction for its own sake, normally but not always kept in check by the texture of his social system.

Of course, hostile forces seek to exploit those feelings, and to turn their manifestation into revolutionary channels—that is, into channels seeking a truly revolutionary transfer of power—or a situation of suicidal chaos, and not simply the acceleration of social change within the pattern of the existing order. And, of course, in the face of such threats governments have to intervene finally to restore and preserve public order. For the first time in many years, we have witnessed demonstrations precipitated by believers in bizarre doctrines of violence as an end in itself. Healthy societies invariably find ways, as they must, to encapsulate such actions, and to treat them for what they are.

But responsible men everywhere would ignore the yearnings behind these events at their peril. Time is running out. The demons of force are slipping their chains. The precarious minimum of order that has been ours since 1945 cannot last indefinitely in the present state of the world community.

If those in Western countries who protest in the name of peace conclude that certain Communist countries are in fact responsible for the absence of peace, the result could be incalculable.[7]

The stupidity, madness, and evil of the generation between 1914 and 1945 did much more than wreck a political system and weaken a culture. It profoundly affected the minds of men. Since the heady days of the Enlightenment, at the end of the eighteenth century, civilized man has believed in reason and in reasonable and automatic processes of science and natural law, which assured

[7] Pp. xvii–xviii.

the general peace and the progress of mankind toward justice and virtue. No man can hold such views today. We know now, and know in our bones, that there is no guarantee of progress, no silent law of natural harmony at work to govern the course of history. We cannot remind ourselves often enough that the two catastrophic wars of this century were unnecessary, as Churchill argued so correctly, and that wise and foresighted policy could have prevented them. But men are fallible. They often hesitate when they should act, and act when they should hesitate. And their folly can release the most evil impulses of our nature, and turn us into Calibans, or worse. In this psychiatric age we tend to avoid the word "evil." But it corresponds to a part of our destiny nonetheless. Hitler's career had more impact on the course of history than all the jostlings of economic rivalry.

What has been lost in this century, as an anonymous critic has remarked, is "not so much a belief in the Christian heaven above the skies" as confidence in the inevitability of "a republic of heaven upon earth." Faith in the benevolence of reason, science, and progress, he wrote, "held the field from the French Revolution at least until the First World War and, with many, until Hiroshima." Today we cannot be sure that even titanic leaders, governors in the stamp of Churchill—if we could find them—could guarantee a decent future for man on earth.

As the preacher said long ago, there is nothing new under the sun. The spectacle of world politics today confirms the appalling wisdom of Sophocles' remark: "Human life in its utmost strength and splendor hangs on the brink of an abyss."

# Index

# Index

# Index

347

# Index

Morgenthau, Hans J., 129, 197–228, 230, 232, 237, 238, 240
alternative foreign policy proposals of, 220–26
author's analysis of, 199–200, 212–214, 218–19
Morgenthau, Henry, 123
Morley, John, 244
Mussolini, Benito, 153, 155, 305
Muste, A. J., 149–51, 152

Nagasaki, 151
Napoleon, 32, 41, 316, 317
Nasser, Gamal Abdel, 256–58, 261, 262, 271, 274–76
Arab unity plans of, 245, 249, 264
NATO, 18, 76, 146, 154, 222, 242
establishment of, 32, 180
Middle East and, 105, 250, 254, 277, 281
Soviet policy and, 325, 326, 328
Netherlands, 29, 261, 293
New Left, 148, 315
New Look policy, 212
New nations, 47
emergence of, 29–30
*New York Times, The,* 57, 64–65, 67
New Zealand, 146, 185, 224, 235, 238, 242
Nietzsche, Friedrich, 226, 287
Nixon, Richard M., 139, 186, 232, 269, 332, 339
Cambodian actions of, 17, 276
China visit of, 54, 133
foreign policy of, 44, 335
Non-Proliferation Treaty, 335
Nonviolence, revolutionary, 152
North Korea, 100, 216, 218, 301–2
North Vietnam, 100, 216
peace negotiations of, 57–63

Oglesby, Carl, 97–144
author's analysis of, 105–7, 127–30, 134–39, 143–44
Oil, 250–51, 254, 259, 281
Ortega y Gasset, José, 289, 293, 304–305

Pacific nations, 136–37, 231
Pacifism, 19, 80–81, 149–50

Pakistan, 189, 237
Palestine, *see* Israel
Parkinson, C. Northcote, 48
Paul, St., 307
Peace, 227, 243, 250
literature on, 11, 21
among nation-states, 42–43, 293–305, 317, 320
through pressure for worldwide integration, 94, 300–5
as problem of law, 20–21, 283–317
social peace within state, 284–93
U.N. Charter and, 20, 34, 301, 320, 330
*Pentagon Papers,* 64–68, 77
Peron, Juan, 237
Pfaff, William, 197, 226–39
alternative foreign policy proposals of, 231–36, 238
author's analysis of, 230–31, 233, 238
Plato, 307
Poland, 110, 111, 120, 159, 217, 281
Marshall Plan offered to, 127
Soviet policy toward, 213
Pompidou, Georges, 281
Portugal, 29, 207
Potsdam Conference, 30, 34, 111, 132, 180
Power, 183, 295, 316
U.S. society and, 291–92
Presidential powers, 263–64, 285
Constitutional, 165–67
Supreme Court decisions on, 168–170
Press, 46, 67–69
Public opinion, 55–57, 65–67, 120, 130, 314, 330–31
foreign policy and, 17–18, 28, 38–39, 52, 82, 276, 319
government manipulation of, 63–71
Vietnam War and, 14, 56–57, 74–75, 238, 263
*Pueblo* incident, 75

Quakers, 80
Quemoy and Matsu, 212

Realpolitik, 87, 91–93, 197–238, 240
Reston, James, 242

349